Michael Rudolph

Ritual Performances as Authenticating Practices

PERFORMANZEN
PERFORMANCES

Interkulturelle Studien
zu Ritual, Spiel und Theater

Intercultural Studies
on Ritual, Play and Theatre

herausgegeben von/edited by

Christopher Balme
Klaus-Peter Köpping
Michael Prager
Christoph Wulf

Band/Volume 14

LIT

Michael Rudolph

Ritual Performances as Authenticating Practices

Cultural representations of Taiwan's aborigines
in times of political change

LIT

Title foto: With kind permission from Pideru Wuga (Liao Jin-sheng), Taiwan.

Publication of this book has been made possible by the generous funding of the DFG (German Research Foundation) within the framework of the Collaborative Research (SFB) 619 "Dynamics of Ritual", University of Heidelberg.

Bibliographic information published by the Deutsche Nationalbibliothek
The Deutsche Nationalbibliothek lists this publication in the Deutsche Nationalbibliografie; detailed bibliographic data are available in the Internet at http://dnb.d-nb.de.

ISBN 978-3-8258-0952-2

A catalogue record for this book is available from the British Library

© LIT VERLAG Dr. W. Hopf Berlin 2008
Auslieferung/Verlagskontakt:
Fresnostr. 2   48159 Münster
Tel. +49 (0)251–62 03 20   Fax +49 (0)251–23 19 72
e-Mail: lit@lit-verlag.de   http://www.lit-verlag.de

Distributed in the UK by: Global Book Marketing, 99B Wallis Rd, London, E9 5LN
Phone: +44 (0) 20 8533 5800 – Fax: +44 (0) 1600 775 663
http://www.centralbooks.co.uk/acatalog/search.html

Distributed in North America by:

Transaction Publishers
New Brunswick (U.S.A.) and London (U.K.)

Transaction Publishers
Rutgers University
35 Berrue Circle
Piscataway, NJ 08854

Phone: +1 (732) 445 - 2280
Fax: + 1 (732) 445 - 3138
for orders (U. S. only):
toll free (888) 999 - 6778
e-mail:
orders@transactionspub.com

TABLE OF CONTENTS

ACKNOWLEDGEMENTS

Publication of this book has been made possible by the generous funding of the DFG (German Research Foundation) within the framework of the Collaborative Research Centre (SFB) 619 "Dynamics of Ritual", University of Heidelberg.

The idea of studying indigenous ritual in contemporary Taiwan developed during my doctoral research on the aboriginal movement of Taiwan's aborigines in the years from 1994-1996. At that time, aboriginal intellectuals increasingly referred to traditional Austronesian culture and religions in order to be recognized. This stood in sharp contrast to earlier years of the movement when Christian metaphors were more popular. As Sun Dachuan (2005) remarks in one of his articles on the issue, each action now "required an assertion that the 'ancestor-spirits' were participating and were present, in order to show that the action represented the volition of the whole ethnic group and that it had a sacred and a legitimate foundation". Similar processes could be observed in the countryside, where local politicians applied for state subsidies for traditional rituals embedded into festivities that could increase their individual power and prestige.

During the five years of my participation in the project on indigenous ritual, I was able to revisit Taiwan's tribal regions eight times to carry out fieldwork on these newly enacted and reinvented rituals. In all these months of participating observation, I was fed and housed in dozens of aboriginal homes. I never cease to be amazed and absolutely delighted by the kindness and hospitality shown to me. In addition, an indispensable basis for all my fieldwork was Hualian's Environmental Protection Association. The association, which is primarily led by Han Chinese intellectuals, not only facilitated my access to the intellectual aboriginal circles who were responsible for the new performances in the tribes, but also provided me with information on the rituals' funding and subsidizing measures under the auspices of Taiwan's nation building process. Deeply indebted to Taiwan's endeavors of "community reconstruction", these friends had themselves at that time – in addition to their environmental activities –started to carry out intensive investigations on aboriginal rituals and their potential for creating solidarity.

Another important source of information were Taiwan's Han anthropologists. In long discussions, Xu Muzhu and Hu Taili provided me with important ideas. Not less important were the inspirations from the younger generation of Han anthropologists such as Huang Guochao, who has been researching aborigines' religious activities for almost a decade. A young aboriginal anthropologist I am indebted to is Gariyi Jihong, who introduced me to the more hidden implications of improvisation and contingency in contemporary Taroko ritual.

Several people have been instrumental in allowing this project to be completed. I would especially like to thank Klaus-Peter Koepping and Susanne Weigelin-Schwiedrzik for their encouragement and patience during the final phase of this project. Many theoretical inspirations for this book came from my colleagues within the interdisciplinary research project „The dynamics of ritual". William Sax's valuable ideas on ritual efficiency, for instance, were most supportive. My colleague Bernhard

Leistle helped me to enlarge my theoretical understanding of embodiment and the synaesthetic dimensions in ritual.

Many thanks go to Janelle Ramaley, who looked closely at the final version of the thesis for English style and grammar, correcting both and offering suggestions for improvement.

Finally, I would like to give special thanks to my wife Fatemeh, whose patient love enabled me to complete this work.

Michael Rudolph, September 2007

INTRODUCTION

1. Cultural and political background

When Li Denghui was officially elected president in 1990 and hence reconfirmed in his role as the first Taiwan-born president in Taiwan's history, a profound cultural transformation took place on the island. After four centuries of domination by foreign powers (the Spanish, the Dutch, the Chinese, the Japanese, and the Mainlanders who imposed forty years of martial law in Taiwan after their arrival in the late forties),[1] the issue of the Taiwanese search for identity became a theme of growing significance in the political arena, tolerated at that time as it did not conflict with Li's endeavor to consolidate his power vis-à-vis the Mainlanders who were still represented in the government and in the military. At the same time, there also occurred a re-evaluation of Taiwan's relationship to the communist mainland whose leadership tried to hinder this development with more and more aggressive emphasis on its claim to sovereignty over Taiwan and who once again stressed the cultural and genetic homogeneity of Taiwan's and China's population.[2]

---

[1] After Japan's capitulation in 1945, Chiang Kais-hek's *Chinese National Party* (KMT) with approximately two million Chinese soldiers took over rule of the island. As a reaction to heavy protests from those Han-Chinese population groups that had inhabited the island before the arrival of the Nationalists, martial law was enacted until 1987. In subsequent years, the rising power of native Taiwanese in Taiwan's government led to an increasing pro-independence stance in the island's official policy and to a Taiwanese search for identity (Rudolph 2004a).

[2] Demographically, Hoklo (*Minnanren*) constitute the majority of the island's population (75%). A second group of Han-Chinese who, like the Hoklo, began to settle on Taiwan about 400 years ago are the Hakka (*Kejiaren*) (10%). The third group of Han-Chinese on Taiwan are the so called "Mainlanders" (*Waishengren*), who fled from the mainland with Chiang Kai-shek after 1945 (14%). The only Non-Han on Taiwan are the Aborigines (*Yuanzhumin*), who in 2000 comprised no more than 1.6% of the population. At least twelve different groups of Aborigines with mutually unintelligible languages are distinguished today. Ethnically, they are considered to be Malayo-Polynesians; linguistically, they all belong to the Austronesian language family, which is dispersed throughout the whole Pacific World from Madagascar in the West to the Easter Islands in the East (Rudolph 2003a).

Figure 1: Map of Taiwan with ethnic groups

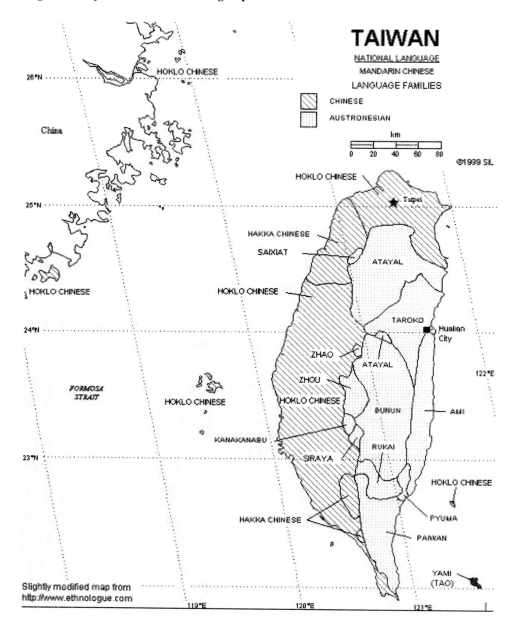

However, even massive intimidation attempts like the missile maneuvers off of Taiwan's coast in 1996 were not able to stop the process of political and cultural reorientation going on in Taiwan. Until the late 1980s, while still claiming the recovery of the mainland that had fallen into the hands of "communist rebels", Taiwan had stressed the position that Taiwan was part of China and that all cultural phenomena on the island represented the "Chinese race". Beginning in the 1990s, however, political leaders propagated the necessity of the establishment of a so called "Taiwanese subjectivity", a concept meant to signal Taiwan's cultural and mental autonomy to the outside world, while supporting the development of a new national consciousness within Taiwan. In order to implement this new policy effectively, institutions were created with the task of examining Taiwanese culture. The history of the island was reinterpreted and schoolbooks were rewritten.[3] All these political modifications were of course also appropriate to make clear that Taiwan's political orientation on fundamental human rights was completely different from that of the mainland.[4] In the following, I will refer to the phenomenon outlined here as "Taiwanese nativism". The term in Chinese is *"Taiwan bentuhua"*, which literally means the "process of Taiwan becoming a homeland". Since the expression is simultaneously used by supporters as well as by opponents of Taiwan's political independence from China, its interpretations range from „Taiwanization endeavours of the Taiwan-

---

[3] The most recent revisions of this kind took place at the end of January 2007. Among the revisions, references to the "mainland" and "our country" were removed and simply replaced with "China". Dr Sun Yat-sen was referred to only by name without previous explanations that he was also the nation's founding father. The revisions were fiercely opposed by those political forces in Taiwan that spoke up against Taiwan's independence (China Times 29.1.2007).

[4] For a discussion of these rather "utilitarian" aims behind the implementation of a multiculturalist policy in Taiwan see Walisi Yougan 1994 and Gao Deyi 1994. In "Development of ethnic relations to a pluralistic entity and aboriginal politics in Taiwan" Gao also names the functions of an adequate aboriginal policy: it served the realization of the equality of nationalities (*minzu*) as provided in the constitution; helped in strengthening Aborigines' loyalty towards the government; assured the healthy development of aboriginal society; strengthened cultural protection and fertilized national culture; raised the international image, and enhanced the peaceful competition with the mainland.

ese in their nativist movement" to "regionalization endeavours in the Chinese province Taiwan". Nevertheless, as I make clear in an earlier work on Taiwan's multi-ethnic society (Rudolph 2003a: 9), it is adequate to consider the ongoing process of "*bentuhua*" as a form of "nativism" or "nativist movement" (*bentuhua yundong*), since it contains the basic characteristics attributed to such movements by leading theorists - that is "the conscious, organized attempt on the part of a society's members to revive or perpetuate selected aspects of its culture" (Linton 1943) as well as the attempt "to construct a more satisfying culture by rapid acceptance of a pattern of multiple innovation" (Wallace 1956).[5] Ostentatiously emphasizing one's own values vis-à-vis those internal and external forces that are deemed as oppressive and imperialist in Taiwan's past and present (Japan, the KMT, as well as Mainland China), one searches for emancipation and autonomy.

The re-negotiation of cultural identities in Taiwan and the construction of a particular history and culture differentiating Taiwan from China also had an impact on Taiwan's indigenous population, that – though consisting of at least twelve Malayo-Polynesian groups – makes up no more than 1,6% of the population of Taiwan. For the first time in the history of interaction between Han and non-Han, the non-Han languages, cultural traditions and value- and moral systems now received growing attention, as they were considered to be the most convincing testimony to Taiwan's "non-Chinese origins".[6] Another reason for the new awareness of these ethnic minorities were the actions and discourses of the small pan-ethnic aboriginal movement (*Taiwan Yuanzhumin shehui yundong*),

---

[5] While Ralph Linton (1943) used the terms nativism and nativistic movements, Wallace (1956) employed the term revitalization movements in his analyses.

[6] Scholars argue that the complete lack of sources about pogroms of the aboriginal population is an indication that Taiwan's Han not only absorbed the cultures but also the genes of those aboriginal groups that were already extinct, i.e., the *Pingpu* peoples (Xie Shizhong 1995). During the nineties, it became increasingly popular to state that "the majority of today's Taiwanese have "Pingpu" genes. People believed that over the past 400 years there had been intermarriage and cultural contact between the Han and "Pingpu" peoples and that few people were exempt from this cultural and biological hybridization process" (Pan Inghai 2000: 85).

a movement that had developed in the mid-eighties as part of the opposition movement against the mainlander regime and that received strong support from intellectual and political Han-elites.[7] Members of different ethnic groups, dressed in colorful traditional costumes, held demonstrations and street performances in which they pointed to the diverse social problems such as girl's prostitution, exploitation of workers, land seizure, ongoing assimilation, as well as the inadequacy of the ethnonym "mountain compatriots" (*shandi tongbao*) – a term that had been used by the government to play down the cultural differences between the island's ethnic groups and that was not changed until 1994 into "Taiwan Aborigines" (*Taiwan Yuanzhumin*). Simultaneously, the activists also fought against such popular terms as "savages" (*fanren*) and "mountain people" (*shandiren*), as well as against the scientific term "high mountain people" (*gaoshanzu*) that had been used by Taiwanese ethnologists and that is still used today by the people on the Chinese mainland when they refer to Taiwan's Aborigines. The demands of the aboriginal movement were presented in manifests written both in Mandarin and in the aboriginal vernaculars and were often additionally emphasized through rituals. Until 1996, most of the demands had been implemented, including the official recognition of Taiwan's Aborigines as indigenous people which was accompanied by the founding of specific cultural institutions.

---

[7] Two years before the *Democratic Progress Party* (DPP) was formed as the first major opposition party in 1986, the *Alliance of Taiwanese Aborigines* (ATA) initiated the aboriginal movement. In its formative years the ATA concentrated on social problems such as child labor, adolescent prostitution, and worker's problems in general, as well as handling individual cases of perceived social injustice. Toward the end of the decade, however, the ATA began to look at issues affecting the indigenous peoples and their continuity as a whole, such as the drive to reclaim their ancestors' lands, the movement for the non-discriminating, pan-ethnic name "Aborigines", or the movement to resume their original family names. Except for a few sporadic demonstrations for ultimate autonomy, the movement stagnated after the establishment of major, ministry-like institutions for Aborigines in 1996. In spite of its high-standing moral claims and standards, the ATA itself was not free from corruption, as studies on the organization reveal (Rudolph 2003a; Hu Defu 2000, Liyijing Yuma 1996).

Due to their role as indexes demonstrating Taiwan's unique culture and history, Taiwan's aboriginal rituals were rediscovered in the 1990s not only by activists, but also by Taiwan's government. After a long period of marginalization and discrimination in the past, these colorful ceremonies were now supported by generous subventions. However, following the suppressive cultural policy of the Japanese Colonial Empire (1895-1945) and the massive assimilation and modernization policy pursued by the *Chinese National Party* (*Guomindang* = KMT) until 1987, the rituals had changed substantially.[8] Furthermore, the religious vacuum that had developed as a consequence of continuing patronization had been filled by Christianity, which after 1945 was extensively propagated in aboriginal society. In some ethnic groups, Christians today make up 90% of the population.[9] Dedicated to monotheism, the Christian churches added the label "superstition" to all traditional indigenous rituals and banned the majority of them. In a study conducted in 1988, anthropologists of the *Academia Sinica* discovered that most types of ritual activities – such as existence or livelihood rites, rites of passage as well as healing rites – had basically disappeared. The only activities that were still pretty much intact were the annual "multifunctional rites of the whole community" (*juluo fuhexing daji*).[10] These, however, were mostly

---

[8] Sun Dachuan (2005) contends that most rituals had died out as early as the end of the Japanese colonial period as a consequence of the intense attempts of the Japanese to subordinate Aborigines to national needs and to integrate them into the modern pecuniary system. Another factor that seems to have accelerated the extinction of rituals at that time was the change in the economic environment and production modes (Hu Taili 2003: 301).

[9] Tung Chunfa (1995: 156ff), who cites a government report from 1991, provides the following data concerning the distribution of religious beliefs in Taiwan's aboriginal society: Protestants 44,43 %, Catholics 32,23%, Buddhists 5,8%, Daoists 4,9%, Atheists 6%. In Taiwan's Han society, only 3-4% of the population are Christians. The rest of the people practice either Taiwanese folk religion (a fusion of Buddhism, Daoism, and Confucianism) or Buddhism.

[10] For this categorization of Taiwan's aboriginal rituals which is based on the sources of Japan's colonial government see Hu Taili (2003: 279-283). Sun (2005) argues that the 1988 research report of Hu and Liu that points to the "continuing" existence of the multifunctional collective rites actually already showed the first results of the Aborigines' awakening, as the situation of Aborigines' rituals before that time had

reduced to mere secular dancing or singing activities that were distanced from traditional religion. In some groups like the Atayal or the Taroko, even this type of ritual had not been handed down.[11] Despite this state of affairs, the government initiative was enthusiastically welcomed by administrative bodies and intellectual elites in aboriginal society and echoed by the claim to represent authentic aboriginal culture or to reproduce it where it had disappeared. Actively supported by governmental bodies, aboriginal rituals in subsequent years gained increasing significance as instruments for the confirmation and legitimation of the cultural and social existence of different aboriginal groups. One of the questions which evolves in the course of the present study is whether the process of cultural reconstruction and retraditionalization observed here in Taiwan's contemporary aboriginal society can itself be referred to as a nativist, revitalist movement in the sense stated above with respect to Taiwanese nativism, or whether it should be regarded as a different phenomenon.

2. Aim of the study

The present study examines the "dynamics" of the contemporary rituals of Taiwanese Aborigines following the change of this people's self-perception in times of Taiwanese nativism. One of the main aims is to scrutinize the efficacy of these rituals within the new religious, socio-cultural, and political context – a context that today is not only impacted by local and national, but also by global influences. Are these rituals mere folkloristic representations of culture, or do they have deeper implications for society and people's identities? Such an examination seems particularly important as no comparable studies have yet been carried out

---

been even more desolate. This, however, could not be proven, no comparable materials from the 1960s and 1970s were available.

[11] Hu Taili 2003; Youlan Duoyou 1995; Youbas Wadan 2005.

in Taiwan.[12] Another aim, however, is to further clarify the role that rituals have regarding the generation, confirmation and transformation of social reality within the context of modernization and globalization processes. Here, special interest is dedicated to the role of ritual in the constitution of socio-cultural identity as well as the performative authentication of political power and social authority.[13]

Subsequent to the introduction of this volume, in which I discuss my theoretical premises, I will analyze the contemporary ritual performances of Taiwanese Aborigines from two perspectives. In Part I, I will examine their role and the discourses connected to them in the wider nativist context, since such contemplation will further illuminate those exigencies of social and political authentication within Han society that helped these rituals to generate their contemporary importance. The examples I give, however, also show quite impressively that these performances, under the circumstances described, sometimes generate effects that – though they may be in tune with the intentions of their initiators – are not always in line with the interests of their supporters. The rituals discussed in this part are mostly performances that explicitly aim at attracting public attention and which are therefore performed either in the big cities inhabited by Han or in the presence of other non-Aborigines. A prominent example is the "pilgrimage" of intellectual Aborigines to Japan in 2005 in order to recover their ancestor souls from the Yasukuni Shrine.

However, the new perception of Taiwan's indigenous peoples and their rituals also has its impacts on the performances held on the local level. In the second part (Part II), I will therefore analyze and compare

---

[12] As for Taiwan's anthropologist's study of aboriginal ritual, the focus has so far been directed to the influence of Christianity (Qiu Yunfang 2004; Huang Guochao 2001; Huang Yinggui 1986, 1992, 2001), and modernity (Hu Taili 2003). Other studies have been made on the influence of tourism and political change on Aborigines' contemporary cultural representations in general (Xie 1992b; 1994a,b,c; Wang Chongshan 2001).

[13] In the following, the term "authentication" denotes the "testification / verification of identity" for the purpose of authorization. For example, societal elites frequently express their identification with certain cultural paradigms in order to enhance the legitimacy of their power(-claims). In this process, they often take up ideals of pure, unchangeable, and unequivocal identities that attract certain groups of supporters.

the contemporary collective rituals of two Austronesian groups in Taiwan, the Taroko and the Ami. In the case of the Taroko – a patri-lineal people in East Taiwan – I will introduce the "ancestor-spirits-rituals" which were revitalized in 1999. These are performances that are integrated into collective yearly festivals and that were not carried out for a long time because they are connected to the former head-hunting religion of the Taroko. Due simply to their problematic background, they caused deep controversies in contemporary Taroko society. These performances, which were constructed according to rituals that are still practiced privately in families, provoked the development of Christian counter-rituals.

In the investigation of the contemporary rituals of the Ami, I also initially focused on the yearly festivals of this ethnic group, the so-called "harvest-festivals". Although these festivals, which usually take several days and which consist of a multitude of different collective rituals (such as ancestor worship, dance rituals, etc.), contain many traditional elements, they are in fact strongly Christianized. Similar to the rituals of other aboriginal groups, they are subject to constant modifications by political elites in the present political climate. And, very much like in the case of the Taroko, nativism also had a "retraditionalizing" influence on some parts of once matri-lineal Ami-society. Here, it enhanced the development of alternative rituals in addition to the official canon, rituals that referred to partly still existing, partly extinguished shamanic traditions. Consequently, the present research does not only analyze the official yearly festivals, but also those ritual performances that developed in the same context and that often embodied the claim of certain social groups to alternative cultural interpretations.

3. Rituals as authenticating practices: Some methodological and theoretical considerations

In his explorations on "Religion and New Taiwanese Identities", Robert P. Weller (2000) gives an example of how ritual serves as a tool for negotiating questions of authenticity and legitimacy in the cross-strait context.[14] He points to the case of community temples in Taiwan that in the early 1990s began to send delegations back to mother temples on the mainland to renew their spiritual authority by taking incense ash back to Taiwan. Superficially, it seems as if this practice recreated the authority of the home temples on the mainland over their Taiwanese descendants, putting the center of authenticity on the mainland and leaving Taiwan as the dependent. In reality, however, the members of these delegations made the trips in order to establish direct ties to the home temple, so that their temple could become independent from intermediate mother temples on Taiwan itself. After their return home, the pilgrims, who usually were the main investors in the mainland temples and their communities, often emphasized that the Taiwanese temples, unlike the mother temples, never broke the stream of incense and actually preserved tradition much better than their mainland counterparts, thus diminishing the authority of the home temples. With such arguments, Weller concludes, the participants in the pilgrimages tried to move the center of authenticity from the mainland back to Taiwan.

In April 2006, the *New York Times* reported a ritual on the other side of the Taiwan Strait in which a similar attempt at authentication was made.[15] On the 5th of that month, a huge crowd assembled at the reputed burial mound of China's first emperor not far away from Xian, one of China's ancient capitals. In a lavish funeral ceremony, leaders from the National People's Congress and top executives from state-controlled Chinese industries joined a Taiwanese opposition leader and 700 invited

---

[14] Weller 2000. When I use "authenticity" in this study, it is predominantly for analytical purposes or in order to mirror discourses in Taiwan. Acknowledging the relationality of identity means assuming the self-definition arrived at by a social group or by an individual at a given moment in time for a temporary synthesis of heterogeneous forces which operate across the boundaries between self and other, inside and outside. In the same sense, "authenticity" must be relational (Köpping, Leistle, Rudolph 2006b: 6f). And, as Clifford (1988) asserts, "if authenticity is relational, there can be no essence except as a political, cultural invention, a local tactic."

[15] Bradsher 2006. The report states that public events had been held at the tomb for the past decade, but that the 2006 ceremony including the big contingent from Taiwan was by far the largest. The author assessed the event as part of the mainland's "charm offensive" toward Taiwan following Taipei's rejection of Beijing's "Trojan pandas" just one week earlier.

businesspeople from Taiwan in paying their respects to Huang Di or the "Yellow Emperor", China's semi-mythical first emperor, who is said to have lived 5,000 years ago. The ceremony took place precisely on Tomb Sweeping Day – one of the most important festivals in Chinese culture in which people traditionally visit the graves of their ancestors. A public holiday in Taiwan and Hong Kong, Tomb Sweeping Day is not a holiday on the mainland, which officially discourages ancestor worship. But Huang Di's legendary role as an ancestor makes it politically easier for Communist officials to bow at his tomb, by somewhat limiting the connotation of ancestor worship. [16] Taiwan's representatives, on the other hand, were expected to rediscover and experience their common cultural roots on mainland China. [17]

The two cases described here may serve as examples for authenticating ritual practices in the broader context of cross-strait cultural and political interaction today. The present study tries to tackle the problem from a narrower perspective and focuses on ritual performances of Taiwan's Aborigines in Taiwan's contemporary nativist setting. The point of departure is the supposition that most rituals publicly performed by Aborigines today amalgamate different levels of meaning. While they articulate and negotiate the identity needs and social exigencies of the respective social group or society (Turner 1969), they simultaneously bear – in the context of the Taiwanese identity search – those often elite-

---

[16] The action was of course highly ambivalent. On one hand, Huang Di is the most popular symbol for the common origin of all Chinese. Since Huang Di is only a symbol, on the other hand, it was easier for the Communist leaders to pay their respects at the tomb. It was, however, even more important for them in this case to occupy the Taiwanese participants on this most important day of ancestor worship with a kowtow in front of the symbol of a common origin, thus preventing the Taiwanese from paying their respects to their own specific ancestors.

[17] Despite their undeniable intermixture with ethnic minorities and foreign peoples that conquered China in the course of Chinese history, all Han-Chinese trace themselves back to Huang Di (2698 B.C.). In Mainland China, the Han ethnic group (one of 55 "nationalities" in China, the other 54 nationalities are ethnic minorities) comprises 93% of the whole population. The Han are made up of many different dialect-groups (official terminology), such as the Cantonese, the Fukianese, the Hakka etc., all of whom have their distinct regional cultures and mutually unintelligible Chinese languages. Different groups of Han-Chinese came to Taiwan as settlers approximately 400 years ago.

dominated mechanisms that are thematized by Hobsbawm and Ranger (1983) or Anderson (1988) in their examinations of processes of cultural invention for the needs of political and cultural entities. In other words, while these rituals may in many cases have efficacy with regard to the constitution of society and identity, they above all serve the authentication exigencies of various elites. In this sense, I will not only examine how social, political and cultural life is influenced by these rituals, but also focus on the cultural and social forces and discourses that have an impact on them.[18] The latter not only include those nativist and traditionalist discourses which are popular today among politicians, cultural workers, and among many members of Taiwan's academic community, but also contending discourses such as those of today's political opposition which pleads for unification with China, or those of representatives and adherents of Christianity in present-day Taiwan.

In addition to analyzing the reinterpretation of text-like organized symbolic contents of meaning that seems to be so characteristic for ritual, the second part of the book in particular will concentrate on the performative construction of meaning by analyzing the iconical significance (performative re-constitution of tradition and "models") and the indexical efficacy (transformation and manifestation of social or political exigencies) of "retraditionalizing" local rituals (Tambiah 1979). The main research methods for the generation of the data analyzed below have been – in addition to participating observation of the rituals themselves – several weeks of qualitative questionairing following the events, a concrete exploration of the political and socio-cultural context and a comparison of the results with the idealtypical practice of the respective rituals as it is described in earlier Japanese and Chinese ethnographic sources.

In the following, I will outline four perspectives which I consider to be crucial for the examination of aboriginal ritual in Taiwan's contempo-

---

[18] My understanding of "discourse" in this context follows Foucault, who defined discourse as an ensemble of utterances and assumptions that produce wisdom which serves the interest of a certain group or class. Stuart Hall points to the fact that Foucault used the concept of "discourse" to avoid the dilemma of having to differentiate between "true and scientific" social discourses und "false and unscientific" ideologies (Hall 1994: 153).

rary nativist context and that will receive special attention in the two main parts of this volume. The first perspective concerns the strategies with which questions of identity and authority are negotiated through ritual. The second one deals with the role of elites in the process of cultural production and the establishment of ritual traditions. The third one looks at how hybridizing and globalizing influences may affect aboriginal performances. Finally, the fourth perspective concerns the question of how authenticating strategies may vary in different aboriginal cultures.

3.1 Vehicles for the negotiation of identity and authority

Inspired by theories derived from the anthropology of performance, this study considers rituals as "transformative practices". Rituals are not only considered as mirrors or as representations of societies, but also as objects and motors of socio-cultural change. In the course of performative practice – in the very moment when structure and event come together – dynamics develop that reorganize social structure and the identity of human beings in a way similar to that which Dell Hymes (1975) described in his epoch-making opus "Breakthrough into performance" or Marshall Sahlins (1981) in his elaborations on the "structure of the conjuncture". As Sahlins remarks:

> Nothing guarantees that the situations encountered in practice will stereotypically follow from the cultural categories by which the circumstances are interpreted and acted upon. Practice, rather, has its own "structure of the conjuncture" – which meaningfully defines the persons and the objects that are parties to it. And these contextual values, if unlike the definitions culturally presupposed, have the capacity of working back on the conventional values (Sahlins 1981: 35).

"Structure", a term referring to culture as a system of behavioral and cognitive orientations, thus can acquire reality (that is: exists) only by way of an enactment as concrete practice.[19] The latter, however, is subjected – and this becomes particularly evident in performance – to the contingencies of the local socio-historic situation as well as to the contingencies of the relationship of actors and audiences (Schieffelin 1996). Simply because of the relationality and intersubjectivity they have in common, performance and human mechanisms of identification are closely related. Performances such as rituals or theatre help individuals as well as groups to see themselves from the perspective of the "other", to mirror themselves in the "other", and to demarcate themselves from him – that is to constitute themselves.[20]

Apart from this identity constituting and identity transforming potential, however, performative practice and particularly ritual are believed to have still another power. Adherents of performance theory emphasize the constitutive and transformative potential for patterns of social organization and authority that rituals have as forums of the negotiation of power positions (Bell 1992; 1997; Butler 1998). Catherine Bell puts it this way:

> "Rituals not only mean something, but also do something, particularly the way they construct and inscribe power relationships" ... "rather than [seeing] ritual as the vehicle for the expression of authority, practice theorists tend to explore how ritual is a vehicle for the construction of relationships of authority and submission."[21]

---

[19] "Structure" I perceive here as a system of behavioral and cognitive orientations that has to do with the respective social group's past. In the present-day meaning of words, categories, and classifications as well as in the structural relations between them, social and cultural history is sedimented and continues to have an influence on the present (Köpping, Leistle, Rudolph 2006: 19f).

[20] Butler 1991.

[21] Bell 1997: 82-83. According to Bell, practice theories see rituals (1) as part of a historical process in which past patterns are not only reproduced, but also reinterpreted or transformed; (2) as processes that not only mean something, but also do something, "particularly the way they construct and inscribe power relationships"; (3) as giving room for individual agency where individuals "acquiesce yet protest, reproduce yet seek to transform their predicament." With this understanding of practice theory, Bell distinguishes herself from Bourdieu (1977, 1987, discussed below) for

The present study will show that the kind of ritual efficacy mentioned here by Bell can also be found in the contemporary rituals of Taiwan's Aborigines. This is in spite of the fact that these rituals are often reconstructions and reinventions whose symbols refer to past traditions and religions and that seem very much detached from present-day Sinisized and Christianized culture and life styles. In the following, I will call these performances that refer to past traditions and religions "retraditionalizing rituals". When in retraditionalizing rituals the past is re-enacted, however, this does not necessarily mean that their denotation is restricted to a mere theatrical representation of the conditions of the former socio-cultural context. It is also possible that such representations, similar to Chinese historical drama (Wagner 1990), allude to themes that have some kind of relevance for the contemporary context. Audiences that have been socialized within this context can easily perceive the connection to certain political or cultural conditions; although, and here lies the special advantage of this modus of representation, this association is not obligatory. When such historical dramas are enacted in the present, they often have "functional indexical uses"; actions and symbols within the drama "point to" circumstances outside of the drama.[22] For instance, they may tell stories of Chinese gods in order to show how a political leader should behave or what might happen to him in the case of continuous immoral leadership.[23] Analogously, we can assume that in the case of retraditionalizing rituals in Taiwan, the respective traditional meanings of a ritual or certain ritual symbols may still be known. Through the ritual's

---

whom practice is merely a realization of behavioral dispositions stored in a group habitus.

[22] In his discussion of the phenomenon of indexicality with respect to ritual, Tambiah distinguishes "semantic and referential meaning" and "functional indexical uses" as two sides of the same coin. He explains: "Thus the value of indexical symbol and indexical icon for us is that they will enable us to appreciate how important parts of a ritual enactment have a symbolic or iconic meaning associated with the cosmological plane of content, and at the same time how those same parts are existentially or indexically related to participants in the ritual, creating, affirming or legitimating their social positions and powers." (Tambiah 1979: 154)

[23] Here, "indexicality" is used in a slightly different sense than Tambiah, who instead focused on participants and social actors who refer to certain cosmological symbols and icons in order to express and enhance their own status and power claims.

performative actualization within the new context, however, it inevitably generates and unfolds new meanings. Hence, we should not restrict ourselves too much to the supposition that retraditionalizing rituals in Taiwan's nativist context merely try to convince people of the cosmological content they represent – even if participants or makers insist that exactly this is the case. Instead, we should recognize that these performances may also deal with contemporary social issues, i.e., a certain attitude of actors and audiences vis-à-vis their past and their culture, a particular status-, power-, or resource- concern of one of the involved or of the group in the contemporary local, national or international context, or a special relationship between different cultural or social groups of the society in question.

Apart from the indexical functions that develop through the integration of traditional models into new frames of reference, however, ritual's indexical functions can also be enhanced through active modification or renovation of traditional models. In his influential article *A Performative Approach to Ritual*, Stanley J. Tambiah (1979), following Grice (1957), points to the phenomenon of conventional and non-conventional implicatures [implicature = what is implicitly meant] being attached to performances by social actors in "ritually involuted" societies.[24] Through the particular emphasis of cosmological symbols caused by repetition, increase in extravagance etc., the understanding of these symbols may be guided in such a way that participants and audiences quite naturally link them to conditions external to ritual.[25] According to Tambiah, the effects of such "conventional implicatures" may further be enhanced by "non-conventional implicatures". Staying in close touch with the already exist-

---

[24] For Tambiah, a "ritually involuted society" is a society in which the "domains of religion, polity, and economy fuse into a single total phenomenon" (Tambiah 1979: 158).

[25] As an example for a "conventional implicature", Tambiah refers to the conventional meanings of the tonsure rite that had to be held on a podium which symbolizing the holy Mount Kailash. The social rank of the person tonsured could be judged from the scale, the magnificence, and the splendor of the rite as well as from the similarity of the podium to the genuine Mount Kailash. According to Tambiah this is a clear indicator for the mutual implication between ritual forms and social privilege (Tambiah 1979: 158).

ing grids of conventional symbolic and indexical meanings, ritual inno-
vators may stretch, modify or even violate particular customs or norms in
order to evoke non-conventional understandings that may help to secure
their own power claims. Tambiah refers to the example of Thailand's
historical King Mongkut (1804-1868). Instead of having the tonsure ritual carried out by his ministers, as prescribed by convention, King
Mongkut, personally and without protection, performed this ritual for his
son in an expensive outdoor ceremony, thereby increasing his own and
his son's reputation. Tambiah benevolently suggests that these agents
were not attempting and are also not viewed as acting to upset the overall framework of customs. In conditions of historical continuity, Tambiah
proposes, "emergent" meanings of this kind are accepted and become
conventional customs in the next round.[26]

In the course of this study, I will refer to a multitude of examples in
which rituals do not generate indexical functions solely through re-
contextualization and conventional implicatures, but also through active
modifications of symbols. What is astonishing in the cases collected and
analyzed by me, however, is the dominating and even monopolizing role
of ethnic elites in matters concerning ritual performances in contemporary aboriginal society. And still another point arouses attention: the allusions and implicatures made in the performances all seem to occur in a
very conscious or, one could say, reflexive manner, evoking the impression that the cosmological contents enacted actually play a less important
role. This seems remarkable in the light of Tambiah's argument that
states that "semantic and referential meaning" and "functional indexical
uses" are actually two sides of the same coin, a duality that "points in two
directions at once – in the semantic direction of cultural presuppositions
and conventional understandings and in the pragmatic direction of the
social and interpersonal context of ritual action, the line-up of the participants and the process by which they establish or infer meanings".[27] Thus,
do we have to realize the possibility that aboriginal ritual has experienced
a thorough qualitative change in today's context of nativism and global-

---

[26] Tambiah 1979: 154-160.
[27] Tambiah 1979: 154.

ization? Is it possible that these rituals are, as Tambiah envisaged in the case of an "ossification" of rituals, instead detached from "whatever semantic meaning they previously had and carry primarily indexical meanings which derive from pragmatic or functional considerations"?[28] In the following section, I will outline why I consider such an understanding of contemporary aboriginal ritual to be partly necessary: even if semantic meanings have not totally vanished, they are today fragmented and ambivalent and therefore function very differently from in the past. This does not mean, however, that these rituals are "ossified" in Tambiah's sense; quite the contrary, they are generally quite new and often have very provocative effects on society. Nor does it mean that they are devoid of (often pre-reflexive) habitual patterns connected to distinctive sociocultural traditions and historical heritages, a point to which I will return at the end of this introduction.

3.2 The role of elites

In his well-known work on ethnicity and nationalism, the political scientist Paul Brass (1991) argues that the survival of ethnic groups does not so much depend on culture, language or religion as such, but rather on the effectiveness of how identity symbols are used by competing elites. He states

> ... ethnic communities are created and transformed by particular elites in modernizing and in post-industrial societies undergoing dramatic social change. The process invariably involves competition and conflict for political power, economic benefits, and social

---

[28] Tambiah was aware that such loss of semantic meaning could happen "during periods of ossification" of rituals: "Cosmological ideas, because they reflect the epistemological and ontological understandings of the particular age in which they originated, and because they are subject to the constraint of remaining accurate and invariant, are condemned to become dated over time and increasingly unable to speak to the minds and hearts of succeeding generations facing change and upheaval (Tambiah 1979: 165).

status between competing elite, class, and leadership both within and among different ethnic categories.[29]

Though elites, according to Brass, often refer to cultural forms in this process, they may fill them with new values and meaning in order to mobilize the members of their particular group. While ethnic leaders can obtain a double-advantage in this process – a deepening of the people's loyalty and trust in their integrity, as well as an improvement of their own political networks – other segments of the society may gain nothing or even be disadvantaged.

With respect to ritual, a very similar evaluation comes from David I. Kertzer (1988). He dismisses the common view that ritual is mainly a religious phenomenon that remains politically significant only in "primitive" small-scale societies since modern societies have presumably separated political affairs from religious life. Instead, he argues that ritual is a ubiquitous part of modern political life. In all political systems, the politically powerful are surrounded by rites that govern their interaction with the public and with each other when they are in the public eye. The modern nation-state has not escaped the need for symbolic representation, but, with its expanded scale and anonymous community, has made its dissemination in ritual all the more imperative. Living in a society that extends well beyond our direct observation, people can relate to the larger political entity only through abstract symbolic means. Since people need to express their social dependence through ritual, political forces that have control over community rites are in a good position to have their authority legitimized. Through such rituals, authority is dramatized and thereby glamorized. This dramatization not only establishes who has authority and who does not; it also defines the degrees of relative authority among the politically influential. Creating a symbol or, more commonly, identifying oneself with a popular symbol, Kertzer argues, can be

---

[29] Brass 1991: 25. For Brass, it is mainly the interaction between the political elites of the central state and the elites of the respective non-dominant ethnic groups, as determined by political and economic factors, which leads to this competition.

a potent means of gaining and keeping power, for the hallmark of power is the construction of reality.[30]

If one looks at the ubiquitous process of cultural reconstruction in contemporary Taiwan, it is widely acknowledged that this development was initiated by ethnic elites at the beginning of the nineties in their endeavor to overthrow old power structures.[31] At that time, closely cooperating elites of the indigenous Taiwanese Han and Malayo-Polynesian Aborigines used cultural discourses of heterogeneity and hybridity in order to undermine the legitimacy of the former Nationalist government that stressed the homogeneity of Taiwan's people with the Chinese and that upheld the claim of reconquering the mainland on the basis of this argument. By the mid-nineties, it became clear that the oppositional movement had been successful, as most of the indigenous Taiwanese Han felt the need to distinguish Taiwan from the mainland, not only culturally and politically, but also economically. Under the claim of bringing about a democratic transformation in a multi-ethnic state, limits and rules were newly determined; newly determined also were the possibilities and the opportunities of the players and the distribution of political and cultural resources, social welfare and compensation and subsidizing measures. In the cultural realm, large sums were invested into the *Plan for Integrated Community Construction* (see Part I Section 3) which was supposed to help Taiwan's different cultural collectives to restore their cultures after several decades of assimilationist cultural politics. However, as only people with the necessary academic competence were able to apply for the resources, cultural development was again largely in the hands of elites, including Han- as well as aboriginal elites.[32]

---

[30] Kertzer 1988: 2-8; 104.

[31] See for instance Chang Mao-kuei (1996), Tien Hung-mao ed. (1996), Tien Hung-mao & Cheng Tun-jen (1997), Bosco (1994).

[32] Rudolph 2003a. Zhang Weiqi 1998: 21f and 136. Zhang criticizes that in today's process of *Integrated Community Construction*, cultural and political resources are totally usurped by elites. A more positive assessment comes from Chan 2006 who states that at least in Taiwan's highly educated Han society, "cultural policymakers, local residents, voluntary cultural workers, intellectuals, elites, entrepreneurs, gov-

Based on the understanding of the dynamics of elites' interaction out-lined above, a major intention of this study is to show how elites' authen-tication strategies not only have a strong impact on Taiwan's aboriginal cultures in general, but also on the contemporary ritual performances of these peoples. In my application of the term "elite", I refer mainly to its use in present-day Taiwan where it is defined very broadly. In general, it comprises all those members of society "who have a certain influence on social, economical, and political processes" (Chen Ruiyun 1990: 29). Thus, it may not only include academics, experts, and politicians, but also all kinds of graduates from technical schools and other kind of col-leges as well as artists and so-called cultural workers, people who initiate or lead projects of cultural protection and reconstruction. A first effort to classify "aboriginal elites" (*Yuanzhumin jingying*) had been made by Taiwan's anthropologist Xie Shizhong (1987a). In 1987, he distinguished between three kinds of elites: (1) The "traditional aboriginal elite" like chiefs and shamans; (2) the "political aboriginal elite", who were loyal to the *Chinese National Party* and only partially coinciding with the tradi-tional elite; and (3) the "intellectual aboriginal elite" that comprised stu-dents and graduates from all kind of colleges and theological institutions, many of whom were at that time organized in the pan-ethnic move-ment.[33] After the beginning of the 1990s, however, political aboriginal elites were no longer necessarily linked to the KMT, but also to the *De-mocratic Progress Party* (DPP) (which until 2000 acted as Taiwan's main political opposition party and since 2000 as the ruling party) and other parties. And as far as the intellectual aboriginal elite was con-cerned, its spectrum was further enriched by the category of the cultural worker (*wenhua gongzuozhe*) who did not necessarily have political, but often economical or ideological ambitions.

---

ernment officials, local leaders and tourists" are all involved in the process of the "nostalgic" restoration of the island's cultures.

[33] Xie 1987a: 75; Xie 1992a: 54.

3.3 Hybridity and its consequences for ritual

In view of the lively cultural exchange Taiwan has experienced over time, it is impossible to perceive cultural developments and phenomena in aboriginal society as isolated. Over the course of the past five centuries, the high degree of attention Taiwan has received from different foreign powers has supported the steady influx of new cultural elements that have been integrated into the local cultures. Growing intra- und international communication, industrialization, democratization, and of course globalization have in recent years further enhanced this influx. Accelerated by increasing electronic mediation, a multiplicity of new concepts is today borrowed from external contexts. In the course of their dissemination through the modern media of mass communication, symbols, pictures, news and ideas get detached from their temporal and spatial dimensions and are free from national or cultural borders. Edwin Ardener (1989) argues that this also includes Western anthropological or political concepts that were once authorized in completely different contexts. In an epistemologically and methodologically confusing way, these concepts today collapse into the space once defined by Western scholars, where they are used as legitimations of persons, actions, and phenomena. In order to understand the strategies of retraditionalization and revitalization that become manifest in contemporary aboriginal rituals in Taiwan, it is therefore necessary to ask about the origin of the paradigms that may have influenced or stimulated a specific arrangement of the performances.

One of the most significant influences on ideas in the last decades has certainly been Christianity. By the beginning of the 1970s, more than 79% of Aborigines had become Protestant or Catholic (Xie 1987a: 34). At that time, even Taiwan's anthropologists expressed worries about the scope of Christianization and warned that a continuation of this situation might eventually lead to cultural confrontations between Han and indigenous people. At a symposium with the title "Studies on the high mountain people in Taiwan: retrospect and future perspectives" (*Gaoshanzu yanjiu huigu yu qianzhan zuotanhui*) held at the Institute of anthropology at *Academia Sinica* in fall 1974, the sociologist Yang Guoshu contended:

If different cultural and racial views are emphasized in the process of missionizing, the identity of the high mountain people (*gaoshanzu*) will become different from that of the majority of the Chinese People. This will be disadvantageous for the assimilation of the *gaoshanzu* to the main culture.[34]

Without any question, Christianity was an important identity shaping force in aboriginal society. Because of its Western origin and its vast distribution, it was considered to be equal or even superior to Han poly-theism,[35] making it an important bastion in times of social and cultural discrimination by Han society.[36] On the other hand, the expansion of Christianity also led, as mentioned above, to the containment of traditional rituals. For this reason, the history of the conversion of the different ethnic groups and the relationship between traditional and Western religion is an important aspect in this study. This relationship not only had a strong impact on the way ritual was arranged and designed, but also on the reactions to ritual innovations.

Furthermore, the nativist traditionalism that became so popular in Taiwan in the 1990s was strongly stimulated by external influences as well.[37] Particularly in circles of ethnic elites, intellectuals were now con-fronted with new culturalist currents and new discourses such as post-colonialism and nationalism, as well as with an increasing variety of po-litical parties and civil society organizations in Han society that had ac-

---

[34] Xie Shizhong 1987b. Even Taiwan's well-known anthropologist Li Yiyuan expressed his worries on this occasion that the expansion of Christianity might be a hindrance to the „integration of the Chinese culture as a whole".

[35] Most of Taiwan's Han are adherents to Taiwanese folk religion (*Taiwan minjian zongjiao*), a fusion of Buddhism, Daoism, and Confucianism with a large pantheon of different gods.

[36] Rubinstein 1991: 259. Rubinstein argues that for paria communities, Christianity and Islam are particularly attractive because they not only give the individual a feeling of moral superiority, but also provide him or her with the impression of belonging to some kind of religious community that treats them as equals.

[37] My understanding of "traditionalism" is not limited to clerical-religious conceptions. In this study, traditionalism is understood as the attempt to revive social structures that have actually already been replaced or at least complemented by new structures.

cess to political and economic resources. In an earlier study on the dynamics of the ethno-political movement of Taiwan's Aborigines (Rudolph 2003a), I showed that the ideology of the leading intellectuals was heavily inspired by Western discourses on culture and ethnicity which they discovered through their close cooperation with Taiwanese anthropologists, Western missionaries, and their contacts with the Fourth World Movement. Enhanced by the reflexivity resulting from this collaboration, many of the discourses and actions of the activists did not directly mirror the premises and categories of the dominant, but were (often subversively) constructed as an antithesis to them, as Roger M. Keesing (1989) stated with regard to intellectual discourses of cultural identity in postcolonial Melanesia and Polynesia.[38] The extent to which the "tendency for globalizing developments through selective, but hybridising incorporation of medially mediated impulses" (Köpping, Leistle, Rudolph 2005: 101) mentioned here also had its impact on aboriginal rituals must be investigated.

In this context, questions of agency and reflexivity become relevant. A focal research interest in ritual studies today is connected to the problem of the extent to which agentive and non-agentive forces (reflexively controlled forces and forces which are inscribed into the habitus) complement each other in ritual. How conscious are ritual actors in the ritual process? Are they autonomous authors of their actions, or are they rather executors of a superimposed program or "structure"? Social scientists are convinced today that the agency and reflexivity of actors can not be perceived as detached from established views and thought patterns. Social behavior is shaped by memory that crystallizes in a cultural repertoire and an embodied knowledge which all members of a collective have more or less in common (Bourdieu 1987; Connerton 1989).[39] Scholars,

---

[38] Keesing (1989: 23) contends that indigenous representations were shaped by colonial domination through "a dialectic in which elements of indigenous culture are selected and valorized (at the levels of both ideology and practice) as *counters to* or *commentaries on* the intrusive colonial culture."

[39] In this study, I refer to Bourdieu's understanding of "habitus". For Bourdieu (1987), the habitus develops in form of a cultural repertoire and a body of knowledge. Earlier experiences coagulate into patterns of cognition, thinking, and action that are

however, have reached no agreement yet in the question of how much room is left for the intentional manipulation of social reality under these conditions. To which degree can people free themselves from a "collective hypnosis" that is supported by social structure? The two major positions discuss whether it is ritual itself which is reflexive (here, agency and reflexivity are perceived to lie in ritual itself), or whether it is rather the reflecting individual who controls the ritual process. Prominent representatives of the first position are Humphrey and Laidlaw (1994) with their volume *The Archetypal Actions of Ritual.* Although they perceive ritual as a "reflective mode of action", as the individual reflects upon the relation between his actual doings and the archetypal act of the ritual, they also contend that there is no real intention in ritual practice. The only intention is to carry the ritual out correctly. Performers have the intention *to* do ritual, but they have no intention *in* doing ritual. Humphrey and Laidlaw even argue that the function of the subject as the author of all its actions is temporarily suspended, the experience of agency being transferred to the cultural prescript. Here, ritual has its own agency, since its dynamics exceed the individual's intention.[40] The advocates of this position, who claim that social reality constitutes itself in ritual, regard rituals where actors obviously intervene into the ritual process with their own constructions with skepticism. They claim that in such "performative" rituals that are – in contrast to the "liturgical" rituals they focus on – enacted for an audience, many actions are not ritualized at all;

---

available as stencils for social action. Members of a common culture, class, or field have a closely related habitus, since their knowledge of action has developed on the foundation of the same objective conditions of existence. These conditions, in turn, are the structure on which the habitus acts back with a stabilizing function.

[40] Bourdieu's (1977; 1987) understanding of habitus and Connerton's (1989) explanations on cultural memory partly support this view. Bourdieu states that that which the individual considers as its own motivations und intentions is in fact only a derivate of dispositions and forms of expression of a collective habitus. And Connerton claims that it is the body that saves and accumulates cultural memory in the form of habitual practices. This means that even experiences and memories that we assume to come from our cognition, are actually part of a more encompassing (mostly preconscious) body of knowledge that is certainly not fully transponable into language.

they are more like theatre, representation, negotiation ... or just politics.[41]

This, however, is the position defended by the second approach – an approach that is strongly inspired by performance theory. If one recognizes that, during ritual, various actors (including non-human actors), worldviews, and interests contingently come together, one can imagine that in the course of such encounters, cognition is intensely stimulated.[42] Ursula Rao (2006) contends that irritations such as conflicts, new developments, unforeseen events, or unintended experiences, provoke reflexions that have a transformative impact on relations, views, and dispositions of acting. Other authors such as Bell, Butler, or Giddens go even further and emphasize the individual's will for conscious creative intervention. Catherine Bell (1992) argues that rituals are forums for negotiation in which the reference to or the adoption of certain symbolic schemata and the inherent cultural meanings is closely connected to the negotiation of social positions of power. And Judith Butler (1998) is concerned with examples of intentional subversion that occurs when existing hierarchical patterns are boycotted by way of performance. Since the boycott or the intentional offence semantically points to the pre-existing status quo and its authorizing context, renegotiations are simply provoked, and structural change becomes possible.[43]

---

[41] Humphrey and Laidlaw hold that performative rituals that stress efficacy in front of an audience are, in contrast to liturgical rituals that have the main concern "Did we do it right"? , only "weakly" ritualized, and therefore neglect them in their analysis. They perceive only liturgical rituals as real rituals, as they are non-intentional, archetypical actions that are held for supernatural institutions (Gaenszle 2000).

[42] See for instance Butler (1991) who argues that the perception of the self is dependent on performances, since it can only constitute itself in and by way of performances.

[43] A prominent example Butler refers to is the black civil rights fighter Rosa Parks, who in the 1960s sat down on a public bus on a seat reserved for white people, a provocation that incited an epoch-making discussion. With such examples and the conclusions she draws, Butler tries to refute Bourdieu's thesis which holds that performative acts can only be successful when they are acted out by authorized actors in authorized contexts. Bourdieu considers the social field to be prestructured and basically devoid of change. For him, the habitus (a practical, embodied knowledge

Butler's examples, however, depict only occurrences in secular, de-mocratic, and multi-culturalist societies that are characterized by plural-ism, where the socio-political context had changed in a way that has made reinterpretations of ritualizations possible and favorable. In this new context, emancipatory voices are no longer ostracized and banished, but rather encouraged and considered to be politically correct. This is also the kind of society Anthony Giddens has in mind when he talks about "post-traditional society". Giddens contends that the reflexive in-spection of tradition under the conditions of modernization and globaliza-tion has entailed a considerable qualitative change in the stance towards ritual, in particular a retreat of the repetitive, the compulsive, the norma-tive, and the belief in authority. Guardians of tradition who proclaimed and embodied *formulaic truth* have now been replaced by the expert, one authority among others who is relied on in a withdrawable *trust* relation-ship. Through abstract systems or "expert systems", the individual in post-traditional society is permanently equipped with information about possible alternatives.[44] Consequently, traditional behavioral patterns and old rituals are freed from the normative restraints of tradition. In Gid-den's words, they become "disembedded". In their collage-like style and with incessant innovations that seem to run counter to documented tradi-tions, contemporary aboriginal rituals often evoke very much the impres-sion that such a disembedment has already taken place on a large scale.

Nevertheless, Giddens also reminds us that there is an interim phase of uncertain duration in which formulaic truth, guardians and compulsive tradition still live on. He remarks:

---

which is a synchronization of a multitude of individual variants) always reproduces the structures from which it stems (Rao 2006).

[44] It is crucial to contemporary society that tradition has been interrogated, problema-tized and undermined to the extent that no social actions can today be carried through solely under the guidance of tradition. Even though we may act from a point of departure in tradition, we are always conscious at some level that it might be done differently. To act in accordance with substantive tradition today, therefore, requires rational justification and a reflexive account of why this is right - that is, it breaks decisively with the form of tradition (Giddens 1994: 62).

When the tie of tradition is loosened and the compulsion to repeat disappears, new opportunities are created for the individual in society, but also risk and the anxiety associated with risk increases, for now decisions have to be made. Thus emancipation from the yoke of tradition is experienced by the subject as a paradoxical vertigo and loss.[45]

This means that, although the conditions of modernization and globalization may support the development of the ability to relativize, the transformation of ritual reflexivity is a gradual process, and not all population groups must be seized by it simultaneously. Because of their higher degree of education and their closer contact with Han and international society, many ethnic elites had distanced themselves faster from binding traditions (including Christianity) than non-elite members of their societies. How does "retraditionalization" as we can observe it in today's nativism and multiculturalism fit into this picture? This study will show that "retraditionalization" in Taiwan only seemingly contradicts "detraditionalization" as described by Giddens. Since, for Giddens, detraditionalization actually does not entail the disappearance of tradition, but rather its reflexive incorporation within modernity (dialogic-discursive and no longer exclusive) or its emergence as a fundamentalism, in opposition to modernity.[46]

3.4 Socio-cultural characteristics of authentication strategies in ritual

Although the reference to „authentic traditions" in Aborigines' contemporary rituals seems to be to a large degree reflexively controlled, we should – keeping in mind the understanding of the dynamic interaction of practice and structure – not neglect the question of to which extent habitual patterns impact these performances as well. As mentioned above, the habitus also comprises the diverse colonial experiences of Aborigines

---

[45] Giddens refers to early modernity in Europe as an example.

[46] Fundamentalism occurs when traditions are defended by traditional means; this is always dogmatism, because tradition relies for its efficacy and authority on the unquestionable status of its premises, which are transmitted as truths through rituals.

that today influence views and behavior on a pre-reflexive level. These experiences and colonial traumata continue to exist in a social group's cultural memory and often express themselves in the form of postcolonial sensibilities, resentments, and ambivalent identifications in people's cultural activities.[47] In the first part of this volume (Part I), I examine this question by analyzing those ritual performances that are enacted by pan-ethnic aboriginal intellectuals for a national or an international audience. In Part II, I will take a closer look at the possible socio-cultural variations of the habitus and its manifestation in contemporary local rituals of the Taroko and the Ami. Here, socio-cultural variations in habitus do not only become apparent in a differing stance towards authority, but also in differences in the choice of authentication strategies, particularly in the way elites of different ethnic groups refer to the available discourses of tradition (autochthonous, Christian, autochthonous / Christian, autochthonous / Chinese etc.) in order to legitimize themselves or their claim for resources. We will see that the strategies in local rituals have certain commonalities with those in the rituals enacted on the supra-local level, especially in respect to the post-colonial consciousness that is expressed here and that has partly reflexive, partly pre-reflexive dimensions.

If we look for the reasons for socio-cultural variations in the local rituals, however, modes of conversion to Christianity become important again. The identification with different Christian denominations has a strong impact on the way rituals are enacted today. In his studies on the conversion experience of another aboriginal group in Taiwan, the Bunun, Huang Yinggui (1992; 2001) argues that this different positioning within Christianity was socio-culturally motivated, as people tended to identify with the particular denomination which had a structure and ideology best fitted to their cultural background. Because of the hierarchical structure of the Catholic church (followers-priest-bishop-Vatican), many Bunun had turned their back on the latter and had converted to the more democratically structured *Presbyterian Church of Taiwan* (PCT), in which each

---

[47] The psychiatrist Frantz Fanon was the first to offer detailed analyses of these psychological processes in "Black skin, white masks" (Fanon 1952) and "The wretched of the earth" (Fanon 1967).

member has more individual voting and partaking rights.[48] These rights
are so extensive that members not only can vote, but can even control the
ministers of their congregations. Similar reasons have led to different
denominational identifications in the cases of the Taroko and the Ami. In
Taroko society today, 70% of the people are followers of Protestantism,
while in Ami society the majority are Catholics. However, difference in
denominational affiliation has not only had direct consequences, resulting
from the churches' differing stances towards ritual, for the respective
cultures and the development of ritual, but also indirect consequences in
the form of political implications. This becomes clear in a statement of
John F. Thorne (1997) who explains that, following the KMT's establishment on Taiwan in 1945,

> many Catholic missionaries arrived, a large number of whom had
> worked and lived on the Mainland for many years and were fluent
> in Chinese languages and were familiar with China and with varie-
> ties of Chinese, mostly Han, culture. Many of these latter were
> virulently anti-communist and were strong supporters of the KMT,
> and they were thus particularly welcomed by the regime. The KMT
> was more suspicious of the *Presbyterian Church* and its primarily-
> Taiwanese membership-base, however, and so curtailed its auton-
> omy, funds, programs and the use of its property, watched its pas-
> tors and monitored their sermons. Thus to Protestant-Catholic ri-
> valry for converts was added several degrees of a political KMT-
> vs.-ethnic-Taiwanese orientational dichotomy.[49]

Last but not least, the ways in which indigenous religious traditions
continue to exist or to exert their influence also have an impact on the

---

[48] Huang Yinggui 1992: 295f; 2001: 35f. In his studies, Huang also points to the case of
   Atayal villages. As modern villages of this ethnic group are compounds of many
   small tribes, these villages are usually characterized by the presence of a multiplicity
   of different denominations.

[49] As we will see in the chapter on the development of ritual under the conditions of
   Taroko Presbyterianism below, Thorne's argument is only accurate with respect to
   the churches' leaderships. Although the PCT's *General Assembly* strongly supported
   the DPP, the presbyters in the rural areas rather supported the KMT.

arrangement, the design and the development of contemporary rituals on the local level. The persistence of indigenous religions, however, largely depends on the room Western religion conceded to the particular culture in the course of the conversion process. Conversion theory distinguishes the pattern of "coexistence" (or "compartmentalization") (Green 1978; Barker 1990; Qiu 2004) from the pattern of the complete "replacement" of the indigenous religion through Christianity as a consequence of holistic change (Kammerer 1990). A third pattern distinguished is syncretism (Abasiattai 1989; Kehoe 1989; Kempf 1992).[50] In the case studies of the Taroko and the Ami presented in Part II, the analyses of the conversion patterns of the respective groups will show why certain styles of representation are more acceptable than others.

---

[50] Kempf (1992) describes a case of replacement due to holistic change in his study on millenarism in Melanesia. Abasiattai's study (1989) on the other hand deals with cases of syncretism. He describes the case of the Nigerian Ibido who adapted Christianity to their traditional religion through the adoption of the Old Testament instead of the New Testament. Qiu (2004) argues that the probability of syncretism rises in cases in which the coexistence of indigenous and Christian religions is not complementary, but competitive.

PART I:

THE NEW ROLE OF ABORIGINES' RITUALS IN TIMES OF CHANGING PARADIGMS

1. Contending definitions of authenticity and
Taiwan's indigenous population

In their introduction to the volume *Syncretism/Anti-Syncretism: The Politics of Religious Synthesis,* Charles Stewart and Rosalind Shaw (1994: 7) give the following explanations concerning the discursive quality of matters as such as authenticity and originality:

> ... 'authenticity' or 'originality' do not necessarily depend on purity. They are claimable as 'uniqueness', and both mixed and pure traditions can be unique. What makes them 'authentic' and valuable is a separate issue, a discursive matter involving power, rhetoric and persuasion. Thus, both putatively pure *and* syncretic traditions can be 'authentic' if people claim that these traditions are unique, and uniquely their (historical) possession. .... Claims of 'authenticity', then, may be disconnected from notions of purity. They depend instead on the political acumen of cultural 'spin doctors' ... who convert given historical particularities and contingencies to valued cultural resources.

If we look at cultural discourses in Taiwan before and after authoritarian rule, we find that Taiwan's people experienced the validity claim of both conceptions distinguished above in very close succession. In the period of authoritarian rule (until 1987) and its aftermath until 1990, ethnic particularities and regional differences were suppressed by the *Chinese National Party* (KMT)-state that proclaimed the ethno-cultural homogeneity of all Chinese in order to gain legitimation to "reconquer the mainland". In that period, cultural authenticity was equated with "purely Chinese", an ideal that the government tried to further reinforce by the promotion of the "Chinese Culture Revitalization movement" (*zhonghua wenhua fuxing yundong).*[1] In the period of thorough Taiwanization[2] and democratization since 1990, however, cultural differences have been fostered and enhanced by the government that now – after a sweeping internal transformation of its "human resources" from Mainlander- to Hoklo-domination – subscribes to building up a multicultural society *vis-à-vis* the mainland and its claims of the ethno-cultural homogeneity of all Chinese. The former discourse of homogeneity has been gradually replaced by a discourse of ethnic heterogeneity and, in order to enhance a feeling of togetherness in the new frame of reference, a discourse of hybridity that points to the mixed ancestry and mixed cultural repertoire of Taiwan's population. Even though the old homogeneity discourse was lived on in Mainland China as well as in parts of Taiwan's Mainlander population, most people in Taiwan from this point on increasingly equated authenticity with "Taiwanese subjectivity" (*Taiwan zhutixing*), an ideal that stands for the uniqueness, the autonomy (or sovereignty) and the self-reflective potential of the Taiwanese and that is to be accomplished with

---

[1] After the May 4th movement of 1919, the KMT was distinguished from anti-traditionalist communists by its traditionalist orientation. In times of authoritarian rule, the KMT's traditionalism was often criticized by Taiwan's political opposition. As a reaction, Chiang Kai-shek in 1960 proclaimed the revitalization of Confucianism and the „Chinese culture revitalization movement", a movement that in times of the Cultural Revolution on the mainland (1966-1976) gained even further momentum. Not only Taiwan's "dialects" (languages that, except for the Aborigines' Austronesian languages, all belonged to the Sino-Tibetan language family), but also all representations of a distinctive Taiwanese culture such as Taiwanese folk religion, Taiwanese opera, or the so called homeland literature that began to develop at the end of the 1960s, were officially banished at that time (Rudolph 2003a; Chang 1994a).

[2] As I pointed out above, Taiwanese nativism (*bentuhua*) can also be translated as "Taiwanization". A "political Taiwanization" (*zhengzhi bentuhua*) – the appointment to government of people from sub-ethnic groups other than the Mainlanders – had actually already started in the early eighties. Since 1990, it was – initiated by mostly native Taiwan politicians as a reaction to the increasing quest of Taiwan's population for political and cultural emancipation from the mainland and Taiwan's Mainlanders – complemented by an ideological and "cultural Taiwanization" which progressively developed into a fully fledged nativism.

the united help of all different ethnic groups on Taiwan in the near future.[3]

In 1996, the newly elected Taipei city mayor, Chen Shuibian, who in 2000 became the first non-KMT president of the ROC (*Republic of China*), held a ritual that was supposed to cement this perception. On March 12, 1996, he announced that the street in front of the president's palace in Taipei – "*Long live Chiang Kai-shek Road*" – had been renamed to "*Ketagalan Boulevard*". The Ketagalan were one of the aboriginal groups in Taiwan that had long before been assimilated into Han society. Members of all aboriginal groups were invited on this day to perform their dances and rituals on "*Ketagalan Boulevard*". In a newspaper article entitled "Should the reason for the "promotion" of the difficult pronounceable street name not yet be clear?" the *China Times* commented on the following day:

> The renaming of the '*Long live Chiang Kai-shek-Street*' into '*Ketagalan Boulevard*' by the Taipei city government in a manner that must have annoyed quite a few people, as well as Chen Shuibian's severe criticism of the opponents as 'supporters of the egoistical cultural superiority thinking of the Han-people / nation', made it clear that the legacy of the KMT was to be abolished. By changing the street name, one could instantly break the authority of the new and old KMT and please socially weak groups such as the Aborigines, which have been neglected by the government for a long time. It further makes clear that if the Taipei city government – at a time when Communist China continuously emphasizes its unshakeable view of 'China's sovereignty over Taiwan' – uses the name of the aboriginal groups of the Taipei basin as street name in front of the President's palace, then the meaning is – on a higher level – to demonstrate the political conviction of the DPP that 'Taiwan is Taiwan and China is China' and to make – for the sake

---

[3] The post-colonial critique of unitary models of subjectivity contends that all such models are based on binary thinking that creates categories like self and other, male and female, first world and third world where the first term is always the privileged term. Rejecting binary models, post-colonial theorists describe both subjectivity as well as experience de-centered and pluralistic (Bhabha 1994).

of its national status – a demarcation from other political influences. After having been renamed, the presidential palace appears in a light symbolizing the 'Taiwanese/Indigenous' (*bentu*) and symbolizing its affiliation to Taiwan.[4]

The event can be seen as a clever attempt of Taiwan's independence movement and the DPP to reinforce Taiwan's authenticity and "subjectivity" against the "Republic-of-China-authenticity" that had been propagated by the KMT during the previous decades. It was supported by hundreds of documents and research records in various media that traced the ancestorship of the Taiwanese back to times when no Han Chinese had yet arrived on the island.[5] After his election as President of Taiwan, Chen Shuibian even founded a Ketagalan Institute in 2003. The motto of the Institute is as follows:

The Ketagalan Institute embodies President Chen's vision of democracy becoming deeply rooted in Taiwan. The name 'Ketagalan' pays tribute to Taiwan's tribal ancestry and recognizes the country's ethnic heritage, while highlighting the diversity of its modern culture — one whose character is interwoven with its indigenous ancestry and the historical remnants of Spanish, Dutch, Japanese, and Chinese influence. Through its advocacy for democratic ideals, the Ketagalan Institute seeks to promote harmony in Taiwan and to integrate Taiwan's voice of democracy with the world.[6]

Apart from ideological considerations, however, there were of course also economical concerns that led Taiwan's national elites to rediscover the island's Austronesian roots. Afraid that Taiwan would become economically too dependant on the PRC, Taiwan's government propagated the so called 'Southward-investment policy' (*nanxiang zhengce*) beginning in the early 1990s, a policy whose main aim it was to make Taiwan

---

[4] China Times 3.3.1996: 14.

[5] See for instance Li Junzhang 1995 who traces back the origins of Taiwan's Austronesian ancestors to 8000 B.C..

[6] The Ketagalan Institute Website. Retrieved on 8.6.2005 from www.ketagalan.org.tw..

more attractive to partners in Southeast Asia and the Pacific World.[7] The most important support for Taiwan's claims of being part of the Pacific World had come from Peter Bellwood, a well-known Australian linguist. In an article in *Scientific American* in July 1991, Bellwood had confirmed an earlier hypothesis that Taiwan was the origin of all peoples of the Austronesian language family (*nandao yuxi minzu*).[8]

Activism, the role of the Church, and Christian symbolism

In this study, I will show how the political paradigm change that slowly started with the lifting of martial law in Taiwan in 1987 also affected the cultural representations as well as the cultural strategies of Taiwan's Aborigines. Although at the beginning of this process, the island's indigenous people had not yet obtained their special status as an important cultural symbol in Taiwan (it took until 1994 for them to be finally recognized as "Aborigines" and as an independent ethnic group), they played an important role in the social movement that aimed at a defeat of mainlander rule on the island. The reason for this engagement was the Aborigines' close alignment with the *Presbyterian Church of Taiwan* (PCT). By the beginning of the 1980s, one third of the PCT's two hundred and ten thousand followers in Taiwan were Aborigines.[9] The PCT

---

[7] Chen Guanxing 1994: 167. Chen analyzes here to what degree cultural discourses supported the government's economic interests in Taiwan in the early 1990s.

[8] Bellwood 1991. Through the application of Bellwood's views, Taiwan not only gained a position as a member, but also a central position in the newly invoked Pacific sphere. The "Austronization" that seized Taiwan beginning in the early 1990s did, of course, not remain unnoticed in the PRC. The new kind of nationalist discourse in Taiwan referring to the hybridity of Taiwan's inhabitants was countered with arguments stressing the Chineseness of Taiwan's Austronesians and tracing back their "racial origins" in Mainland China (Rudolph 2004a).

[9] When the Japanese rulers left the island, they also left a deep spiritual vacuum in aboriginal society. Quite differently from Taiwan's Han, who had never really relinquished their folk religion in spite of compulsory Shintoism after 1938, the animist belief systems of the Aborigines had almost totally crumbled at that time. Thus most of them happily converted to Christianity, which seemed strong and prestigious enough to them to help them in times of uncertainty. Even the more doubtful among

was not only one of the strongest defenders of human rights in Taiwan during the seventies and the eighties, but it also maintained its own powerful organizational network with hospitals and colleges on the island. Many Aborigines received part of their education in PCT-institutions. The influence of the PCT in aboriginal society further increased after the Church's indigenization endeavors in the 1970s and the implementation of the practice of spreading the Gospel in the various aboriginal vernaculars. Therefore, it was only natural that Aborigines also actively took part in the Church's liberation struggle. The *Alliance of Taiwanese Aborigines* (ATA), which in the mid-eighties initiated the aboriginal movement, was largely dependent on the PCT's support; its main leaders came from the PCT network. Michael Stainton (1995), who served as a PCT- missionary from 1981 to 1990, described the Church-dependency of the movement this way:

> Though the ATA seemed to be the main actor to the outside, it only played a minor role as an executor. To the extent that the aboriginal movement had an organization, it was the *Presbyterian Church*, which provided an ideology, a multi-level organizational network [for instance own colleges and hospitals, but also *Urban Rural Mission* training in Japan and Canada], trained and paid workers [both clergy and staff at the national offices] and financial access to the Taiwanese donors and foreign grants through the *World Church Council Program* to combat racism.[10]

As Stainton shows in his master's thesis, *Return our Land: Counterhegemonic Presbyterian Aboriginality in Taiwan*, a major motivating force behind the aboriginal movement's activities was the Church's ideology, which was strongly orientated towards liberation theology. Since the leading members of the aboriginal movement had been trained in

---

them were finally convinced by means of food donations and other sorts of presents. As a consequence, more than 80% of aboriginal society had become Christian by the 1980s, most of them Presbyterian or Roman Catholic, but other denominations were represented as well.

[10] Unpublished statement from personal communication with Stainton in 1998.

Church institutions and Church programs, they were thoroughly influenced by this ideology and conveyed messages linked to it in most of their demonstrations and petition manifests. Prominent examples are those demonstrations that were held from 1987-1989 with the request for the return of the Aborigines' ancestral lands. In these demonstrations, metaphors like "God's chosen people" and "promised land" played a crucial role. With such metaphors, the primordialization of aboriginal land rights, which was otherwise difficult to legitimize, received a philosophical basis. They suggested that it was not a historical coincidence that the Aborigines had owned Taiwan's land, but that it was a legacy from God to the ancestors. The Aborigines had a responsibility towards the land given to them by God for the prosperity of all further generations.[11]

The Church-dependency of the aboriginal movement, but also the use of Christian ideology and metaphors described here faded in the 1990s with the strengthening of culturalist tendencies in the movement, a trend which also becomes visible in the development of ritual revitalization after 1990. After 1990, ancestor-gods and -spirits became much more popular as legitimizing authorities in the activities of aboriginal activists than symbolism connected to a Christian God.

Representation rituals, local rituals, and their audiences

Much of the revival of aboriginal tradition and religion that has occurred in Taiwan since the lifting of martial law has been initiated and guided by young intellectuals who were in one way or another linked to the aboriginal movement. These people, however, hardly ever came from a traditional milieu, but rather had a hybrid cultural background in modern Western, Christian and Chinese education.[12] Furthermore, they had a

---

[11] For a concise description and analysis of Christian metaphors and poster titles in these demonstrations (for instance "Land is life"; "Land: a lost heritage" and "Return our land") see Stainton 1995 and Rudolph 2003a.

[12] Although Taiwan's school system is very much westernized, children in general also get some sort of traditional Chinese education in so far as they have to read and learn the Chinese Classics (for instance the Confucian Analects).

very clear understanding of their political and social possibilities. This gave them the opportunity to separate ritual practices from their original context and transfer them into new political or cultural contexts, thereby causing these practices to have a particular, often impressive efficacy for non-aboriginal audiences. Re-adaptation of ritual elements occurred on a wide range of occasions. We can distinguish rituals whose addressees were mainly Han and to a lesser degree Aborigines, and on the other hand rituals whose audiences were mainly Aborigines and only to a lesser degree Han. In this first part (Part I) where I examine the role and the discourses connected to aboriginal rituals in the wider nativist context, I will mostly deal with the former type, which encompasses activist rituals of resistance, rituals of status representation and pragmatic political rituals. In comparison to the second type of rituals dealt with in Part II, yearly collective rituals that were mainly held in the local areas where they negotiated local concerns, the first type was most often performed in the bigger cities or in places where publicity and media coverage were guaranteed. A common feature of both types, however, is the recourse of aboriginal elites to ancient religions as a tool for self-authentication and particularization vis-à-vis political opponents and rivals.

2. Ritual and resistance before nativism: The Tao example

One of the first examples of the re-adaptation of ritual elements in a political ritual were the so called "Exorcising evil spirits"–actions conducted as a protest against the continued storage of medium-level nuclear waste on Lanyu (also "Orchid Island"), a small island southeast of Taiwan which belongs to the *Republic of China* and which is inhabited by approximately three-thousand indigenous Tao. [13] As the Tao's actions

---

[13] The population of the "Tao" of Lanyu – an ethnic group that until 1996 was officially called "Yami"– no longer exceeds 3100 individuals. After retrocession, the island was used as a prison. In the 1960s, Taiwan's government chopped down what was

started immediately after the lifting of martial law in a period when the PCTs influence on the social movement was still very strong, the integration of traditional religious elements in the protests still occurred in a rather careful and modest way, trying not to challenge the monotheistic ideal of the PCT.

At the beginning of the 1980s, the government-owned utility, *Tai Power Corporation,* had built what was said to be "a fish cannery" on Lanyu with its own port facilities. No one opposed the dump until 1987 when Guan Xiaorong, a well-known Han-photographer and social critic, went to the small island and spent a year there.[14] Living in close contact with the people, he also informed them about the dangers of the waste storage facility and the harmful effects of nuclear waste on human life. While most young people were easily persuaded by Guan's arguments, it was difficult to work against the more conservative positions of the older people, who did not understand his reasoning and who were afraid to openly confront the government.[15] However being told that the barrels regularly shipped to the island contained "evil spirits" and that the increasing rate of cancer among the elderly at that time was caused by these invaders eventually convinced them to join the protests.[16] "Evil spirits", or *"anito"* as they were called in the Tao- language, originally were the spirits of the ancestors which could inflict damage on the afterworld if not properly handled. Traditionally, there were numerous ways to scare away or exorcise *anito*, for instance by using spears or by making appalling gestures. In recent years, however, a new type of exorcism service has come to Lanyu - practices that have been greatly inspired by Christianity, in which *anito* today is translated as "Satan". In an anthro-

---

left of Lanyu's tropical rain forest. At the same time, the Tao were obliged to leave their traditional houses, which were subterranean, and had to move into modern cement houses. As the latter were built with sea sand, they were affected by severe erosion by the 1990s (Guan Xiaorong 1992).

[14] Guan Xiaorong worked as photographer for Renjian. Chief editor of this social-critical journal (1985-1989) was Chen Yingzhen, a neo-marxist intellectual. Chen and Guan are both Mainlanders.

[15] Guan Xiaorong 1992: 8ff.

[16] Guan Xiaorong 2000. Huang Meiying 1995.

pological account of the change of Tao-identity in the last decades, we
learn the following about the new understanding of *anito*:

> The exorcism service is performed by members of the *Presbyterian
> Church*; they invoke the power of Jesus to cast Satan and his min-
> ions out of the possessed (in the style of Jesus' Gospel exorcisms).
> (…) In the Presbyterian ceremony, it is not spirits of the dead that
> are being cast out of the possessed, but Satan's minions.[17]

**Figure 2: Tao performing "Exorcising evil spirits"-ritual. Left side: Traditional ritual
(Photo from Renjian Magazine No. 36, 10/1988). Right side: Protest in Taiwan's parliament
1995 (Photo taken from video tape provided by Huang Guochao).**

On February 20, 1988, only months after the lifting of martial law in
Taiwan, the first "Exorcise the evil spirits" -action (*quzhu e'ling*) took
place on Orchid Island. Led by young pastors of the *Presbyterian
Church*, large groups of people in traditional armour and equipped with
protest banners and large puppets that represented the "evil spirits" left
their villages and gathered near the nuclear waste dump, where they performed the ritual that had once only been conducted in connection with

---

[17] Limond 2002: 11.

the warding off of evil ancestors spirits. Similar processions on Lanyu were held in 1989 and 1991.

Even more impressive for the Taiwanese public, however, were those protests and demonstrations that were held in Taipei in front of the *Tai-power* building and the Taiwanese Parliament, many of them together with the *Alliance of Taiwan Aborigines* (ATA), the *Presbyterian Church of Taiwan* (PCT) and Taiwanese anti-nuclear activists, who assisted the Tao not only in their street protests, but also in personal appeals to the legislature.[18] The most attention was received by an action staged in 1995 by the Tao elders at Taiwan's parliament. On June 19, 1995, thirty-six elderly Tao-men in traditional armour appeared in front of the parliament where they were received by a number of well known politicians from the oppositional movement of that time. In a moving ceremony, they stepped into the building and held a long press conference on the dangers of nuclear waste on Lanyu. Again and again, the elderly emphasized their opposition to the continued dumping of waste and claimed that if the government again ignored their demands, they would resort to their traditional warfare practices in order to fight the Han government.[19] The accusations and threats made by two young Tao ministers were emphasized by traditional chants and the typical gestures that were used to exorcise evil spirits – menacing grimaces, strained neck muscles, strained arms and clenched fists. The performance was so impressive that the chair of the press conference, a female Han-politician from the DPP, was overwhelmed, broke out into tears and was temporarily not able to continue with the program.

In the protests described, the young people claimed to have mobilized the older people by referring to traditional concepts. If one investigates the issue more deeply, however, it soon becomes evident that the elder's acceptance of the explanation that barrels shipped in from abroad contained invading *anito* was rather the result of an amalgamation of traditional and Christian beliefs. *Anito* in this case were obviously not equated

---

[18] For many years Tao youth were at the forefront of the anti-nuclear movement. (Arrigo 2002).

[19] Wei Yijun 1997: 29f; Video tape of the press conference on 19.6.1995.

with one's own ancestors, but rather with the devil. The extent to which traditional and Christian convictions are in fact synthesized in the Tao's cosmology today, is also pointed out by Andrew Limond, the author of the anthropological report on Tao-identity cited above:

> After questioning several members of the congregation, it became clear that since exorcism terminology is so similar in traditional and in Christian ceremonies, many people (who have not received a theological education) mix up Lanyu's traditions with Christian ideology. Thus in some respects, Christianity is seen as an extension of traditional beliefs.[20]

The blurriness of religious convictions referred to here – one of the consequences of recombination and reintegration of the many often contradicting data inscribed in the complex palimpsest of contemporary aboriginal identity – will be a key theme in the subsequent chapters. In many of the cases described by me, religious ambiguity is linked to a phenomenon which is widespread throughout the global dispersal of Christianity, i.e., the unintended syncretism through translation. In their attempt to assimilate local meanings in their translation, missionaries identified the local spirits with "the devil", thereby causing an, albeit deformed and negatively connotated, continuity of past concepts.[21] Remarkable in the case of the missionaries in the Tao case, however, was not only that these missionaries were indigenous Tao themselves, but that they were able to apply their own creation in such a way that it fitted into the contemporary political agenda. In spite of profound Christianization (with respect to the

---

[20] Limond 2002: 12.

[21] As Birgit Meyers (1994: 63) remarks in her study on a very similar dynamic in the evangelization process among the Ewe in Ghana, it was this specific kind of diabolization which caused the spiritual beings of the old religion to become part of Protestantism: "God's dark counterpart, who stands for the shadowy side of Christian belief which is open for fantasy and speculation, is the intermediary between the missionaries' variant of Protestantism and the pre-Christian Ewe religion. Through him, the old could be integrated into the new, and together with vernacularization this makes for the peculiarity of Ewe Protestantism."

belief system as well as to the actions themselves), the Tao had made themselves convincingly appear to be attached to traditional beliefs following a different logic than that of the Han.

The way that ritual and resistance are linked in the case of the Tao strongly recalls the results in Jean Comaroff's (1985) study of the Zionist movement among the Tshidi in the South Africa-Botswana borderland. Comaroff argues that the Zionist synthesis of Tshidi tradition and Christian rites of healing is not a passive accommodation of colonialism but rather a set of highly coded efforts to control key symbols and defy the hegemonic order of colonialism. In Zionism, Christian messages are adopted but given new meaning through a re-contextualization that connects them to meanings in traditional Tshidi religion. Thereby the Zionist Church incorporates a source of power associated with the dominant and transforms it into a tool for the transformation of the condition of the subaltern group. Comaroff considers re-interpretation to be an effective tool in the struggle for human liberation, because it effectively re-shapes the consciousness of the oppressed and re-creates their self-respect. "Ritual provides an appropriate medium through which the values of a contradictory world may be addressed and manipulated", she notes.[22] In her view, the ability to address and to manipulate these values is the power to define what is real and to shape how people behave.

It was this very power of ritual that aboriginal elites gradually discovered in the interim period between the lifting of martial law and the beginning of democratization in 1990. And although the aboriginal movement of that time was only loosely linked to the movement of the Tao, it was the Tao example that gave way to this realization. The success of the Tao made the young intellectuals realize that a paramount technique for guaranteeing efficacy for aboriginal representation in Taiwanese society was to allude to aboriginal religious traditions, an aspect of these traditions that could best be illustrated in ritual performance. Efficacy ap-

---

[22] Comaroff 1985: 196. "Ritual", Comaroff contends here "is a struggle for the sign". For a discussion see also Bell 1997: 79.

peared to be at least twofold: [23] On one hand side, the allusion to religion seemed to impress Han-Taiwanese, because they could now compare the Aborigines' predicament to their own situation. (Indeed, many people now felt "pity" with the Aborigines who were so different in their cultural modes and whom nobody allowed to live according to their cultural particularities. It became increasingly popular to speak of "guilt feelings" towards Aborigines.) Although the ritualized actions did not manage to provoke an immediate reaction from the government, [24] they led to an increase in emotional support from the oppositional movement, whose members were themselves fighting for the recognition of an alternative identity and world view. The first "Exorcising evil spirits" –actions occurred at a time when consciousness about the ecological limitations of one's own life world and a general thoughtfulness about alternative cultural possibilities, wisdoms and cosmologies were just beginning to blossom in Taiwan's Han-dominated society. As mentioned above, this new awareness also led to the close alliance of Taiwan's anti-nuclear power movement with the Tao's movement.

On the other hand, the performances and the positive feedback from the Han society had direct effects on aboriginal identity. One effect was that the elders who participated in the actions suddenly recognized that the police no longer interfered the way they had done before the lifting of martial law, when demonstrations by political activists had often been broken up violently using batons. This change caused them to act with an increased self-consciousness and courage. [25] Another even more important effect, however, was that the actions supported the re-establishment of a

---

[23] A third sense in which the performances were efficacious was with respect to elite's careers. The success of the pastors in the Tao's mobilization contributed to their influence both on Lanyu and in the *Presbyterian Church of Taiwan* in general. In 1998, one of the pastors, Guo Jianping, was elected as County Councillor, a success that had only been made possible with the help of the PCT, which strongly encouraged members of its congregation to vote for the Church's preferred choice of candidate in island elections (Limond 2002: 14).

[24] The Tao had to wait until the mid-nineties for Taiwan's government to finally make concessions concerning the nuclear waste problem: Nuclear waste is no longer shipped to Lanyu.

[25] Lin Jianxiang 15.4.1996, personal interview.

distinct Tao identity. They not only led to the coming together of old and young people in a unified christianized Tao identity vis-à-vis Taiwan's Han and Taiwan's globalizing economy, but also enhanced the formation of a new confidence of Aborigines regarding their (albeit altered) cultural and religious traditions. The latter especially had been subject to severe discrimination for decades. During the 1980s, the legend of Wu Feng was the most well-known symbol of the civil inferiority and backwardness of Taiwanese Aborigines. The legend, which formed a chapter in Taiwan's school books, told of the honorable death of a Han Chinese who, loyal to his Confucian principles, had dedicated himself to the task of moral improvement (*ganhua*) among the Aborigines. To protect his Han compatriots, he finally sacrificed himself as a prey to the head-hunters. Studies of Taiwanese ethnologists show that although the legend already existed in Taiwan during the Qing dynasty (1683-1895), it was first propagated extensively in the period of Japanese colonial rule, during which Wu Feng was reinterpreted as a symbol of martyrdom and as "Christ of the East". After 1945, Chiang Kai-shek ordered the legend to be part of the curriculum in elementary schools, and a memorial statue with an inscription in honour of the martyr was built in Jiayi.

It was the anthropologist Chen Qinan, later vice-head of the *Council for Cultural Affairs* (CCA), who in 1980 first expressed doubts about the verifiability as well as of the adequateness of the story reprinted in schoolbooks. This initiated a hot debate, in which not only anthropologists but also members of the opposition, the *Presbyterian Church of Taiwan* (PCT) and the *Alliance of Taiwanese Aborigines* (ATA) were to take part. Most severely criticized was the representation of Aborigines as 'raw, wild and morally rotten', as was suggested in the legend through its emphasis on their indulging in head-hunting and the mean murder of the noble-minded Confucian Wu Feng. When protests did not cease, the story was taken out of the schoolbooks in 1988; in the same year, the Wu Feng memorial statue in Jiayi was torn down and smashed by a group of aboriginal activists. The attending police did not interfere in this happening that was again led and organized be the PCT. Subsequently, it was regarded as more or less politically incorrect to mention head-hunting in relation to Aborigines, and even anthropologists seldom referred to it.[26]

After all, there were clear signs that a major change in Han attitudes to aboriginal religious traditions and to Aborigines in general was taking place; a change that not only had its implications for Aborigines' self-esteem, but also for performances staged by the members of the aboriginal movement. Before I deal with this aspect, however, I will first describe some of the main features of political transformation in Taiwan in the 1990s and show how they affected the development of aboriginal rituals in general.

3. Taiwanese multiculturalism and its impacts on aboriginal rituals

The "ethnification" of Taiwan's society as an integrating measure

At the end of the eighties, the Mainlanders' influence on Taiwan's military and the KMT steadily decreased – a phenomenon that had mainly biological causes as intermarriage between mainlander Han and Taiwanese Han was still rare and there were not enough qualified second generation Mainlanders to replace their elders.[27] Simultaneously, an increasing "ethnification" of the island's population was observed. After it

---

[26] In an article on "multicultural education in Taiwan's elementary schools", ethnologist Wu Tiantai asserts that fights and disagreements between Taiwan's different peoples (for example, the debates surrounding the Wu Feng story) should best not be no longer mentioned in the curricula for multicultural education in order to avoid the generation of negative stereotypes (Wu Tiantai 1993).

[27] By the late 1980s, 70% of the KMT membership of 2.4 million was Taiwanese, and by 1993 the very highest posts in the government were filled by Taiwanese, including that of President (Li Denghui), Premier (Lian Zhan), and President of the Judicial Yuan (Congress) (Lin Yanggang) (Song Xiaokun 2002). While this process of co-option from sub-ethnic groups other than the Mainlanders is often called political Taiwanization, cultural Taiwanization started in 1990 with the election of Li Denghui as president.

was legalized in 1989, the opposition DPP had to find a way to appeal to those groups in Taiwan who were different in language, culture, social needs and problems and for whom a direct identification with the Hoklo and their understanding of national identity was difficult. Not only Hakka, but also members of the aboriginal groups were afraid that a sudden seizure of power of those people who called themselves "Taiwanese" would only bring about another period of suppression and domination. In order to convince these groups of the common nationalist project and to win their votes, the DPP introduced the concept of "Taiwan's four great ethnic groups" (*Taiwan si da zuqun*) in 1989.[28] This concept not only emphasized cultural differences, differences in experience and the particularities of the different cultural groups with equal rights in Taiwan, but also pointed to a multitude of commonalties especially in terms of historical experience. Besides its integrating function, however, the concept of "Taiwan's four great ethnic groups" was also useful for contradicting the former KMT definition, according to which Taiwan's populace was entirely made up of members of the "Chinese nation" or "Chinese people" (*zhonghua minzu*) distinguished only by different "provincial origins" (*shengji*).[29] Although three of these "four great ethnic

---

[28] see Rudolph 2004a where I describe how Taiwan's ethnologists and oppositional Han-intellectuals created, at the end of the eighties, the Chinese term "*zuqun*" as a direct translation of the English term "ethnic group", a term which implied a group's distinct descent. In a second step, all groups that had formerly been termed "dialect groups" such as the Hoklo, Hakka, and Aborigines were retermed into "ethnic groups", emphasizing that members of each of the groups spoke different and mutually unintelligible languages. In order not to exclude Taiwan's mainlanders, they also received the label "ethnic group". The concept of "Taiwan's four ethnic groups" from now on formed a contrast to the former concept "Chinese race / nation" (*zhonghua minzu*) which is still used on the mainland today and which implies the common descent of all the category's members.

[29] see Zhang 1993, 1996a; Chang 1994; 1996. Until 1991, the origin either from one of the mainland provinces or from "Taiwan province" was still typed in the identity cards of Taiwanese citizens. This definition suggested that all people on the island were members of the Chinese race / nation (*zhonghua minzu*) or "Children and grandchildren of the [common ancestor of all Chinese, the] Yellow Emperor" (*Yanhuang zisun*), as the propaganda machine of the state often emphasized. After 1991,

groups" were undeniably of Han-origin, the fourth group, which comprised the island's Austronesians, had a completely different linguistic and socio-cultural background.[30] As a result, the new definition was apt to suggest ethnocultural differences between all of these four "ethnic" groups and consequently also between them and the "Chinese people".

Solidarization of the members of Taiwan's life community through encouragement for active participation in local cultural life

Because the discourse referring to the "four great ethnic groups" was suitable for strengthening the position of Taiwan's Han in general, it soon spread beyond the political opposition. It even received increasing approval within the mainstream-wing of the KMT-government around Li Denghui in the early 1990s.,[31] Leaders in the KMT-government as well as the DPP were aware that at a time when the homogenizing national frame of the "Chinese nation/people" imported by the Mainlanders was being undermined with all its symbols, another solidarity-endowing political concept that would keep the people of Taiwan together and that would encourage them to form a new "nation/people" was desirable. A concept that seemed capable of uniting the "four ethnic groups" (and that was less provocative than the direct verbalization of a Taiwanese na-

---

    however, a new regulation was introduced according to which only the birth place was mentioned in the identity cards.

[30] Actually, all of the four groups can be further divided into subgroups or smaller ethnic groups. In 2005, 12 distinct aboriginal ethnic groups were distinguished in Taiwan. As far as Taiwan's Mainlanders are concerned, they also originate from a multitude of different regions on the Chinese mainland with – and this also pertains to the Hoko- and Hakka-groups on Taiwan – mutually unintelligible Chinese languages (categorized as "dialects" by the Communist state).

[31] In the course of the formation of the *New China Party* in 1993, it became evident that even Taiwan's second- and third generation Mainlander-Han, who had developed an increasing "consciousness of crisis" (*weiji yyishi*) in the years following Li Denghui's election, had largely accepted the new categorization. In order to be elected, they called themselves "the party that represented the interests of the "Mainlanders ethnic group" (*waishengren zuqun*)" (Zhang Maogui 1996).

tion/people (*Taiwan minzu*)) was "Taiwan's fate-community" (*Taiwan mingyun gongtongti*) or "Taiwan's life-community" (*Taiwan shengming gongtongti*).[32] A couple of Li Denghui's additional directives and slogans in 1993 and 1994 furthered this trend and intensified the impression that now even the official side appealed to Taiwan's inhabitants to form an autonomous national community with an autonomous national identity. Notably, the emphasis on the necessity of a "Management of Great Taiwan and the Construction of a New Centre of Chinese Culture" (*jingying da Taiwan, jianli xin zhongyuan*) or the appeal to form a "New Taiwanese" seemed to leave no doubt about Li's real intention. At the same time, there were changes in the official cultural politics to provide the infrastructure foundation for such a development. Statements made by the minister of the interior and the education minister in 1993 indicated that the KMT wanted to compensate for its mistakes in the past and that it was now not only willing to recognize Taiwan's multi-culturality, but that it also wanted to offer opportunities for the further development of the different cultures and languages in Taiwan.[33] Specialists were appointed to work out specific school curricula for Hoklo- and Hakka-

---

[32] Shortly after the first term's creation by the opposition party in 1990, it was taken up by President Li Denghui, modified slightly as "Taiwan's life-community".

[33] By the beginning of the 1990s, not only politicians from the opposition party, but also governmental institutions such as the *Council for Cultural Affairs* referred more and more often to Taiwanese society as a "multicultural society" (*duoyuan wenhua shehui*). The new self-description "multicultural" not only added a new dimension to Taiwan's democratization discourse, but also caused an inherent dilemma of democratic systems, i.e., the precarious dialectic of "universalism" and "particularism", to become even more salient. It now had to be asked to what extent the claim of equal rights, equal respect and non-discrimination could be satisfied by a politics of "recognition of universal human dignity", or whether cultural difference should be recognized to a much larger degree than before in order to give non-mainstream members of the "life-community" in Taiwan the feeling of a more respected existence. Under such circumstances, their "cultural difference" would be taken as the basis for a differential practice. They would be guaranteed certain rights and authorities which did not apply to other Taiwanese, and, as multiculturalism in its deepest sense also suggested, attention would be paid to those interests which aimed at the cultural survival of a group and the generation of further members.

speakers as well as for the different aboriginal groups.[34] New five-year-plans were set up to meet the particular educational needs of different ethnic groups. In 1994 the government even proclaimed a plan for the implementation of elementary and junior school education in preferential zones, which was supposed to counteract disparities in education between rural and urban areas by means of "active reverse discrimination". The "recognition of difference" was however not limited to the field of education. Important concessions were also made in general policy, for instance, concerning the recognition of the self-chosen name of the Aborigines, *Yuanzhumin*, in 1994, the right for rehabilitation of traditional first and last names in 1995, and the establishment of *Aboriginal Affairs Committees*. Such committees were established not only in the two metropoles Taipei and Gaoxiong, but by late 1996 also on the central level with representatives of twelve different ethnic groups, including the Peipohuan (*pingpu*) who had been gradually reappearing since the beginning of the nineties.[35] Furthermore, long-term projects were established such as the *"Plan for [re]construction of the local communities"* (*shequ jianshe jihua*) which in 1995 was continued as the *Plan for Integrated Community Construction* (*shequ zongti yingzao jihua*). The most important aim of this plan was to 'diminish the negative results of industrialization, cultural homogenization and over-emphasis on individual development and lead people back to a feeling of responsibility towards their fellow-citizens and their community'. However, the politicians believed that the latter would not be attainable without the individual's re-identification with the surrounding local culture.[36] As ethnologist Chen Qinan, who in 1992 became vice president of the *Council for Cultural Affairs,* declared, "only through participation in cultural activities in one's own community could civil consciousness and responsibility be

---

[34] First efforts to implement multicultural education could be discerned in 1990/91. At that time, the DPP began to introduce lessons in the different Taiwanese vernacular languages in schools of all counties ruled by the opposition party.

[35] In the early 1990s, already influenced by claims for multiculturalism, the movement of the so-called *"Pingpu"* (i.e., those aboriginal groups, who were thought to have been assimilated since the early years of the 20th century) came into existence.

[36] Council for Cultural Affairs 1995.

developed and finally be adapted to a national level".[37] The government thus offered funds and resources to encourage all communities in Taiwan – ethnic, rural and urban communities, most of which were either Hoklo, Hakka or Aboriginal – to participate actively in local cultural life, to organize rites and festivals, and to engage in the preservation of local culture and the collection of oral history.[38] In these endeavors, however, aboriginal cultural representations played a rather unique role and were thus particularly fostered.[39]

The Aborigines' function as nutrient, fertilizer and stimulus for Taiwanese culture

With the of rise of Taiwanese nativism in the 1990s, the Aborigines' image had gradually shifted from that of a pitied minority to that of a societal group symbolizing Taiwan's uniqueness in terms of the island's historical, cultural, demographical and political development. The new role and status that was now given to Aborigines with respect to the construction of a distinct Taiwanese culture versus Chinese culture is illustrated by a commentary of Wu Micha, a member of the *Taiwan Association of University Professors* (TAUP), in a publication of this association that actively supported Taiwan's independence in the early nineties. Pondering the question of how the island could wholly free itself from internal and external colonialism, Wu states that the reconstruction of an own

---

[37] Chen Hua 1998: 3f.

[38] Chen Hua 1998; Council for Cultural Affairs 1995. Lacking other symbols for identification - such as a Taiwanese nation, a homogeneous China, or an anti-Communist ideology - the reorganization of Taiwanese society along regional and cultural identificatory symbols appeared to be an adequate method to prevent society from further disintegrating. Thus, it does not surprise that the initiative against an 'orientation- and identity-vacuum' coincides exactly with the period of time in which Taiwan first relinquished its claim to recover the mainland (in 1992) as well as its claim to be the sole representative of China (in 1994 by emphasizing that countries which had established diplomatic ties to China were welcome to establish diplomatic ties with Taiwan as well).

[39] Republic of China Association for Cultural Development of Taiwan's Aboriginal Peoples 1994: 55ff.

national culture by putting oneself into antithesis to one's oppressors – a method that had been successfully applied by post-colonial nations like India – was difficult in Taiwan, as many of the island's cultural symbols were identical with those in the various provinces of Taiwan's main oppressor China (Wu points to examples of the Taiwanese puppet show or the Taiwanese opera that have very similar counterparts in South China).[40] For this reason, Wu pleads for the valorization of "Taiwan's Aborigines as a nutrient" (*Yuanzhumin de yangfen*) – only by stronger emphasis on this "nutrient", could the differences between Taiwan and China be made more clearly discernable.[41] Other Han intellectuals also pointed to the stimulating effects, the chances and the opportunities inherent in the different value systems of Aborigines. In his article "The hunter of Chinese characters in the forest of Han rascals", the social critic Fu Dawei (1993) emphasizes the subversive potential of aboriginal discourse in Taiwanese literature and its helpfulness for the development of an overarching Taiwanese subjectivity vis-à-vis a Hoklo-dominated perspective:

> Crucial are perhaps those effects of irony, challenge, subversion and seduction that this writing culture can generate when it succeeds to enter, settle and develop within the writing culture of the

---

[40] Wu's skepticism also included the culture of Taiwan's Hakka, a South-Chinese minority that had been discriminated against by other Han-Chinese over a long period and who also asked to be more respected in their particularities. In a well organized "Return our mother-language" movement (*huan wo muyu yundong*) in 1988, representatives of this group argued that they spoke their own Chinese language and that their ancestors had immigrated to Taiwan at least as early as Taiwan's Hoklo. Actually, their culture was even closer to the centre of the 5000- year-old Chinese culture (*zhongyuan*) than the culture of most other Han, a fact that should cause Hakka culture to be revered and respected as much as Hoklo culture. What the members of the Hakka movement failed to realize was that this very "closeness to the '*zhongyuan*'" they appealed to had lost much of its former attractiveness by the end of the 1980s; accordingly, their movement did not get much support from the Hoklo.

[41] Wu Micha 1994: 119, in "Taiwan nationalism". Other authors in this volume that has been edited by the Taiwan Association of University Professors (TAUP) in 1994 express very similar convictions.

bailang (Han rascals).[42] (...) Wouldn't it be possible that the latent explosive potential which is inherent to the grammatical displacements and subversions undertaken by the "character-hunter" of the Atayal can evoke a new politics, a new history and even a new geography within the language and the scripture of the *bailang*?[43]

As Fu Dawei further makes clear, the manifestation of the "subversive" power of Aborigines was particularly necessary in times of growing influence of Taiwan's Hoklo and the rising danger of some sort of new hegemony that could evolve in the course of a redefinition of Taiwanese culture and the accompanying reallocation of power and resources. Such a development was believed to have very negative implications for Taiwan's nation building process as a whole and was therefore devotedly discussed by many other Han intellectuals of that time. It was argued that, in the case of Hoklo hegemony, there would be a high risk that Han-centered and Han-chauvinist value-orientations would continue to exist unaltered, and different groups in society might again be culturally, politically and economically suppressed or discriminated against because of their cultural or physical differences. The project of the liberalization of Taiwanese society would then be bound to fail, because, within Taiwan, suppression still prevailed, and Taiwan would lose legitimacy for the claim that because of its different socio-cultural conditions and predispositions, it had to take a different path than mainland China. An adequate strategy for preventing this scenario from coming true was to foster and encourage the development of alternative subjectivities in Taiwan.[44]

---

[42] "*Bailang*" is the Mandarin transcription for the Atayal-pronounciation of the Fujian-dialect-term "bad person".

[43] vgl. Fu Dawei 1993: 35. Fu here particularly points at the example of the bilingual reader "Selection of Atayal legends" composed by the two Atayal intellectuals Duo Ao und Adong (1991). The book expresses a rather open and uninhibited relationship towards sexuality and sometimes looks like a parody of the Han way of life (vgl. Fu Dawei 1993: 33f).

[44] Chen Zhaoying 1995. Because of their thorough identification with Chinese culture and their ancestral linkage to the "Centre of Chinese Culture" (*zhongyuan*), neither Mainlanders not Hakka were believed to be able to support the deconstruction of si-

Fu Dawei therefore appeals to Aborigines that "if they wanted to maintain a certain independence and subjectivity in their opposition against
suppression, they would have to show incessantly and actively strategies
and initiatives in the future".[45]

Other Han intellectuals engaged themselves in attempting to thoroughly re-evaluate the moral- and value system of the Aborigines. An
impressive account is the comic *The Wushe Incident* produced by Han
caricaturist Qiu Ruolong (1990) after a five-year stay with the Atayal of
Wushe. The work was greatly praised by aboriginal elites because of its
glorifying attitude towards head-hunting. In order to elucidate the sophisticated and elaborate nature of aboriginal religion, Qiu here works with
representations of the tattooing and head-hunting culture of the Atayal
which are as fascinating as they are shocking. While it had already become evident in commentaries during the Wu Feng debate that there was
a willingness not just to falsify the "savageness and meanness" of the
Aborigines, but to relativize it as a style of representation also inherent to
the Confucian value-system,[46] Qiu (1994) goes even a step further and
thus elucidates the romanticism felt by many Han Chinese in connection
with Aborigines. In a commentary on his successful comic, Qiu explains
that the inner logic of head-hunting and tattooing had been in fact the
impulse felt by natural man to keep up the equilibrium of a complex ecological system. He contends:

---

nocentrism and Han-chauvinism in Taiwan. In the eyes of Hoklo intellectuals, Aborigines seemed to be the only people eligible for this task.

[45] vgl. Fu Dawei 1993: 45. Fu's concern that the Hoklo could establish a new kind of
hegemony was actually a view held not only by critical Han intellectuals; it was one
of the main reasons why most common people in aboriginal society kept up close
ties with the KMT.

[46] Although cultural relativism of this kind had existed in the eighties during the Wu
Feng debate - the historian Dai Guojun for instance argued that the Han also killed
human beings in war or skirmishes and that it was thus unfair to label Taiwanese
Aborigines as raw-natured and wild just because they reacted with head-hunting
when threatened by the Han –, it did not become popular until the beginning of nativism (Alliance of Taiwanese Aborigines 1987: 153-160).

When you look at the destruction caused by modern civilization in Taiwan, you ask yourself how long mankind can still live here. Thus, the old people with facial tattoos are not only a national treasure witnessing old culture. They are outstanding personalities in which abilities, virtues, art, philosophy and practice are concentrated......

Rise of interest in aboriginal ritual activities

Due to the attitudes and motivations depicted above, a new occupation with aboriginal rituals began at the beginning of the 1990s. Not only so called "cultural workers" from Han society, but also Han anthropologists as well as aboriginal intellectuals began to focus on the remnants of Taiwan's aboriginal ritual culture.[47] Had aboriginal culture in past decades mainly served the leisure and amusement interests of domestic and foreign tourists (mostly Japanese and Koreans),[48] traditional aboriginal customs and rituals were now re-evaluated in order to understand their inherent logic, especially their logic regarding environmental protection and sustainable development.[49] At the same time, questions of "authenticity" became increasingly important. Cultural representations were now scrutinized in a new way, asking how ethnic particularities had, under the impact of colonialization, discrimination, exotization, and commercialization, possibly been fused and blended with foreign and non-indigenous cultural elements.

---

[47] Because of its nativist motivational background, this kind of occupation was different from the commodification, erotization, and disneyfication that had – albeit on a smaller scale - started as early as the 1960s (Munsterhjelm 2002; Friedman 2005; Thorne 1997). Aboriginal dance became an important part of domestic tourism at the time when Atayal dancers at Sun-Moon Lake in the West, and Wulai in Northern Taiwan would dance for tourists. The vast majority of such tourists, however, were American soldiers coming and going from Vietnam (Thorne 1997: 214).

[48] Hsieh Shih-chung 1994. Until the mid-eighties, the main location for tourists interested in Aborigines was Wulai, a mountain resort in North Taiwan near to Taipei inhabited by Atayal. As Xie shows in his article, the culture exhibited here was a mixture of all kinds of aboriginal cultures, including foreign ones.

[49] Sun Dachuan 2005.

Important foundations for this engagement, however, had been laid even earlier. Although many anthropologists who were interested in Aborigines had, at least since the beginning of the pan-ethnic aboriginal movement in 1984, focused on the social problems of these minorities, some of them were also engaged in projects that tried to detect and to salvage the cultural resources of Taiwan's indigenous peoples. From 1986-1988, *Taiwan's Provincial Government* engaged two anthropologists from the *Academia Sinica*, Hu Taili and Liu Binxiong (1987), in a large scale research project that investigated and evaluated the situation of the Aborigines' rituals and their singing and dancing cultures.[50] Further, both in the establishment of the *Aboriginal Culture Village* at Sun Moon Lake in 1986 as well as in the planning and the establishment of the *Aboriginal Culture Park* in Pingdong in 1988, anthropologists worked as advisers and as organizers. The exposition of authentic aboriginal culture was a common ideal in these projects. As we learn from Xie Shizhong (Xie 2000: 14f), official support for this kind of research was at that time still very much motivated by the perception that "aboriginal culture was about to be extinguished" and that the remnants had to be salvaged and documented before their complete assimilation into "Chinese culture". The success of the two parks, however, pointed to a public interest in this formerly rather disregarded aspect of Taiwanese cultural life. It was this experience that gave rise to the idea of exporting the local rituals "from the tribes to the stage" (*cong buluo dao juchang*).[51] Not only anthropologists like Hu Taili and Ming Liguo, but also film directors and music researchers like Yu Kanping and Li Daoming were pioneers in this kind of representation of aboriginal culture. From 1990 to 1994, they produced dance anthologies of different ethnic groups and transposed the results directly into staged performances. Since the ideal in this case was again "authenticity", the rituals and dances shown were mostly reconstructions of cultural activities as

---

[50] The study suggested that the government should not only subsidize the ritual activities of Taiwan's Aborigines, but that it should also help to reduce political and religious pressure in order to give the rituals a new vitality (Hu Taili 2003: 311).

[51] Sun Dachuan 2005. A conference with the same title took place at Dongwu University in December 1994 (Liao Baoyi 1994).

they might have looked in the pre-colonial and pre-Christian past. Among the most well-known examples for this approach are the performances of the aboriginal dance group *Yuanwuzhe,* which was established in 1991 under the guidance of Hu Taili. In the years following their foundation, *Yuanwuzhe* studied the rituals of almost all aboriginal groups and performed them on the stages of Taiwan's metropoles, for instance the "Ceremony of the Dwarfs" ,the collective festival of the Saixiat, or the "Harvest festival" of the Ami of Taibalang (see Part II on the contemporary local rituals below), a performance into which even former head-hunting dances were integrated.[52] The direction of the Han experts concern was highlighted by a remark by anthropologist and documentary filmmaker Hu Taili in 1994. At a conference discussing the implications of the transfer of performances "from the tribes to the stage", she contended that a crucial question was how these rituals that had been so properly reconstructed and preserved could be integrated into the tribes again, where they could then continue to develop in a way unaffected by the blurring and distorting influences of Han culture.[53] A critical response to this kind of traditionalist devotion could be read in a newspaper commentary the day after the conference. Here, the author expresses her doubts about such

> commitment to preserve culture and to pass on traditions, which motivates not only the directly participating dance ensemble *Yuanwuzhe,* but also the ethnologists and documentary filmmakers who have shown concern for Aborigines for many years to go to much effort to save the traditional cultures at risk of disappearing. However, they never face or never want to face the fact that aboriginal culture has already been integrated into modern society. In this way,

---

[52] In spite of the intentional inclusion of past traditions, *Yuanwuzhe* 1993 interestingly avoided the rehearsal of any ritual elements that were linked to the shamanist traditions of the Ami. As one of the aboriginal leaders of the group explained in 1998, this was because of the horror common people felt whenever this aspect of traditional religion (especially frightening were obviously the shamanist songs and dances) was touched (Shanhai zhuanji 1998: 16).

[53] Liao Baoyi 1994.

the discussions on Aborigines always fall into formalist thinking. Shall those young Aborigines who have been in contact with Han society for a long time identify with an image of Aborigines that has stagnated for several decades or centuries? Or shall they identify with a culture that has – as a result of inevitable historical development – interacted with other ethnic groups? And what kind of "Aborigines" shall non-Aborigines identify with? Is it possible that [these experts] – in order to redress the Han's former hegemony or for reasons of political correctness – unconsciously bring all possibility for the Aborigines' pluralist cultural development to an end, or maybe even force Aborigines – among all these cries for "return" – re-disintegrate into a people that has to lock itself away into the mountains again?[54]

However, no such critique was publicly heard from the natives themselves. Instead, an indispensable resource that Han-experts could count on in their efforts to reconstruct the "authentic" were young intellectual Aborigines whose interest in their own cultures had risen not only because of the stimulation brought about by the aboriginal movement, but also because of the interest Han intellectuals showed in the Aborigines' formerly stigmatized culture.[55] This human resource even increased in the following years when a growing number of young aboriginal intellectuals returned from the cities to the tribes. As a consequence of aboriginal activists' repeated failure in parliamentary elections, the pan-ethnic *Yuanzhumin* movement had split up into two branches in 1989, a branch that continued to fight for aboriginal social rights in the metropoles and another whose members went back to the countryside and dedicated themselves to the preservation and the reconstruction of the foundations of their cultures.[56] Many of these young intellectuals were later also engaged in the state "*Integrated Community Construction*" projects men-

---

[54] Lai Shuya 1994.

[55] Sun 2005. Sun here talks about the inspirations coming from those Han who came into the tribes to make film and music documentaries. A further motivation mentioned by Sun was the feeling of loss of cultural identity faced by the post-war youth who found themselves in midst the ruins of their cultures.

[56] Xie Shizhong 1992a.

tioned above, together with more and more aboriginal workers who had to leave the metropoles as a consequence of the increasing influx of cheap labour from South East Asia.[57]

4. The role of aboriginal rituals in times of Taiwanization and nation building

After the change of political paradigms in Taiwan, there could also be observed an increasing tendency by the central and local governments as well as by individual politicians not only to highlight the cultural particularities of their populations, but also to emphasize the respect they paid to these traditions. Primarily because of their strong feeling of authenticity, aboriginal vernaculars and rituals were assigned a prominent role in these endeavors.[58] Below, I will look at contemporary aboriginal ritual from the perspective of four critical discourses in Taiwan that seem to be helpful for an assessment of the role these rituals play in today's political and cultural climate. They raise the question of whether aboriginal rituals are to be considered to be mere "appropriations" by the nation-state, or whether they are rather "media for (post)colonial emancipation", "instruments in the competition of elites", or "a means for reflexion and self-examination". It is remarkable that all these discourses, instead of describing contemporary culture as if it were still the same as in the past and insisting on authenticity, acknowledge that aboriginal traditions had

---

[57] By 2000, the percentage of unemployment among Aborigines had risen to approx. 10% (Pan Meiling 2001).

[58] Walisi Yougan 1994. In a critical discussion on aboriginal vernacular education this Atayal writer argues that the phenomenon of multiculturalism in Taiwan has to be seen in close relationship to the efforts of "Taiwanization", the "deconstruction of the authoritarian system", the "discovery of Taiwan", the "return to the homeland" and the "search for Taiwanese subjectivity". As Walisi points out, even the initiative to implement vernacular language classes was not so much due to the latent ethnic consciousness of the Aborigines but to the endeavor of local DPP and KMT governments to show their willingness and fervor for Taiwanization.

undergone some kind of substantial, qualitative, and irreversible structural change – a change that resulted from constant ethnic interaction and
that had equipped these traditions with new functions.

4.1 National appropriations?

Financial subsidies and "symbolic violence"

In his account on ritual revival, Sun Dachuan (2005) makes the following remark concerning the new political importance of the rituals of
Taiwan's Aborigines:

> The ten years from 1990 to 2000 were the time when amendments
> were made in Taiwan's constitution and frequent big and small
> elections were held. Taiwanese Aborigines, who had become a pro-
> totype and a model in Taiwan's ethnic politics, now of course also
> became an instrument in election campaigns and propaganda. In
> these 10 years – no matter whether it was in the cities or in the
> countryside - elections went hand in hand with all sorts of rituals,
> which were often unworthy of the title or simply invented" (…)
> "The tribes were suddenly full of performing groups that gave per-
> formances at many events sponsored by government bodies or pri-
> vate persons, and rituals were always also part of the program.
> Quite often the tribes even had the opportunity to give perform-
> ances in foreign countries. To some point, ritual performances were
> already running rampant to an unfavorable degree.

A similar concern is expressed by Taiwan's well-known cultural
worker Liu Huanyue (2001) in his introduction to *A Comprehensive
Guide to the Rituals of Taiwan's Aborigines*. Liu writes:

> Funding the localities for their cultural activities may originally
> have been a good approach. Later, however, the donor became
> the greatest and was able to control everything, and the locality in

its poverty could only yield to this oppression. No wonder most aboriginal rituals became reduced to theatrical performance activities in this way. When all rituals lose their original meaning and are only held because of the cultural subsidies, who believes that such rituals will live on for generations?[59]

It is highly remarkable that, after 2000, such pessimistic assessments concerning aboriginal rituals were heard even from cultural workers and aboriginal intellectuals who themselves had a strong interest in propagating the originality of Taiwan's native cultures'. If one investigates the issue further, however, one discovers that initial worries that aboriginal rituals were endangered by the new cultural policy were uttered much earlier.[60] In 1996, Taiwanese anthropologist Xie Shizhong (1996), today head of the *Institute of Anthropology* at *National Taiwan University*, published the second piece in a series of articles on the development of aboriginal festivals and rituals. *"The Control and the Management of 'Traditional Culture': Aboriginal Culture under the National Culture System"* first appeared in the aboriginal magazine *Taiwan Indigenous Voice Bimonthly* and, in spite of many tables and evaluation lists, it looks more like a warning to aboriginal elites than a mere academic paper.[61] One of its core arguments is that aboriginal culture in the 1990s endured a sort of new "symbolic violence" as a consequence of massive financial subsidies.[62] Xie points to the danger that this culture, after having been thor-

---

[59] Liu Huanyue 2001: 5. When Liu here speaks of rituals as "only held because of the cultural subsidies", this statement has of course a subtext: Since the beginning of Taiwan's nativism in the early nineties, cultural associations relying on governmental subsidies mushroomed in aboriginal settlements. Much of the money raised for activities, however, was tacitly spent in election campaigns, and many of the activities themselves became instruments of local politicians to demonstrate and to increase individual power.

[60] See also Ming Liguo (1991: 159) for this kind of skepticism.

[61] The same article was later also published in Xie 2004: 115-132. Xie discusses similar problems in 1994c; Xie 2000; Xie2004.

[62] In his reflections on "symbolic violence", Xie cites Katherine Verdery, 1993, "Wither "nation" and "nationalism"?", in: Daedalus 122 (3): 37-46. The article provides use-

oughly exposed by Taiwan's national leadership, was now not only fully under the control of national politics, but also that it might be relinquished again as soon as the usefulness of Aborigines in the nation building process should fade. After all, subsidies from governmental bodies would not last forever. As a consequence of the subsidizing policy, however, any further cultural production and development of aboriginal culture stagnated because of the Han's decision only to protect "authentic", "traditional" and "old" culture. Once the practice to subsidize ritual performances and festivals had been established, any organization of rituals depended on the successful application for resources for "traditional culture" events. Whether the application was successful, however, was dependent on subjective decisions within the central and the local Han governments. Xie writes:

> "Over the course of time, Aborigines have learnt the strategies of applying for subsidies from the governmental bodies right before the activities. Those who prove to be most traditional, also have the largest chances to be subsidized. (…) The Aborigines know this logic very well and act exactly according to this policy. When putting the yearly rituals into practice, they do this by thoroughly reproducing or emphasizing culture and tradition."[63]

In a later article in 2000, Xie (2000) slightly relativizes his point that only "old traditions" were supported in Taiwan's nation building process. He points out that, in the beginning, the main reaso+n for the search for ‚authentic Taiwanese traditions' had been to establish a culture that was different from China and from the Mainlanders. Later, as a consequence of the protests of the smaller, less influential cultures in a multicultural

---

ful tables of the kinds of government sponsored ritual activities and the budgets offered for aboriginal festivities in the mid-nineties.

[63] Xie 1996: 99. Xie adds that such behaviour looked as if Aborigines were in the dominant position again, in so far as they successfully made use of the governmental resources to give their own traditional culture the possibility to live on. In reality, however, Xie emphasizes, Taiwan's pluralist cultural policy was also a pretence for indirect cultural oppression and domestication in times when direct cultural oppression was no longer a practical choice.

society, the main aim became to create a common national culture that was not only a collage of the island's different colonial cultures, but that had its own subjectivity (*zhutixing*). These new conditions led to an increase in creative activities in aboriginal society in which young cultural workers searched for new market opportunities (for instance the selling of handicrafts in Taiwan's Han-dominated society). This development led to a further "mutation" (*tuobian*) of national culture. With the exception of pure traditions, new creations and new traditions (*xin chuantong*) now received increasing recognition, and there also developed a view that the commercialization of culture was to be accepted. Under the influence of these two processes, i.e., the endeavors of Aborigines and a mutating national culture, almost all kinds of handicraft activities were massively supported by governmental bodies (Xie 2000: 34). As Xie puts it, at least aboriginal material culture from 1996 on "increasingly awoke from the dream of pure tradition". This was mainly due to the rising awareness of aboriginal cultural workers of the necessity of finding new market opportunities. Many private museums began to exhibit these new products, thereby helping Aborigines' to establish a new cultural identity (Xie 2000: 35).[64] Pointing out the fact that most public museums still continued to display genuine old treasures, Xie however also makes clear that the two different approaches (the ostentatious exhibition of new traditions as well as that of old traditions) actually coexisted.[65]

---

[64] Xie argues that this development culminated in a new overarching aboriginal cultural movement (*Yuanzhumin quanmin wenhua yundong*) which followed the Aborigines' ethno-political movement of the 1980s. The new cultural movement was a result of three factors: (1) Taiwan's national multiculturalist movement, which had developed as a reaction to the homogenization policy of the past and which eventually also promoted new pluralist [hybrid] creations; (2) aboriginal endeavors to create a cultural identity; and (3) the "Return to the Tribes Movement" that searched for new market opportunities (for instance the selling of handicrafts in Taiwan's Han-dominated society) and that saw its products as manifestations of a new worldview.

[65] Xie's description is revealing in so far as it shows that the whole process of national culture development was obviously not planned in advance, but was much more characterized by a series of reactions.

Rain rituals and purification rites

In the following, I want to refer to several examples of aboriginal ritual representation that seem to give support to Xie's argument of aboriginal rituals' incorporation into the national culture system.[66] There are several cases mentioned by Xie himself, for instance the inclusion of aboriginal rituals into the celebrations of Taiwan's national day or mass weddings like that one arranged by the *Taipei City Government* in 1995 where 115 Han couples were married with the help of the chiefs of different aboriginal groups.[67] Another example in this context which seems to fit into Xie's argumentation is the official cultural propaganda on the Internet. From 1994 on, the *Central Information Bureau* employed, from each ethnic group, aboriginal reporters who had undergone special training in film and documentation work. Their main task was to record all political and cultural events including the festivals and rituals of their particular ethnic groups and to make these materials accessible to the public in a regular program. In order to give even Chinese-speaking audiences outside the broadcasting zone, for instance on the mainland, access to this program, the texts of the program were also digitalized and emitted through the Internet.[68] Here, the propagandist function of the Internet was used in at least two ways: While, on the one hand, such websites served as an effective medium for cultural propaganda, they

---

[66] As Sun above already mentioned, financial support and subsidizing measures by party politicians pertained not only to representation rituals that were mostly held for the media and for Han audiences, but also had implications for the annual local rituals. The latter, however, will be dealt with in a subsequent chapter. In this section, I want to further concentrate on those rituals that had representative value in a political and cultural surrounding perceived mostly by Han.

[67] Xie 1996: 92 and 96.

[68] See Wang Yawei 1999. As the producer of the program "Aborigines' News Magazine" (*Yuanzhumin xinwen zazhi*) Wang makes clear, this method not only guaranteed that the program could be received by Aborigines in remote mountain-areas without Cable-TV: It also guaranteed that the program's messages would be "state-encroaching" (*kuaguo*). The underlying meaning of the carefully chosen term "state-encroaching" instead of "internationally receivable" becomes transparent when it is added that all materials of this program are in Chinese language.

also pointed to the political differences between the Mainland and Taiwan, where the Internet had already become a symbol of democratic interaction and freedom of speech in comparison to the constant interferences and crackdowns undertaken by the KPCh against this medium.[69] In 1996, the *Taiwan's Ministry of Education* also started a special project with the name "Web for materials on the culture of Taiwan's Aborigines", which sponsored the establishment of internationally receivable aboriginal websites, which from that point on – of course all in Chinese language – flourished on the web.[70] Government bodies themselves spared no costs in creating colorful websites displaying aboriginal culture as a national asset, often referring to the traditional rituals and religions of these peoples in their introductions and in special video files.[71]

Directives from within the "national culture system" obviously also affected ritual performances of the kind described below. In spring 2002, Taiwan's northern and southern regions were plagued by an unusually long period of drought. On May 17 of that year, the *Council for Indigenous Peoples* (CIP), a quasi-ministerial institution which is part of Taiwan's central government, launched a campaign that assigned all aboriginal groups to hold traditional ‚rain rituals' in order to show Aborigines' "care for the life of Taiwan's different ethnic groups". Even in those regions of the island that were not affected by the drought, Aborigines performed these rituals – rituals that had not been held for many decades and the contents of which had been mostly forgotten, as the participants admitted. Although the performers were well remunerated for their commitment, some subtle undertones were also heard in these rituals. In one case, the ancestor-spirits were implored to no longer bear a grudge against Aborigines and to let it rain again for it was not the Aborigines' fault that they had to live with the Han people. In another case, perform-

---

[69] On this issue see for instance Peters 2002.

[70] For these efforts see Lee 1997.

[71] Impressive examples are the websites of the Taiwan International Film Festival (TIEFF) and the Cultural Park of the *Council of Indigenous Peoples*. (Again, the video files of the latter page are only accessible for readers of Chinese) (Taiwan International Film Festival 2004; Bureau of Cultural Park of the *Council of Indigenous Peoples* 2004).

ers announced that the ancestors did not appreciate the rice wine provided by the *Taiwan Tobacco and Wine Board* and used this as an opportunity to rehabilitate self-brewed millet wine, the selling of which was
illegal.[72] As aboriginal writer Walisi Yougan makes clear in a newspaper
comment, the rituals were a testification to Aborigines' submission to
"the state's control machinery".

**Figure 3: Ami shamans cleansing the atmosphere of bad spirits at a Hualian sports
ground 2001 (Photo taken from video file provided by Banai Gumu).**

According to his viewpoint, the main function of the rituals in this machinery was to propagate a well-integrated, multi-cultural society. At the
same time, the incident was apt to reconfirm the authority of the CIP
(which in the years since its establishment in 1996 had often been criticized for its inactivity).[73]

---

[72] Jian Dongyuan et al 2002.
[73] Walisi Yougan 2002.

Some material I collected in 2001 seems to confirm this concern about the incorporation of aboriginal rituals into Taiwan's "national culture system." After a series of serious accidents on a public sports field in Hualian on Taiwan's East Coast, the local government gathered Ami shamans from various surrounding villages to perform a purification rite. Although purification rituals – called *daladuas* – had actually taken place in former times, they had never been conducted by different tribes collectively.[74] Waving around bundles of ginger and spitting rice wine into the air, the shamans cleansed the location and then sacrificed several pigs. The ritual, which took place on September 1, 2001, was initiated by a local politician from the *People First Party* (PFP), who campaigned successfully in the elections for county parliament two months later.[75] As the newspapers reported, Ami from Hualian had suggested the cleansing measures in order to appease the Ami's ancestor-spirits who were dissatisfied with the Han's invasion of the region 100 years ago. At the same time, however, pressure was put on the politicians responsible for the area by emphasizing that "if the spirits were not consoled, this would bring bad luck on them."[76]

Not surprisingly, the conveyer of these messages, an assimilated Ami school director, was a member of the *People First Party*. The school director, however, also had a very personal interest in the issue. According to his own explanation, he wished to help his son, who was trying to become a member in the group of Hualian shamans.[77] (As I learned later, this young man was a student at *National Donghua University* and wrote an academic thesis on the shamans). At the end of the ceremony at the

---

[74] This was simply not possible since pantheons were too different (Banai 3.4.2003., personal interview).

[75] PFP parliamentarian Zeng Yuxia was re-elected on December 17, 2001.

[76] China Times, Hualian edition, 2.9.2001.

[77] Li 19.10.2002, personal interview. I refer to the Ami- school director as "assimilated" due to three reasons: He had passed into the cultural system with respect to kinship, religion, and language. After marriage to a Han-woman, he had adopted Taiwanese folk religion (after the experience of being teased because having allegedly obtained aiding goods from the Catholic missionaries) and raised his son in Chinese. Only recently – mainly because of his son's endeavors with respect to tradition – had he rediscovered his own culture.

sports field, the young man (who, shortly after arriving at the location in the morning, could no longer move his legs) was involved in a healing ritual by the shamans. He was healed of his afflictions and was from then on qualified to participate in the shamans' activities. After the performance, the politicians gave the shamans money in red envelopes. Participants later told me that, with the subsidies the politician had acquired for the traditional event, he had not only been able to demonstrate his individual agency (for instance by paying the shamans), but was also able to finance his election campaign.[78]

4.2 Rituals as media for (post)colonial emancipation?

"Reverse symbolic violence" or "part of the game"?

All together, the examples listed above can easily evoke the impression that any kind of ritual representation in aboriginal society today is in one way or the other subordinated to Taiwan's national cultural politics. The last two cases mentioned above, however, point to still another phenomenon. In both incidences, there are indications that the kind of repression and symbolic violence mentioned by Xie Shizhong is answered with subtle undertones of post-colonial subversion and rebellion. Whether we think of the rain rituals, in which the ancestor-spirits were implored to bring rain despite the Aborigines' accommodation with the Han, or of the purification rite on the sports field, in which aboriginal shamans helped to redress the earlier misdeeds of the Han – in this case the Han's invasion of aboriginal land – Aborigines are obviously trying to demonstrate who the real master is. Indeed, subversion seems to be a frequent element in contemporary aboriginal rituals in Taiwan. The scope of undertones ranges from ridicule, mockery, derision, and a gloating humiliation of the alleged oppressors to the active subversion of the Han's moral and political system. Interestingly, the same kind of mockery and derision can also be observed in rituals at the local level; how-

---

[78] Banai 19.10.2002, personal interview. Because of the habit of vote-buying, election campaigns are extremely expensive in Taiwan.

ever, here again it comes from cosmopolitan aboriginal elites. One incident I will refer to in the chapter on the local rituals of the Taroko in Part II is the distribution of raw liver of the ritually killed animal not only to Taroko participants, but also to Han representatives. Since the latter do not have the custom of eating raw liver, they reacted with embarrassment when they were asked to taste it, provoking uninhibited laughter in the Taroko audience. Can this and related phenomena perhaps be explained as a kind of "reverse violence", a way of coping with (post)-colonial traumata and discrimination?

Numerous ethnographies from other contexts confirm the possibility of such a dynamic. Well-known examples are Taussig's (1980) gloss of the hybrid fetish god in Bolivian tin mines, Comaroff's (1985) study of the subversivity of Zionist Churches, Cohen's (1993) work on carnival, as well as Stoller's analysis of Hauka spirit obsession (1995). In his documentary "The Mad Masters", Jean Rouch (1957) describes the therapeutic efficacy of performances in which the colonial regime is parodied. The documentary produced by Jean Rouch in 1954 in colonial Ghana shows the members of the Hauka sect in a syncretist ritual in which they savagely jump up and down and mime and parody their Western masters with Western requisites, portraying their alleged order and civilizedness as chaotic and uncivilized. The following day, the same actors who, the day before, had been filmed with foaming mouths, appear with completely relaxed faces. As Rouch alludes, the main reason for this transformation was the performance that enabled them to release for their suppressed aggressions and frustrations. Through the symbolic humiliation of their suppressers, they were collectively cured of the psychological disharmony that had been a consequence of discrimination and oppression.[79] Frantz Fanon's work also points in this direction, as Fanon (1967) suggested violence as the way to liberty - violence as an equaliza-

---

[79] Rouch further explains that this kind of mimesis also served as a therapy for individual psychosis. The performance also helped the actors to find relief of their individual problems and psychological complexes. (For more detailed information also see Stoller 1995).

tion for the violence one had endured in receiving the negative self-image.

Such assessments seem to underline the possibility that the subversiveness observed in the ritual representations of Taiwan's Aborigines might also have the function of a kind of psychological sublimation or psychological pressure valve. In the accounts mentioned above, ritual subversion and rebellion are depicted in a way that make them appear as acts belonging very much to the realm of the subconscious or preconscious – a behavior that is somehow linked to the people's past, their historical experiences and their socialization and that has therefore become part of their (structure dominated) habitus. If we look at the history and the life experiences, characterized by hegemonic subjugation and social frustration, of Taiwan's Aborigines it is not hard to imagine that there are certain dispositions that would support the development of such compensation behavior. While rural Aborigines could generally still find shelter and protection within their communities, elites were much more exposed to Han society and were thus much more likely to have negative experiences in their urban surroundings. Cosmopolitan Aborigines, who had generally left their communities at a very early age and who often could hardly speak the language of their ethnic group, experienced to a much greater extent particularly the loss of tradition, religion and the own self . Further, many of them became detached from Christianity in the course of their life with the Han and thereby often had even greater problems in coping with the humiliations they were subjected to by members of Taiwan's Han society. The main cause for such humiliation and disdain had often been jealousy on the part of Han colleagues because of the Aborigines' enjoyment of the grade-bonus-system (*jiafen zhidu*) in high schools and in universities as a consequence of the Aborigines' status as "citizens of remote areas" (*pianyuan diqu jumin*).[80]

---

[80] This regulation also pertained for Han citizens of the small offshore islands Jinmen and Matsu.

Aboriginal subjectivity: The re-emergence of head-hunting

On the other hand, there are also indications that seem to suggest that subversive actions in aboriginal rituals are not merely part of a pre-reflexive or a subconscious habitus, but rather that they are consciously integrated into the rituals because they are "part of the game" in contemporary Taiwan, where emancipation and self-determination are valued ideals. In a previous contribution, I described the emphasis Han intellectuals had put on the necessity of the development of a "new aboriginal subjectivity" starting at the beginning of the nineties. They argued that this was the only way for Aborigines to become free from the psychological domination to which they were still submitted. One of the recipes for manifesting subjectivity was – besides the ostentatious representation of aboriginal cultures – the subversion of the order and the moral system established by the Han (Fu Dawei 1993; Liu Shaohua 1993). The concept of "subjectivity" – the call for a self-determined identity – of course stemmed from post-colonial discourse, an approach that was extremely popular in circles of Taiwanese intellectuals as of the beginning of the nineties, because it seemed to indicate ways and strategies that could help not only to deal with previous hegemonic experiences, but also to construct a national identity independent from the "colonized" identity of the past and from the conservative forces within the KMT-government that was still in power until 2000.[81] Being in close contact with these Han intellectuals who had their roots either in the Taiwanese oppositional

---

[81] Closely related to neo-Marxist theories that became popular in Taiwanese opposition circles as early as the 1970s, post colonial studies gained rising popularity at the end of the 1980s, since these theories could be well applied to Taiwan's situation in general. Frantz Fanon, Edward Said, and Stuart Hall became trendy authors at that time because they pointed to the different ways in which postcolonial (and colonial) individuals and collectives could liberate themselves from the mental chains of their "masters" (until 2000, many Hoklo considered continuous KMT rule as a form of ongoing colonialization by the Mainlanders). Equally popular were theories on nationalism and nation-building from authors such as Eric Hobsbawm, Terence Ranger, or Benedict Anderson, since they offered information on the techniques of the construction of culture and the nation state.

movement or in communist-orientated circles of the mainlander-elite, young aboriginal elites who participated in the aboriginal movement adapted these theoretical notions to their own ideology and used them as a strategy for aboriginal liberation from Han domination and dependency. The first signs of such an adaptation can be detected in aboriginal literature in 1992. In *Drawing the Savages' Knife*, aboriginal writer Walisi Yougan appeals to aboriginal elites to stand up against the "enslavement" by the state: in order to be successful, one should be "equipped with the will of the hunter who takes revenge for former humiliations", otherwise one would be thoroughly "civilized" and corrupted by "civilized society" which had built its civilization on exploitation.[82] Walisi Yougan, who was to be one of the main initiators of the "Cultural Head-Hunting Raid" at the *Aboriginal Culture Congress* two years later, clearly makes here an argument in line with the perspective of colonial and postcolonial discourse: in order to reach complete emancipation one must liberate oneself from the negative self-image that the dominators had forced upon the dominated.[83]

One of the first open manifestations of aboriginal subjectivity was observed at the end of 1993. On December 10, 1993, International Human Rights Day, various groups of the aboriginal movement gathered in a demonstration in front of the Ministry of the Exterior. As the leaders of the demonstration emphasized, the main aim of the protest was to point out the "inter-national" relationship of Han people and aboriginal people and to call on the government to improve the treatment of Aborigines for the sake of international recognition.[84] This event was closely followed

---

[82] Walisi Yougan 1992.

[83] Walisi was strongly influenced by Han intellectuals such as the psychiatrist Wang Haowei, a friend of Walisi, who was one of the main introducers of postcolonial discourse in Taiwan in the late 1980s (see for instance *Isle Margin*, a leftist magazine edited by Wang).

[84] The manifest of the demonstration that was entitled "Fight of Taiwan's Aborigines against occupation and for existential continuity: Give us back our land" contained the following statement: "Before the Han government does not recognize Taiwan's Aborigines' fundamental human rights, it has no right to request international right of existence in the face of the international community". Chiang Kai-shek had signed the UN convention for the protection of indigenous peoples as early as in

by another incident that aimed at an even more imposing display of self-determined aboriginal identity. In April 1994, the *First Aboriginal Culture Congress* convened in the newly established *Aboriginal Culture Park* in southern Taiwan – a congress that was organized and funded by the Taiwanese government and in which not only aboriginal activists and anthropologists, but also politicians including the Taiwanese President himself participated.[85] The day the congress began, a group of ten aboriginal activists in traditional costumes suddenly marched on to the stage and - rudely interrupting the speech of a high-ranking politician - solemnly presented the "cultural head-hunting raid proclamation".[86] Although the proclamation started in aboriginal language, the language soon switched to Mandarin after annoyed interjections from the audience. In general, the content of the manifest was a catalogue of demands in which Aborigines requested to be taken more seriously with respect to their sovereignty (Jiang 1994). The participating cadres were asked to intensify their co-operative efforts regarding the correction of the ethnonym from "mountain compatriots" to "Taiwan Aborigines"[87] as well as the implementation of aboriginal institutions and autonomous zones. In addition, the anthropologists who had been the main planners of the congress were blamed not only for wasting too much time on academic questions, but also for their Han-centered world-view, demonstrated by the under-representation of Aborigines at the congress, ... and in fact, the

---

1963 ...without ever caring for Taiwan's Aborigines. Until 1996, the latter were not officially recognized as indigenous peoples, since their recognition would have endangered the alleged homogeneity of the Chinese people as well as the legitimacy of the Han's occupation of Taiwan.

[85] President Li Denghui attended the third day of the congress and became, that day, the first politician of the ROC government who officially recognized the Aborigines' self-chosen ethnonym *"Yuanzhumin"*.

[86] *"Yuanzhumin wenhua chucao xuanyan"* in Chinese. With the exception of the Tao, all of Taiwan's aboriginal groups practiced head-hunting (*'chucao'* in Chinese, literally "launching an attack out of the grass") until the beginning of the 20th century.

[87] The first official recognition of the ethnonym *"Yuanzhumin"* occurred during the speech Li Denghui gave on the last day of the congress. For a more detailed description of the event see Rudolph 1996.

whole agenda of the congress should be changed in accordance with Aborigines' perspectives. The manifest finished with a gentle menace:

> Since our feelings of helplessness, sadness, anger, heavy-heartedness and agony seem not to be able to change our people's fate, our ancestor-spirits tell us to severely denounce those people who tread on this land.

Compared to its audacious title – a title that, in combination with the intellectuals' rude behavior, functioned as a kind of "frame" – the proclamation's content appeared rather moderate. It soon became clear, however, that it was this very frame that counted. Security regulations for the President's visit over the next days were immediately intensified, and the newspapers indulged in speculations on the meaning of "head-hunting" (*chucao*). In its coverage of the incident the following morning, the *United Daily News* published the following comment on "head-hunting":

> "Head-hunting" is an important cultural particularity of Taiwan's Aborigines. In traditional tribal society, each tribe had its fixed territory and culture, so head-hunting towards the outside marked the territorial boundaries. To the inside, head-hunting was an important ritual in order for the aboriginal warrior to be recognized as a "person" by the tribe. For this reason, head-hunting has been sacred … . Formally, head-hunting originally denoted the hunting of human heads, later it simply stood for the hunting of wild pigs etc.; therefore, it can not be called barbarian, because they never ruthlessly killed, but always symbolically killed just one. This "cultural head-hunting raid" is therefore just a formal, pan-ethnically launched assault to demonstrate aboriginal subjectivity … .[88]

Many of those Han intellectuals who advocated an independent and multicultural Taiwan enthusiastically welcomed the incident. In her article "*Preliminary attempt of an theoretical evaluation of ‚High mountain*

---

[88] "Yuanzhumin wenhua chucao" [The Aborigines' cultural head-hunting]. In: United Daily News 10.4.1994.

people'-research in Taiwan's ethnology", journalist Chen Zhaoru (1994) writes with satisfaction that, at the Culture Congress in 1994, aboriginal intellectuals had finally demonstrated their subjectivity by openly doubting the function of the gathering and by expressing their unwillingness to remain 'discussed' and 'researched' objects of the ethnologists. In a publication entitled *"The head-hunting raid proclamation is the beginning of a dialogue between Aborigines and Han"*, documentary filmer Jiang Guanming stresses the importance of Aborigines developing their own strategies and discourses for the sake of cultural survival and cultural dignity. In no case should they depend on the decisions and interpretations of the government or of ethnologists. In the same text, Jiang however also explicitly mentions the positive implications of Aborigines' cultural interpretations and subversions for the development of Taiwanese discourse and subjectivity.[89]

The symbolic "head-hunting" action at the *Aboriginal Culture Congress*, however, did not remain the only reference to a theme which had originally been banned from public discussion some years before. In the mid-nineties when I did my research on the aboriginal movement, it was very popular in circles of intellectual elites to theorize on the possibility of the continuing the *gaya* – the laws of the Atayal that members of the group had to follow in order to not annoy the ancestor-spirits and to receive the right to cross the rainbow bridge into the realm of ancestors.[90] For instance, young intellectuals told me many details about the mysterious death of Duo Ao, a local Atayal politician who allegedly did not simply die in a car accident but rather who, by throwing himself in front of a car to prove his virtuousness in a quarrel with a friend, had actually acted in accordance with the *gaya*. I was also told stories about the last head-hunting incidents on the east coast in the fifties. Ample examples of symbolic head-hunting as a form of open revenge can also be found in the internet. An impressive example is the website of Pideru Wuga, a Taroko-Singer who performs "traditional aboriginal music" and who

---

[89] Jiang Guanming 1994: 44.

[90] From 1994 until 1996 I conducted field research in Taiwan on the impact of the aboriginal movement on the attitudes in local areas.

appears in full, albeit false, tattoo on the site.[91] At least for the male members of the Atayal and Taroko tribes, the application of facial tattoos had once been possible only after the successful accomplishment of the most important *gaya*, i.e., head-hunting. In the first song entitled "Head-hunting", Pideru sings in Taroko-language:

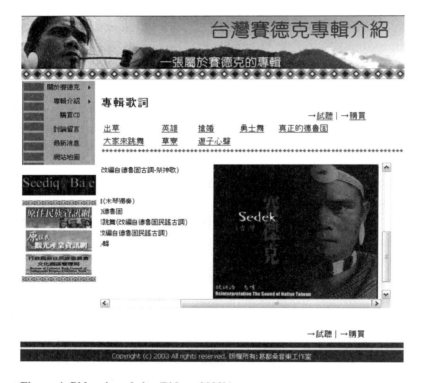

Figure 4: Pideru's website (Pideru 2002b)

I am a son of the Taroko-Sedek, I don't fear any trouble.
I only remember the lesson from our ancestors - I have not forgotten it until the present day.

---

[91] Pideru Wuga 2002. In personal interviews Pideru admitted that the theme of his song was in fact inspired by the commemorative head-hunting rituals of the Church elites. However, he simultaneously pointed out that he does not ideologically support – and this is also indicated by the title of his CD – the Taroko-independence-movement of these elites (personal interviews with Pideru 14.4.2003).

Look: Don't provoke me, don't make fun of me. If you provoke
me, I will chop off your head and take it to worship the ancestor-
spirits. Look at the mark on my head, that's a real man. Don't act
wantonly! See! Taroko-Sedek. Uh!
I invite you to come here. This is the place where my ancestors
live. Here you will rest in peace. I also invite your forefathers,
brothers and sisters to live here. Uh!

Additionally, in order to prevent any misunderstandings that he had
learnt his lesson well, Pideru provides an "additional interpretation" below the Chinese translation of the song:

When your blood flows out of your body, all hatred between you
and me will vanish. I invite your soul to live here by my side, and I
will feed you with millet wine and food. After you have become
one of us, you will protect our people together with our ancestor-
spirits.[92]

To find out more details about the philosophy alluded to here by
Pideru Wuga, we must look at a Power Point file provided by the Taroko
teacher Gariyi on the website of his elementary school.[93] In the document
entitled "Head-Hunting, Tattoos and Head-hunting Cloth" we seem to be
carried back to the former times of traditional religion. In several video
clips integrated into the presentation, tattooed people perform wild
dances and whirl around sculls, which they subsequently feed and hail in
the way depicted by Pideru above. The underlying text explains the

---

[92] Pideru Wuga 2002a, b. Not only the melody, but also the comments to the head-
hunting ritual are almost identical to the contents of the head-hunting ritual organized by PCT-elites. However, as Pideru does not refer to "Taroko", but only to
"Sedek" in his main title, this caused some annoyance from the side of the head-
hunting ritual's re-inventor Imi (personal interviews with Pideru 14.4. 2003 and with
Imi 16.4.2003).

[93] Gariyi 2000. The document was to be found on the webpage of the Fu-shih Elementary School until August 2003.

deeper meaning of the ritual practices performed here and the utensils and colors used.[94]

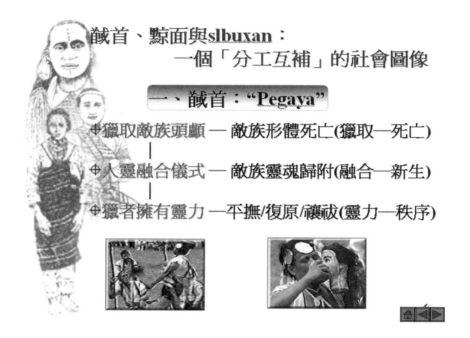

Figure 5: Website displaying Taroko head-hunting-rituals (Gariyi 2000)

4.3 Rituals as instruments in the competition among elites?

While it seems hard to tell in the cases mentioned above whether references to head-hunting and ancestor-spirits were manifestations of "reverse symbolic violence" or rather reactions to the Han's call for "subjectivity" (*zhutixing*), they can all be explained very well as a special stage

---

[94] What is not mentioned in the presentation, however, is the origin of these scenes. They were filmed at an open cultural event of the Taroko in 1991, the second year of Taiwanese nativism, at "Buluowan", the site of an ancient Taroko-Tribe. (The site is situated in the Taroko Gorge on the east coast of Taiwan). The title of the festival was "Cultural artistry of the Aborigines of Hualian County" (*Hualian xian yuanzhumin wenhua jiyi huodong*).

in the process of the Aborigines' psychological emancipation in contemporary Taiwanese society.

A slightly different intepretation for the increasingly popular use of evocative symbols such as ancestor-spirits is provided by the Puyuma intellectual Sun Dachuan (2005). In an article entitled *"The return of the sacred: contemporary situation and revitalization of the rituals of Taiwan's Aborigines."*, the former vice president of the *Council for Indigenous Peoples* (CIP) remarks:

> The activities of the aboriginal movement increasingly depended on the support from ritual symbols. Each action required an assertion that the "ancestor-spirits" were participating and were present, in order to show that the action represented the volition of the whole ethnic group and that it had a sacred and a legitimate foundation. (…) Each gathering and assembly that had to do something with Aborigines now began with prayers conducted by elders or shamans, in a way that it was unbearable.[95]

Sun's statement suggests that allusions to sacred symbols such as ancestor-spirits also fulfilled legitimizing functions for aboriginal elites, legitimizing functions especially vis-à-vis the Han, who were the main addressees and supporters of their performances. As I have stated before, 80% of Taiwanese Aborigines today are Christians, and my own research in aboriginal villages has shown that the people there were not eager to thematize the ancestor-spirits at all, even if they continued to exist in their minds as so called "superstition" (I will come back to this complicated and ambivalent religious mindset of the common people in Part II of my study). By contrast, for intellectual and political aboriginal elites, who since the early nineties had been heavily influenced by postcolonial discourse and global Fourth World discourses, Christianity had generally

---

[95] Other motivations were the inspirations coming from those Han who came into the tribes to make film and music documentaries as well as the feeling of loss of cultural identity faced by the post-war youth who found themselves in midst the ruins of their cultures.

lost its normative brackets. They often emphasized that Christianity was a foreign and not an indigenous religion, making it easier for them to break certain taboos.

In Taiwan's Han society, however, aboriginal ancestor-spirits have still another connotation. As a consequence of the revision of history, which started after the lifting of martial law, ancestor-spirits today not only represent aboriginal "authenticity", but also call up an association with the suppression of Taiwan's non-Han cultures and religions, a historical burden of which Taiwan's Han are constantly reminded in the age of multiculturalism and the rewriting of the island's historical records.

It is this meta-discourse which is effectively instrumentalized today by ethnic elites for their own authentication and authorization. By reference to the ancestor-spirits and to certain elements of aboriginal religions, aboriginal elites can simultaneously point to an unquestionable religious identification as well as to the century-long history of stigmatization, both sensitive points in the conscience of Taiwan's Han. In a political climate in which national politicians are eager to demonstrate "political correctness", aboriginal elites who refer to the sacredness of their actions gain a discursive space where they are unassailable and which they can use to attack and discredit political rivals.

This multivocal potential of ancestor-spirits and aboriginal traditional religions, which has actually become slightly visible in some of the examples mentioned above, becomes particularly apparent in two cases related below. In 2004 – ten years after the *Aboriginal Culture Congress* of 1994 – another "Head-hunting raid proclamation" was published. The author of the new manifest was Gao Jin Sumei (Gao 2004),[96] an aboriginal parliamentarian supported by Taiwan's pan-blue camp, which advocates Taiwan's reunification with China. The main purpose of this proclamation (which interestingly lacked the prefix "cultural" found in its precedent from 1994) was to mobilize Aborigines for a demonstration

---

[96] The father of Gao Jin Shumei is mainlander, her mother Atayal. Only after starting her political carreer, did Gao Jin add her mother's last name to her original name (a measure which has been possible possible since 1996) and officially became an Aborigine. Many people suspect that the main reason for this change of identity was to increase her electorate.

against Vice-President Lü Xiulian, a female politician from the ruling *Democratic Progress Party* (DPP). Lü had dared to doubt the "indigenity" of Taiwan's Aborigines by openly referring to the Negrito-population that probably inhabited the island before the Malayo-Polynesians, thereby killing a holy cow of the aboriginal movement, which had fought for the recognition of aboriginal originality for over ten years (i.e., from 1984 until 1994).[97] The aboriginal manifest that was decorated with a picture of the "savage's knife" (*fandao*) read like this:

Think about the homeless compatriots in the areas of catastrophe![98]
Think about the 420 thousand compatriots that have no future!

Think about the instructions of our ancestor-spirits! Think about our next generation! We should feel ashamed! If we don't act now, how shall we face our ancestor-spirits when we come to the rainbow bridge? (...) [99]

---

[97] The most provoking argument of Taiwan's aboriginal movement was that today's Aborigines were the first inhabitants on the island and thus had primordial rights on this soil, which had been invaded by Han Chinese only 400 years before. This argument was hard for the KMT to accept as they propagated that Taiwan belonged in fact to the Chinese. They therefore refused the Aborigines' request to be retermed into ab-originals – original inhabitants of Taiwan – until 1994, pointing among other things to the fact that Non-Malayo-Polynesians might have inhabited the island even before today's Aborigines.

[98] Gao Jin Sumei here refers to those areas affected by the disastrous earthquake of September 1999 as well as by frequent avalanches which are a consequence of the destruction of Taiwan's natural rainforests.

[99] In the traditional religion of the Atayal, the rainbow bridge is the place where the ancestor-spirits judge whether a person is qualified to pass into the realm of ancestors. One of the most important qualifications was the tattoo, which for males could at one time only be applied after successful head-hunting. The manifest that was published on July 16, 2004 further reads: "Our opinion is: Even if Lü Xiulian apologizes, the wounds of continuing oral genocide can not be healed. (...) We propagate: Hunger-strike until the colonial government offers Aborigines a reasonable treatment! We speak out the warning: No foreign government [denoting Taiwan's government that comes from the outside] can ever exploit the Aborigine's right to return on the soil of the Ketagalan."

The call for the rally against Vice-President Lü was followed by more than 4,000 Aborigines of different ethnic groups, many of them wearing red headbands reading "oppose racism" and "head-hunting raid".[100]

出草宣言

2004/07/16

作者:吉娃斯. 阿麗（立委高金素梅）

今天，我們回到凱達格蘭母土！天氣雖然炎熱，但我們心情沈重！先讓我們以肅穆的心情沈默三分鐘。

想一想災區一無所有的同胞！
想一想四十二萬沒有明天的同胞！
想一想祖靈的訓示！
想一想我們的下一代！
我們是否應該慚愧！
再不行動，將來我們如何在彩虹橋上面對祖靈？

出草宣言

我們認為：即使呂秀蓮道歉，也無法撫平原住民族被連續語言滅族的傷痛！

我們堅信：由行動所產生的道德意義，是原住民族的尊嚴與美學！

我們宣佈：無限期絕食！直到殖民政權給原住民族一個合理交待！

我們警告：任何外來政權都不能剝奪原住民族回到凱達格蘭母土的權利！

我們期待：平等待我之各族同胞，展現制裁種族岐視的力量！

吉娃斯. 阿麗（高金素梅）2004/7/16

Figure 6: Gao Jin Sumei's Head-hunting manifest in 2004 (Gao 2004)

Another action also initiated by Gao Jin Sumei occurred in mid-June 2005. Under the guidance of the young and attractive female parliamentarian, sixty representatives from twelve aboriginal ethnic groups made a protest trip to Japan in order to recover several thousand aboriginal souls that were enshrined in the *Yasukuni Shrine* and transport them back to Taiwan. The ancestor souls were stored here after the Pacific War (1941-1945) together with 2.4 million souls of Japanese war-dead. During a press conference held by the delegation at the *High Court of Osaka,* furi-

---

[100] See Taipei Times of 25.7.2004: 1.

ous reproaches against Premier Koizumi, who, by his repeated visits to the shrine, had sent false signals, were uttered. After all, the shrine also contained the souls of numerous war criminals, showing that perpetrators and victims were not carefully differentiated. A further reproach was that, by enshrinement together with millions of Shintoist Japanese, the souls of members of other religions were not properly respected.

Figure 7: Gao Jin Sumei's Protest in Japan 2005 (Gao 2007)

The protesters also resolutely articulated their disapproval of the preceding actions of the chair of the *Taiwan Solidarity Union*, a party from the pan-green camp, which advocates Taiwan's independence from China, who had visited *Yasukuni Shrine* in April to honor Taiwan's twenty-eight thousand war-dead who were enshrined here during the Japanese period. In order to enhance the protest's efficacy, Aborigines not only showed pictures of their head-hunting ancestors, but also performed traditional rituals before and after the press conference. In the process of worshipping the different ancestor-spirits, Aborigines beseeched them to punish their respectless oppressors in the appropriate way … .[101]

Similar to the three former trips to Japan undertaken by Gao in this matter since 2002, this protest was also without success: After the delegation's arrival in Japan, the excursion to the *Yasukuni Shrine* was diverted by the Japanese police, who explained that it had "to protect the visitors from attacks by Japanese right-wing radicals".

Figure 8: Taiwan's Aborigines at their 2005 protest in Japan holding up Anti-Japanese transparencies (Gao 2007)

However, the incident was sensational enough to bring Taiwan's Aborigines into the headlines of the Japanese and the Chinese media for some days. Most interesting in the case of Gao Jin Sumei's actions is the way that head-hunting and other symbols connected to traditional aboriginal religions were integrated into these political rituals in order to gain political advantage and to combat rival political forces. In both cases, the authority of Taiwan's pan-green camp and its politicians was questioned

---

[101] Wu Gufeng 2005.

and attacked. Particularly in the last example, a major aim was to compromise Taiwan's government in front of an international community, by pointing to the government's lack of assistance with regard to religious belonging and its complicity with a country that did not repent its war crimes.

In his analysis of the incident, Scott Simon (2006) also discusses the allusive and compromising potential of Gao's pilgrimages, arguing that they were an attempt to instigate a thorough re-interpretation of the role of Japanese colonialism in Taiwan suitable to please the People's Republic of China (PRC). By portraying Aborigines as suppressed and suffering colonial subjects and not as "fierce" fighters as they used to see themselves, Gao tried to reorganize the attitude of Taiwan's citizens towards the Japanese, who were usually well thought of even by those who had fought against them. The incident aimed at a manipulation of collective memory exactly at a moment when individual memories of the colonial time were vanishing. Simon writes:

> "Through her protests at the *Yasukuni Shrine* over several years, May Chin [the English name of Gao Jin Sumei] brought Japan's Formosan aboriginal soldiers into Taiwanese social memory as symbols of Taiwanese, and particularly aboriginal, suffering and injustice during the colonial period."

In any case, the subtle messages of Gao's ritualized political performances could neither be proved nor be prosecuted. This is also a consequence of ritual's ambivalence and multivocality. As Stanley Tambiah already made clear in his elucidating analysis of the performative quality of rituals, ritual agents can always make themselves appear to be referring to cosmological patterns, thereby avoiding a clear political statement. This is surely one of the reasons why ritual has such a prominent role in political life. A similar dynamic has been pointed out by Catherine Bell (1997) in her reflections on the efficacy of invented rituals. Referring to the Olympics as a new international ritual that successfully forges a new common identity and negotiates between different political positions, she contends:

> The ambiguity of the Olympics is one of its most striking features. Various scholars of ritual have examined ... the way it simultaneously combines sports, games, warfare, and ritual. ... Heavy on the rhetoric of common values while open to a great deal of variation in each participant's purposes, ritual makes few of the pragmatic or substantive statements so vulnerable to disagreement and contention.[102]

And, as far the use of sacral symbols is concerned, Bell continues:

> Appeals to an ancient tradition, like the model of the Greek games, provide a more faceless, external, and neutral sort of authority. It suggests a type of canonicity, to return to Roy Rappaport's terms, that can downplay the indexical nature of the activities [or: underscore the non-utilitarian nature of the activities, as Bell emphasizes on page 145]; in other words, the authority of "ancient tradition" can reassure potential but uneasy participants that their coming together is equally empowering.[103]

While almost all of the incidents mentioned so far refer to representational or political rituals of aboriginal elites in urban areas, local rituals are not spared political instrumentalization by ethnic elites. An account which shows to which extent the traditionalist endeavors in contemporary local aboriginal rituals are also connected to elites' competion and elites' power ambitions is offered by Zhang Weiqi (1998) – a young Taiwanese anthropologist who has herself participated as a cultural and social worker in the new government policy of "*Integrated Community Construction*".[104] As Zhang remarks,

---

[102] Bell 1997: 231.
[103] Bell 1997: 235.
[104] Zhang Weiqi 1998: 138; 126; and Zhang 1999.

The majority of the tribes-people (...) understand better than the tribes' elites and the scholars with their wishful thinking that straw huts, old cultural relics, and traditional cloth are things that in reality no longer "exist". But they also understand that this is exactly what the government and the scholars want to see. Following the requests from the tribe's elites and the [Han] colonialists, they not only have to give the performances [for some money (Zhang 1998: 128,138)], but also have to make the audience believe that this is the culture of their everyday life. Simultaneously, their performances give the people from the outside the wrong impression of "tribal solidarity". (...) The *Integrated Community Construction* which is promoted by an alliance of government, scholars, and tribal elites, is on the one hand – by upholding the cultural idea of de-politization – concealing the elites' strive for overall control. On the other hand, it enforces – through the affirmation which is given from outside forces – the authority these elites have in the tribes.[105] (...) Since the reappearance of this authority is produced by the government's fostering of "culture" or "traditional culture", and since these cultural activities can not be supported by the present economy of the tribe, the *Integrated Community Construction* is not capable of revitalizing these "cultures" within the vein of modern life, and the residents never get any advantages from this kind of cultural performances. This is why I argue – speaking with Fanon – that this desire to lean on the past and trying to revive already sublated traditions, not only runs counter to the historical development, but also violates the wish of the tribes-people. Those who use traditional culture to establish their authority within and without the communities, simultaneously also establish a relationship of domination in the tribe.[106]

Because of this phenomenon, Zhang argues, the government's ambitious policy of *Integrated Community Construction* was in fact a kind of

---

[105] Zhang Weiqi here cites the example of the East-Rukai who in recent years participated in every kind of cultural revitalization activity sponsored by the *Council for Cultural Affairs*. These revitalizations finally lead to a reinforcement of the symbolic authority of the tribe's chief.

[106] Zhang Weiqi 1998: 138; 143.

"re-colonialization" and consequently "a failure" – "symbolic 'culture' had become a bargaining counter for different elites in their competition."[107] Zhang's account seems to confirm a dynamic which we have already inferred from some of the examples above: in order to win the support of Han elites, certain ethnic elites exhibit "authentic culture" on a large scale. With the financial support they receive, they are able to finance election campaigns and to dominate and defeat other ethnic elites. As my own research has shown, ideology did not count very much in this game. Despite their alleged "China-unification" stance, elites particularly from the pan-blue-camp were very talented in getting hold of resources that were part of the multiculturalist plan for "*Integrated Community Construction*", and many of the most traditionalist performances and representations observed or documented by me were arranged by pan-blue-camp-adherents. I will come back to this point in Part II of this volume, where I describe the political background of the local rituals.

4.4 Ritual as a means for reflexion and self-examination?

The observations made above suggest that the contemporary ritual performances of Taiwan's Aborigines can neither be reduced to Xie's thesis of thorough "incorporation of aboriginal rituals into the Han's national culture system" nor to their psychological functions with respect to post-colonial emancipation and identity reconstitution. They also – and perhaps even more importantly – have a function as instruments in the competition among elites.

Despite his allusion that reference to the ancestor-spirits had "mainly legitimizing functions", another kind of social function of contemporary aboriginal rituals is however discussed by Sun Dachuan (2005) in "*The return of the sacred.*" From Sun's perspective, it was not so much the Han government's manipulation but the Aborigines' own identity ambivalence that caused an increasing politization, commercialization and – as the author admits – "vulgarization" of aboriginal rituals. This process,

---

[107] Zhang 1998: 134; 126; 129.

however, entailed an important means for identity constitution, a dimension that had been neglected during the political and legal reforms for Aborigines. For Sun, the revitalization of traditional rituals took over the role of a re-confrontation of one's own traditional values:

> The Aborigines' entire movement of ritual revitalization was from the beginning to the end characterized by worries between the sacred and the profane: On the one hand, one relied on political elections, official state support, tourist entertainment and market mechanisms to manifest the vitality and valor of one's culture; on the other hand, one feared that exactly these secular factors might blur one's already variegated traditional face.

It was this dilemma, Sun suggests, that created the chance to re-adapt to the new living environment:

> ... no matter whether it was for the requirements of the political movement, the requirements of tourist entertainment, the requirements of the policy of *Integrated Community Construction*, or the requirements of stage art, all of these different styles of cultural reproduction wavered between the sacred and the profane. Secularization was meant to adapt to the new conditions and to give the withering traditions new vitality; and sacralization was meant to avoid a rupture in the foundations of one's tradition and one's existence. Sacralization here also had the function of reuniting the secular world in which one was living.

Thus, Aborigines had to go through the revitalization and the re-performing of ritual in order to find a way back to themselves and to re-discover the second half of their existence – the cosmic dimension – "just in a way as indicated by Mircea Eliade 2000 [1968] in *The Sacred and the Profane : The Nature of Religion*", Sun suggests. For Sun, the eventization, the synthetization with contemporary art, and even the staging of aboriginal rituals had the advantage of letting Aborigines communicate with their past self:

Modern man believes that after the "removal of superstition" and the "elimination of the sacred", he is also set free from the obscuration, the ignorance and the fear in which his ancestors dwelled. Any religious representation of a religion or cosmology is no more for him than a preceding historical stage or pre-modern hangover; man depends on his logos, he can explain his own existence as well as the cosmos. (...) [However,] Every secular person today is the descendant of religious persons, man can not completely destroy his own history. The actions of his religious ancestors have formed each man into what he is today. (...). From this perspective, the revitalization of aboriginal rituals is not just a problem of social adaptation or a mere cultural-economic calculation, nor does it merely satisfy the subjective identity or a nostalgic worry created by Aborigines' wishful thinking. It is more like a chance to enter into a dialogue with our existential foundations, face to face, as our ancestors did before ... .[108]

5. Concluding remarks

Due to the identity search triggered by Taiwanese nativism, aboriginal "authentic" culture and the manifestation of "aboriginal subjectivity" has received increasing attention since the early nineties. This also had its impact on the way in which aboriginal religions were represented in the public sphere. Compared to the period before 1990, there was a clear change in the practice of strategic reference to aboriginal traditions. A major change could be observed in the attitude towards the ancestor-spirits. Rather than being identified as "evil spirits" who had to be chased away (as for instance in the example of the Tao where the Han invaders were symbolically equated with the satanic spirits frequently exorcized by the Church), ancestor spirits from this point on were represented as benign authorities that came to take revenge and help Aborigines. In this new pattern, allusions to the ancient religion and to the spirits not only served as a testification for inalienable collective religious identifications,

---

[108] Sun Dachuan 2005: 13.

but also often as a menace and a provocation: they expressed the intention to subvert Han-made cultural values or at least to question these values, thereby gaining an advantageous discursive space in Taiwan's new multiculturalism.

At the same time, however, such provocations had even further "indexical functional uses" with solid political implications. In most cases mentioned, the challenges were also actually connected to power contests between different groups of elites, parties etc. While the cultural head-hunting raid of 1994 was meant as an assault against the ruling KMT – an assault that was also very much welcomed by the DPP at that time –, the main target of the head-hunting raid by aboriginal parliamentarian Gao Jin Sumei against Lü Xiulian in 2004 was the ruling DPP. Similarly, the visits of Gao Jin Sumei to Japan signaled an affiliation to all pro-unification forces inside and outside Taiwan. And as far as the head-hunting representations of Pideru and Garyi described above are concerned, they were part of a quarrel between different positions vis-à-vis the Taroko independence movement in the local areas (notice that Pideru refers to Sedek and only secondarily to Taroko on his website. I will give more detailed information on this movement in Part II, in which one chapter is dedicated to the development of contemporary rituals among the Taroko).

Since the initial quest for "aboriginal subjectivity" had come from Han intellectuals who needed it for their own authentication, it is questionable whether the propagated goal – i.e. the emancipation from the oppressor's values and power sphere – was really achieved. Even if there had taken place a certain empowerment, Aborigines were actually not free in their actions, but thoroughly interconnected with intellectual and political currents in Han society. Although aboriginal rituals were apparently used to subvert Han morals and policies, the same actions were simulteanously instrumentalized by political factions or currents within Han society. This phenomenon suggests that the original power relations were in fact not altered. A similar problem has been described by Keesing (1989) in his study on cultural identity in postcolonial Melanesia and Polynesia. As Keesing shows, the categories of the dominators were extensively internalized by native intellectual elites in this region, not only because the discourse of domination had created the objective conditions in which struggles had to be fought, but also because it defined the semiology in which claims to power had to be expressed. This problem was actually discussed by *Academia Sinica* scholars as early as 1994 in the course of the name correction movement of Taiwan's Aborigines. In a defense for the aboriginal struggle to change the ethnonym from mountain compatriots to Aborigines (*Yuanzhumin*), they wrote that the way in which the claims were made mirrored in fact the mental dependency and cultural dominatedness of these peoples. At their own choice, Aborigines neither tried to link themselves to superordinate ethnic movements like the Great Movement of Malaian Peoples, nor did they express a wish to leave the lingual boundaries established by Taiwan's Han government (they had chosen a Chinese-language term as their ethnonym). After 400 years of Han domination, Aborigines thought and acted completely within the categories assigned to them by the Han, the scholars contended.[109]

There might, however, have been one tiny change in the relationship between the Aborigines and Han. Although Aborigines were still mentally dominated by the Han, their traditionalism did no longer necessarily support those who had empowered them for their own needs. Instead, this traditionalism often went its own unpredictable ways, because it was enacted by people who not only had their particular historical and cultural experiences, but also their individual power ambitions.

An interrelated issue that became problematized particularily through the account of Sun Dachuan is that contemporary aboriginal culture and especially ritual vacillates between "instrumental" material endeavors (as manipulation by Han elites and instrumentalization by aboriginal elites) and "expressive" identity exigencies (as post-colonial, often rebellious, demarcation or the thrust felt by Aborigines to identify with their cultural and religious roots). Sun's account is in so far exceptional as it tries not only to handle the first, but also the second dimension, the expressive dimension. For Sun, ritual helps Aborigines to communicate with their

---

[109] Huang Yinggui et al. 1993.

supernatural, with their spiritual selves – i.e., their ancestor(-spirit)s who help them to find a way back to themselves. What is also interesting in Sun's account is that he makes it very clear that a Christian God can not adapt, or can not be adapted to, this very role of the ancestors. For him, it was Christianity that caused the "desacralization" of aboriginal society. Christianity was the deadly blow for all sorts of traditional rituals. After its invasion, rituals were suddenly not "sacred" anymore, but were defined as rudiments of "superstition" and testimonies of "blasphemic polytheism". Christian ministers replaced the role of the shamans and chiefs, and members of former ritual groups were torn apart as a consequence of the disagreement between different denominations.

The attitude that Christianity was not necessarily a helping hand for aboriginal society, but rather further aggravated the problems, especially identity problems, caused by modernity sharply contrasts with the view of most Han scholars (Huang Yinggui 1992; 2001; Xie Shizhong 1987a, Qiu Yunfang 2003) and Western scholars (Rubinstein 1991; Stainton 1995), but has its parallels in the accounts of other aboriginal intellectuals (Youbas Wadan 2005; Tian Zheyi 2001: 161f.). What also becomes quite clear in Sun's account, however, is that he is not necessarily speaking for ordinary people in the tribes, who usually lead a very religious life, embracing not only Christianity but also rudimental traditional beliefs at the same time. Instead, Sun's objects of study very obviously were aboriginal intellectuals, who are confronted to a greater extent with the problem of the loss of tradition, religion and the own self than their rural counterparts. The view from the countryside, however, will be the theme of the next section.

At a closer look, Sun's idealistic assessment of contemporary aboriginal ritual activities is very much in line with the convictions of performance and practice theories that claim that it is through practice and bodily experience that social reality is constituted. By carrying out rituals, a person can reach the inner and hidden states of his self; the bodily experience will help him to reactivate the social memory of his group and adapt it to contemporary exigencies, exactly in the way Catherine Bell (1997) paraphrases Marshall Sahlins' approach:

ritual enables enduring patterns of social organization and cultural symbolic systems to be brought to bear on real events; in the course of this process, real situations are assessed and negotiated in a way that can transform these traditional patterns or structures in turn.[110]

By taking a very similar stance towards contemporary aboriginal ritual performances, Sun not only tries to emphasize the self-determined nature of aboriginal activities. He also demonstrates his conviction that carrying out ritual – despite the strange development of rituals in times of nativism – will be of some help to Aborigines and lead them back to their real selves. This view is very different from Xie's pessimistic contention of Aborigines' "thorough incorporation" into the Han's national system and social structure, as Suns vision still takes an individual, self-determined development of these rituals into account. It also goes far beyond the view that contemporary rituals are only held for political benefits and competition advantages, where "cultural and political spin doctors" (Stewart & Shaw 1994) convert "given" economical capital into cultural and symbolic capital in the sense as William S. Sax (2002) – citing Bourdieu – puts it:

> not only accumulated (i.e., conventional economic) capital but also educational capital embodied in qualifications, cultural capital acquired through one's class and upbringing, and symbolic capital, which often takes the form of public rituals, dramas, parades, and other forms of display, ... are interconvertible, so that educational capital can be converted into economic capital in the form of a high paying job, and an expenditure of symbolic capital in a ritual performance can be recaptured as cultural capital in the form of enhanced marriage alliances.[111]

Although Sax refers to Bourdieu in order to criticize "the expressive-instrumental dichotomy", the conscious management of such interconvertability by intellectual members of a society is, at least to my view,

---

[110] Bell 1997: 77.
[111] Sax 2002: 6.

thoroughly instrumentalist. I will elucidate this point in my explorations into the local ritual events. What seems impressive to me in Sun's account is his enthusiasm, which may, after a period of time, prove to be correct. When people enact certain themes over and over again, they are also socialized by these themes in some form, or they develop, as children of modernity, some kind of reflexive stance towards these themes.[112] This seems especially probable in the contemporary religious situation of Taiwan's Aborigines, who linger between a Christian God and traditional ancestor-spirits. Although it is not clear yet what decision will be taken in the future, ritual performance will – as a consequence of the contradictions enhanced by them – surely have an effect on people's minds.

The tendency to think of ritual as essentially unchanging has gone hand in hand with the assumption that effective rituals cannot be invented (Bell 1997).[113] This is also the case in Taiwan, where aboriginal traditionalists defy any intermixture of traditional ritual with non-aboriginal religious elements.[114] Sun, however, seems to offer a new perspective. Although not totally dismissing traditionalism (in so far as he himself sees the "Christian" religion as opposed to aboriginal "sacrality"), he emphasizes the potential of efficacy in Aborigines' self-consciously revitalized rituals. To him, it is not necessarily the question of whether a tradition is real or invented that seems to be crucial, but rather the way in which ritual makes man reflect upon his destiny. With this intellectual perspective, Sun is representative for a global trend that sees ritual as

> a medium of emotional, intuitive expression that is able to express the spiritual states, alternative realities, and the incipient connectedness in which individuals and communities are embedded. While ritual once stood for the status quo and the authority of the dominant social institutions, for many it has become anti-structural,

---

[112] Bell 1997: 75: "Indeed, the processes of creative socialization seen in cultural patterns of play may be particularly relevant to understanding ritual. Some analysts of the meta-communication patterns in play and ritual have stressed the similarity of "make believe" and "let us believe"."

[113] Bell 1997: 223.

[114] Pan Chaocheng 2003.

revolutionary, and capable of deconstructing inhuman institutions and generating alternative structures. [...] The older conviction that increasing modernization, rational utilitarianism, and individualism would inevitably do away with most forms of traditional ritual life has given way to a heroic championing of ritual as the way to remain human in an increasingly inhumanized world.[115]

In Sun's arguments we can clearly see that this Puyuma intellectual embraces secularism in a way that is typical for Taiwan's Han society in general, a society that is far removed from Tambiah's "ritually involuted society" in so far as religious thinking is detached from most other aspects of social life such as politics, education, economy and even family. C. Bell puts it like this:

> In a secularized or secularizing society, religious activities increasingly become a matter of personal choice and voluntary affiliation instead of an automatic cultural assumption or obligatory public duty.[116]

In Part II, we will see to what extent this feature also pertains to rural aboriginal society.

---

[115] Bell 1997: 257f.
[116] Bell 1997: 223.

PART II:

AUTHENTICATION THROUGH 'OLD' OR 'NEW' TRADITIONS?

ANNUAL FESTIVALS OF TWO AUSTRONESIAN PEOPLES IN TAIWAN

1. The Taroko's "revitalized" rituals:
Traditionalist and Christian conceptions

1.1 The emergence of collective ancestor-spirits-rituals

Since local rituals of Taiwan's Aborigines today are, for the most part, also designed by ethnic elites, they bear very similar dynamics to those representational rituals described above. They are thoroughly influenced by the external global, geopolitical, and political frame; they play a decisive role in the authenticating endeavours and in the power struggles of various elites. Nevertheless, they are also efficacious in terms of identity constitution in so far as they negotiate current identity exigencies and social hierarchies. I will illustrate this by referring to the yearly rituals of the Taroko and the Ami where I did most of my fieldwork.

Figure 9: Academic Classification of Taiwan's Taroko (until 2004)

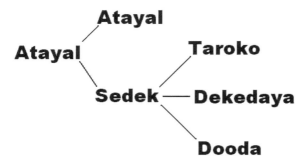

This chapter focuses on processes of identity constitution and construction manifested in the contemporary rituals of the Taroko, one of Taiwan's twelve Austronesian groups. After a description of the main traits of this group's revitalized annual rituals, I will give an account of how representatives of two competing traditions – i.e. traditionalism and Protestantism – structure and organize cultural symbols in the events to demonstrate their respective authority.

Figure 10: Distribution of Atayal and Sedek (slightly modified map taken from Ma 1998)

Most Taroko today live on Taiwan's east coast near Hualian. Anthropologically categorized as a dialect-group of the Sedek, one of the two subgroups of the Atayal, the Taroko (approx. 25.000 individuals) were not officially recognized as an independent ethnic group until 2004. Before recognition occurred, however, the question of the adequate display of this group's culture was a constant bone of contention among various ethnic elites, with ritual playing a crucial role in the process.[1]

Figure 11: Photographs of elderly tattooed Taroko from the mid-nineties (Photos: M. Rudolph and Ma Teng-yueh)

As older Taroko confirm, head-hunting had once been an integral part of Taroko tradition – a way to prove one's own skills, legitimacy, and righteousness in the face of the ancestors. Only men with these qualities could acquire their full facial tattoo; likewise, only men who had the facial tattoo were able to get married, to father children and to return to the realm of ancestors after death. Only people with blood on their hands

---

[1] According to the anthropological classification, the officially recognized Atayal are divided into Atayal Proper and Sedek. The latter are again divided into Dooda, Dekedaya and Taroko (Rudolph 2003a: 305f). The Taroko claim of independence from the Atayal was finally granted in the course of the presidential election of 2004, a success due to concessions by the ruling DPP to *Presbyterian Church* elites, but which is not yet fully accepted by the Taroko population.

were believed to be able to cross the "rainbow bridge" into the realm of the deceased, because in the eyes of the ancestor-spirits, only blood was meaningful – it was the precondition for all reproduction and status change.[2]

Since all rituals in Taroko society were once closely connected to the Taroko's ancestor-spirits-belief and to certain traditions linked to it, such as tattooing and head-hunting, the practice of collective rituals had been strongly discouraged during Japanese colonial rule in Taiwan. After Japan's surrender in 1945, a collective return to the ancestor-spirits-belief seemed impossible: The former ritual groups who once worshipped common ancestor-spirits had been torn apart in the course of the resettlement policy of the Japanese. Furthermore, the rapid spread of Christianity hindered any open practice of rituals connected to the old religious beliefs. By the end of the sixties, most Taroko had become Christians. And, last but not least, the homogenization policy practiced by the *Chinese National Party* (KMT) and the concomitant discrimination of most Han people towards the "barbarians in the mountains" did not encourage the Taroko to display any of their cultural traditions, but rather made them try to conceal their ethnic origins.[3] As a result, this group – similar to the Atayal – did not practice any collective rituals for a long time.[4]

A sudden change occurred in 1999. With the financial support of local government bodies, a group of politicians and educational elites arranged in Tongmen, a Taroko-village near to Hualian, the first collective and inter-village ritual. As the organizers of the *Taroko Cultural Construc-*

---

[2] Rudolph 2003b. See also the documentary of Qiu Ruolong of 1999 "GaYa".

[3] The stigma felt by most Aborigines because of their cultural background as "savages", "mountain people", and poorly educated "Chinese" was not only expressed in strong feelings of inferiority towards the outside, but also in "passing behavior" when exposed to Han society, as well as in different kinds of anomie, like alcohol abuse, prostitution, and a high divorce rate (Xie Shizhong 1987).

[4] It must be added that "collectives" in the past were constituted differently from collectives today, as Taroko tribes usually consisted of only one ritual group (often no more than 40-50 people) with its own spirits (*utux*) and norms (*gaya*). Therefore, collective rituals in which whole village or ethnic communities participated had never existed before.

tion Association[5] emphasized, their so called "ancestor-spirits-ritual" was supposed to serve as a model for all further activities of this kind. In their view, an overarching Taroko identity could only be forged and consolidated with the help of a common ritual celebrated collectively at least once a year – a habit that could be observed in all other aboriginal groups except the Atayal and the Taroko. If the Taroko wanted to receive their own financial resources in the future, they would have to engage in a common culture.[6]

Figure 12: Animal sacrifice at a Taroko's ancestor-spirits-ritual

The "revitalized" ritual itself was reconstructed with the help of the oral accounts of elderly and of Japanese sources from the colonial period. As nobody could remember its original name, even the Taroko term for the ritual *"megay bari"* had to be taken from the Japanese materials. The term was discovered by a Church minister in a book by the ethnologist

---

[5] This association (*Hualianxian Tailuge jianshe xiehui*) was established in 1992 as an organization of Taroko teachers, politicians and one PCT minister.
[6] Gariyi Jihong 2003: 11-12.

Sayama Yukichi (1917), and it meant as much as "to feed the spirits". As it seemed more neutral than another term suggested by some of the educational elites – i.e. *"mekan hadul"*, which had once been used for collective head-hunting rituals – it was finally adopted as the official name for the ritual.[7]

Figure 13: The Taroko's ancestor-spirits-ritual and its frame

The ritual's most salient characteristic was that sequences that originally would have lasted several days were now put together as if in "fast motion", compacting it to a one-hour-event.[8] One of its central elements was a blood sacrifice before hunting. The throat of a chicken was carefully cut, and the blood of the still living animal was collected in a bowl. Subsequently, the ritual leader, whose role was played by a Church intellectual, spread some of this blood on the weapons and on the soil. According to traditional beliefs, such blood contained supernatural power and ensured victory and success. Other sequences performed in the collective ancestor-spirits-ritual were the killing of the prey (usually raised "wild" pigs), as well as a thanksgiving sacrifice after hunting that was

---

[7] Gariyi Jihong 2002. The primary school teacher Gariyi lives in Tongmen, a Taroko village near to Hualian, and is one of the few aboriginal academics who continue to live in the tribes in close contact with the people. According to the findings of Gariyi, *"mekan hadul"* once stood for "the yearly celebration that was held for the hunted heads in order to let them be happy in their new surroundings".

[8] For instance, the sequence of the ritual hunting was omitted and only commented on by the moderator, while the scenes before and after it were performed.

conducted with parts of the prey. As the organizers of the ritual emphasized in long commentaries in Chinese and in the Taroko language, there
was one main idea central to all these sequences, i.e., the idea of the fore-
father's close observation of the *"gaya"* – the organizational rules and
norms of the Taroko that had once guaranteed discipline and solidarity in
the Taroko tribes and whose ethical and spiritual value should, for the
sake of ethnic survival, not be forgotten.[9]

Figure 14: Ritual leader of an animal sacrifice organized by traditionalists

The model ritual described here was framed in a way typical for most
collective aboriginal rituals in Taiwan today: speeches by politicians and
Protestant church ministers preceded the performance, and after its com-
pletion there were collective games, competitions and dancing. Before
2001, the ancestor-spirits-ritual was performed four times at collective

---

[9] Unang-Kasaw 22.11.2002, personal interview.

festivals;[10] thereafter it was gradually replaced by other forms of collective rituals organized by Church elites, for instance a head-hunting-ritual in one case, a wedding-ritual in another, or a hunting ritual in still another case. A common feature of all these later performances was that they no longer involved any real blood sacrifices. While the props used in the head-hunting-ritual were a plastic head and red paint, the sacrifice in the wedding-ritual, a pig waiting in an iron cage next to the ritual place, was simply omitted. In the hunting ritual I observed in 2004, the pig was played by a boy who was finally hunted down by other boys with paper sticks. The sacrifice before hunting was not shown in this case. As the Church members declared, the main function of these rituals was to remember the achievements of the ancestors and not to revive any customs from the past. In order to leave no doubt about the rituals' Christian orientation, the official name for the events was changed in 2004 to "festivals of gratefulness" (gan'enjie).[11] Remarkably, even the term "(worship)-ritual" (ji) as in "zulingji" had been changed to the worldly expression "festival" (jie).[12]Although political and educational elites continued performing animal sacrifices in individually organized "ancestor-spirits-rituals" even after 2001, these events were no longer given the status of the yearly collective festivals of whole communities.

1.2 Conflicting perspectives

There are a number of factors responsible for the difficulties in canonizing the ancestor-spirits-ritual as the Taroko's main ritual, the most im-

---

[10] The first occasion was in May 1999 in Wanrong, the second on the eve of the new millennium in Xiulin, the third 2000 in Wenlan, and the fourth 2001 in Tongmen. As the Xiulin-township-administration decided to support only village-festivals instead of village-overarching festivals from 2001 on, the subsequent festivals were organized by individual villages.

[11] This was also the term used in 2006 in the official announcement of Taroko events by the County and National governments.

[12] This antipathy toward all things that were connected to traditional forms of worship (in Chinese "ji") actually derived from the Protestant Han parishes, where ministers tried to fight ancestor worship.

portant ones being its incompatibility with Christianity on the one hand and elites' competition on the other.

Figure 15: Theatrical head-hunting ritual organized by the Church

Though not practiced openly and collectively until the end of the 1990s, ancestor-spirits-worship had in fact never ceased to be an essential part of the Taroko's religious life. Wherever things were suspected to be outside of the range of competence of the Christian God, or where the ancient gods' competence was considered to be stronger (as after certain kinds of social transgressions or in times of passage within a man's life-cycle), people still practiced the "old superstitions", as they pejoratively referred to their own habits in Chinese. This is why animal sacrifices like those mentioned above were still frequently carried out before hunting, at weddings, after child birth, or even after the purchase of a new car.

After each performance of the collective ancestor-spirits-rituals, however, the traditionalist organizers were confronted with profound criticism, particularly from the more fervent adherents of Taiwan's *Presbyte-*

rian Church, who denounced the sacrifices in the ritual not only as "blaspheme" and "dangerous" acts, but also as "negligently provoking supernatural powers".[13] One reason for the broad uneasiness felt by many common people was the frequent use of the expression *"gaya"* in the rituals, a term that in Taroko-language means "rules/law of the *utux*". While the organizers understood this expression in a positive way in times of degenerating social morals, many common people perceived it instead in its traditional sense, in which it also had the connotation of "punishment" and "responsibility for a crime".[14] The greatest suspicion, however, was aroused by the "instrumentalization" of the Church intellectual as "ritual leader" in the sacrifices. Shortly after the first enactment of the ritual, a letter was circulated in the Taroko-branch of the *Presbyterian Church of Taiwan* (PCT), in which the ritual and particularly the Church intellectual's participation were severely attacked as "misleading".[15] In short, there was a subtle fear that the collective ancestor-spirits-rituals might still be, or might still be perceived as, efficacious in a religious sense – a situation that was totally intolerable for devoted Christians in Taroko society. This concern sharply contrasted with the attitude of the traditionalists who contended that people should "face their common culture and their commonalities" in order to find their common identity and who criticized the "mental colonization" exercised by the Church.[16] In postcolonial Taiwan, such reasoning actually was not uncommon and could, though with a different connotation, even be found in the self-criticism of intellectual circles within the Christian churches, who discussed the question of further indigenization of the Christian re-

---

[13] Personal Interviews with Nanang 23.11.02; Jiro 15.04.03; Imy and Gu 10.04.03. Also see Qiu Yunfang 2002: 9; Qiu Yunfang 2004.

[14] Cao Qiuqin 1998: 22; Qiu Yunfang 2002: 14.

[15] Most people were convinced that Hayu Yudaw – a Taroko-minister and PCT-College teacher, who had participated in the ancestor-spirits-rituals several times as a ritual leader, had been "misused" by the political elites. Hayu Yudaw himself dismissed these accusations, arguing that his only aim had been to "intervene" and "mediate" between Christian and non-Christian traditions. The motive of the traditionalists in allowing the minister to participate, however, can only be explained as an attempt to "borrow his authority".

[16] Lodi 2.12.2002; Gariyi Jihong 7.12.2003, personal interviews.

ligion with the aim of stopping the incessant decrease of followers in recent years.

Figure 16: Taroko performers "absorbing supernatural power" at a theatrical head-hunting ritual organized by the Church

1.3 Church elites vs. political elites

Apart from the differences in their cultural attitudes, there were also certain political experiences and an ideological gap dividing Christians and traditionalists in Taroko society. Many of the opponents of the revived ancestor-spirits-ritual were Church ministers themselves or persons who were closely linked to the *Presbyterian Church* (PCT), which had once built the foundations for Taiwan's nativist movement.[17]

---

[17] Rudolph 2004b: 243. Beginning in the mid-seventies, the *Presbyterian Church of Taiwan* (PCT), was always the most active institution in terms of protection of aboriginal cultures in Taiwan. About half of the 84% Christians in Taroko society belong to the PCT. Although the *Roman Catholic Church* and the *True Jesus Church*

At the high tide of nativism in the second half of the nineties, however, the fruits of this former commitment were increasingly monopolized by other ethnic elites, for instance local politicians, who boasted of being the saviors and protectors of aboriginal culture, as well as Taroko school teachers and directors who were now officially assigned with the organization of aboriginal mother language curricula.

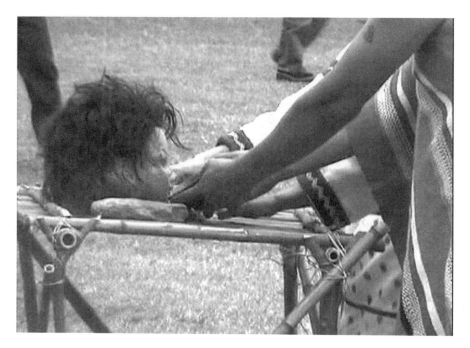

Figure 17: Taroko performers "feeding the enemy spirits in order to convince them to become the tribe's own ancestor-spirits" at a theatrical ritual organized by the Church

From the perspective of Presbyterian ministers, the success of these elites was often regarded with much suspicion, as most of them formerly had been loyal to the authoritarian regime and still belonged to political circles in Taiwan today called "conservative influences". As their devotion to local culture had only begun after the spread of nativism, it was sus-

---

also have large congregations in Taroko society, they very rarely engage in cultural activities and even advise their followers to stay away from the revitalized ritual events.

pected that their interest in the rituals mainly stemmed from their wish to dominate official cultural resources and to exert better control over the people.

In terms of ideology, both elites actually had a common goal, i.e. the establishment of a common ethnic identity in order to increase the Taroko's opportunities in Taiwan's multiculturalism. There was, however, also an important difference. The main goal of the traditionalist politicians was the acquisition of financial support under the ethnic name "Sedek": By presenting oneself as "Sedek" or "Sedek-Taroko" in authentic rituals and not as "Atayal", one could acquire funding. Despite their attempts at cultural particularization, these politicians did not really aim at an ethnic separation from the Sedek or the Atayal, since they profited from an intact Atayal political network, in which the KMT was still the dominant force. Politicians close to the KMT thus did not anticipate any advantages from secession and instead petitioned for the maintenance of the *status quo*.

The majority of Taroko PCT ministers, on the other hand, participated in the "Taroko-recognition-movement" that advocated independence not only from the Atayal, but also from the Sedek, claiming that the latter were culturally different.[18] This, of course, was a sensitive argument, as

---

[18] Actually, the Taroko's - or better the "Sedek's" - independence from the Atayal had long been recognized by the PCT, which had always distinguished between an Atayal and a Taroko congregation, the latter also including the Sedek. This was justified with the immense difference between the Atayal and the Sedek languages in which sermons were held. As Qiu Yunfang points out, the real "Taroko-recognition-movement" began in 1996 after the issue of a "Taroko-ethnie" had been made the subject of a symposium within the Taroko congregation of the PCT. At that time, the West Sedek on the other side of the central mountain range reacted with great discontent, as their population consisted of equal proportions of the three Sedek subgroups, Dooda, Dekedaya and Taroko. As a consequence, they split away from the Taroko congregation and established their own Sedek congregation in 1998, which in turn provoked the Taroko of Hualian to radicalize their "Taroko-recognition-movement". Qiu makes clear that the engagement in the revitalization of the Taroko's collective rituals was actually only one of the endeavors of this movement. Another was the commemoration of a martyr's incident particular only to the Taroko, i.e., the anti-Japanese "Taroko incident" of 1914 instead of the anti-

smaller populations of the two other Sedek groups, the Dooda and the Dekedaya,[19] lived in common villages with the Taroko.[20] In addition to cultural considerations, however, there was a very rational calculation behind the PCT-intellectuals' request to be recognized as an independent group – with its own political representatives, the PCT hoped to be able to break the monopoly of the *Chinese National Party* (KMT) in the region. Also, if the new DPP government[21] really did establish "autonomous zones for Aborigines" within the next few years, as it had announced, the Taroko too would have to be dealt with as an independent ethnic group with its own zone and administration system, thus also bringing new opportunities for PCT adherents close to the DPP.[22]

1.4 Authenticating Strategies

In the following, I will show how social tensions as those pointed out above were not only very clearly manifested in the Taroko's reinvented rituals, but were also efficaciously negotiated during the performances. By way of the strategic arrangement of certain ritual symbols and actions, ethnic elites succeeded in conveying messages that went far beyond the cosmological meaning of the ritual enacted and that had not only the aim of providing villagers with alternative identity symbols, but also of establishing, renewing or consolidating their own authority. Most

---

Japanese "Wushe incident" of 1930, which was representative for the Sedek and even for the Atayal as a whole.

[19] The Taroko of the east coast pejoratively call the Dekedaya "Bleibao", which means "Foreskin" (= unimportant).

[20] Although the argument applied better to the Taroko's relationship to the West Sedek who lived on the western side of the mountain range and from whom the East Sedek had separated some hundred years ago, it caused much discontent among those Sedek who had no or only partial Taroko background.

[21] Since May 2000, Taiwan has been governed by the *Democratic Progress Party* (DPP), whose adherents are mainly Taiwan-born Chinese. The DPP was officially acknowledged after the end of the authoritarian rule of the *Chinese National Party* (KMT) in 1987 and functioned as Taiwan's main political opposition until 2000.

[22] See "Delugu zhi sheng–The Voice of Truku", No.6, 17.10.2002, a monthly magazine published by the *Truku Youth Association*, where this perspective is articulated.

of these arrangements were improvisations that were neither documented in the ritual script prepared and published by the educational elites, nor were they mentioned in the Japanese sources or in the old people's accounts.[23]

Framing techniques of traditionalists and Church elites

Let me start with the second sequence from the reconstructed ancestor-spirits-ritual summarized above. Traditionally, an animal sacrifice (*bouda* in Taroko language) is conducted by two or three people, viz. the ritual leader and those who help him while he communicates with the ancestor-spirits. In all the performances of the "model-ancestor-spirits-ritual", however, there were two ritual leaders participating in the sacrifice, one of them being the big chief (or better the person who played the role of the big chief in the ritual),[24] the other being a Church intellectual who took over the task of open communication with the transcendental powers – begging for strength and success in hymn-like verses murmured into the microphone, he addressed the supernatural with a multitude of confusing expressions, including titles like "god of all gods" (*utux kana utux*), "weaving (= creating) god" (*utux tminun*), "old ancestors" (*utux rudan nami sbiyaw*), as well as "god of all our ancestors" (*utux kana rudan nami*), to mention only a few.[25] Another sacrifice performed by the Church intellectual was the thanksgiving sacrifice, which took place later during the model-ritual. In this latter sacrifice, however, an interesting modification was made as a reaction to the severe criticism that had followed the first enactment of the ancestor-spirits-ritual. While, in the first performance, tiny pieces of the prey's intestines and extremities that had been wrapped into leaves were collectively offered to the ancestor-spirits (this was the way that the ancestor-spirits-sacrifice was still carried out

---

[23] The ritual scenes described below are well documented in diverse documentaries and film clips that I was able to collect in the last couple of years. A reproduction of the script can be viewed in Gariyi Jihong 2004: 72-77.

[24] In the first ritual performed in May 1999 in Wanrong, the big chief was played by the village head of Wanrong.

[25] Gariyi Jihong 2003: 26.

when domestic animals were slaughtered in private households),[26] only harvested fruit and vegetables were offered in subsequent performances, a strategy by which the organizers were obviously trying to suggest that the possibility of the sacrifices' misinterpretation by supernatural powers was now reduced. No such concessions, however, were made with regard to the animal sacrifice in the second sequence of the model ritual, i.e., the blood sacrifice before hunting.

The improvisations in the sacrifices described above point to two kinds of competition among elites in contemporary Taroko society. As far as the integration of the Church intellectual into the ritual and the modification of the thanksgiving sacrifice are concerned, they were clearly motivated by the traditionalists' endeavor to make their "model ritual" more resistant to attacks and doubts from the part of Christians. Particularly the employment of a man from the Church as a "ritual leader" must be understood as an attempt to "borrow" the authority of the Church – an authority that was almost absolute in aboriginal communities – in order to legitimize the new ritual.[27]

The confusing participation of the Church intellectual as "ritual leader" on the other hand also points a dispute between two different wings of the *Presbyterian Church of Taiwan* (PCT). In order to adapt the Christian religion to the specific needs and aesthetical perceptions of Taiwanese Aborigines, intellectuals close to the PCT's General Assembly (*zonghui*) had begun to proclaim the necessity of a "third path"[28] – a

---

[26] The Taroko were convinced that only creatures raised by human toil would work as sacrifices.

[27] Here, "borrowed authority" is used in a slightly different sense than pointed out by Klaus-Peter Köpping 2004: In his article "Borrowed Authority", Köpping not only shows how leaders may achieve special effects with symbolical ritual actions by way of "borrowing" or referring to the authority of others (often transcendental powers), but that this borrowing may in turn also enlarge the counterpart's authority, similar to citation processes in academic writing. However, such a reverberation was surely not intended by the traditionalists in Taroko society.

[28] In December 2002, I had the opportunity to attend a conference entitled "The third path" organized by the PCT's Yushan Theology College. Very similar conferences with the title "Encounter of the Aborigines' traditional culture and rituals with

policy that was well-meant in times of declining numbers of followers,[29] but that was increasingly criticized by PCT-ministers and presbyters in the countryside, who did not believe in the functionality and the religious legitimacy of such a proceeding.[30] As a member of a PCT college, the Christian intellectual who had played the "ritual leader" in all the ancestor-spirits-rituals had in fact always been one of the most fervent advocates of the "third path".[31] This did not mean that he really wanted to revive traditional religion or that he was truly cooperating with the traditionalists. As he made clear in personal interviews, his participation in the ritual was just his own individual way of promoting the kind of indigenization that was welcomed by the intellectual superstructure of his Church. It had also been motivated by the wish to "attract the Taroko Christians who generally attended hardly any collective festivals at all". During the rituals he had of course always spoken to his Christian God, and he had made clear that this God was "on the highest level".[32]

Christianity" were subsequently organized by Taiwan World Vision in cooperation with the PCT in July 2003 in Hualian and in February 2004 in Pingdong.

[29] According to some PCT intellectuals I talked to at Yushan Theology College, the "smithy" of aboriginal intellectuals in Taiwan, the "third path" was also a measure of containment against the traditionalist currents in aboriginal society. Although the PCT intellectuals looked upon these endeavors with great concern, they finally saw no other choice but "to jump on the bandwagon and to join the development" in order not to lose control completely.

[30] Since aboriginal ministers who lived in the villages were in permanent contact with the people, they did not only have the deepest knowledge of the psychology of the people, but also had to cope with any negative results of "cultural experiments" (Jiro 15.04.03). Quite to the contrary, Church intellectuals who advocated the "third path" as well as most of the traditionalists were usually very much assimilated into the corresponding social and intellectual strata in modern Han society.

[31] In May 1999, Hayu Yudaw (1999) handed in a Master's thesis at the Vancouver School of Theology, in which he discusses the possibility of an indigenization of Christianity in Taroko society. In this study, Hayu also calls for the adaptation of the Eucharist to the aesthetical perceptions of the Taroko (for instance to serve millet cakes and millet wine instead of bread and wine etc.).

[32] Hayu Yudaw 15.11.2002, personal interview; see also the interview in Gariyi Jihong 2003: 25. In these accounts, Hayu not only emphasizes that he had actually prayed to his Christian God during the rituals, but also admits that he has sometimes been afraid during the rituals, as he was not sure how the 'utux' would react.

Remarkable in the account above is that both elites, traditionalists as well as Church elites, had very similar perceptions of how the "real life" status of an actor could be used to "frame" a ritual action in a way that it evoked associations different from the cosmological meaning it stood for. While the traditionalists expected that the juxtaposition of the real and the cosmological role conveyed the implicit message "look, even a Church man can participate in the ritual", the Church intellectual was convinced that his participation (as well as his ambivalent speech) would make the ritual look like "a Christian activity celebrated in honor of God". The placement of the Christian ministers' speeches before the rituals of the traditionalists was in fact motivated by the same expectations.[33] As we will see below, the pattern described here – the manipulation of ritual symbols and their strategic juxtaposition in relation to certain aspects from real life – was a common feature in the Taroko's reinvented rituals.

Local politicians and rituals of status inversion

Another example for such a strategic juxtaposition of real and ritual roles could be observed in the interaction of politicians and ordinary people in the reinvented ancestor-spirits-rituals.

The most influential people in Taroko society today are the township heads, each one of whom governs approximately ten to twelve thousand Taroko in his township.[34] At the time when the Taroko lived in acephalous tribes, the most capable person had been considered to be the leader – a status that had to be constantly earned and re-earned. Hunting and especially risky head-hunting had once played an important role in this context. Vested with the capability to assert his authority over all other Taroko in the township, a modern township head surely had, at least in the eyes of the common people, the qualities of a traditional leader. In the reinvented collective rituals, however, such politicians did not necessar-

---

[33] Qiu Yunfang 2002: 5.

[34] Most of the Sedek inhabitants of the two townships Wanrong and Xiulin on the east coast of Taiwan are Taroko. Only very small percentages are Dooda and Dekedaya.

ily play a role equivalent to their real social status. In the ancestor-spirits-ritual performed on the eve of the new millennium in Xiulin, for instance, the township head was dressed in the traditional cloth of the ordinary people – cloth that is characterized by a very simple black and white pattern and that is easy to weave. Contrastingly, a person of much lower social status in contemporary Taroko society played the big chief in the ritual.[35] He was dressed in the so-called *slbuxan*, a cloth that, woven by the most skilful women, could originally only be worn by the successful head-hunter.[36] Ordinary people commented on the switching of social roles indicated here with delight and ridicule, as for them the township head was by no means the most well-liked person, but rather a man whose influence they feared and envied at the same time. In the improvisation described here we can easily see a "status inversion" in the Turnerian sense – a rite that mediates between the upper and the lower strata of a society. As this improvisation was, however, intentionally designed by the elites, it clearly also had the function of consolidating the politician's authority within the group.[37]

Subversion and ridiculing of Han authority

A multitude of improvisations in the new rituals demonstrated the underlying conflict between Taroko and Han. While it was difficult for the Taroko to express their dissatisfaction and frustration, which had accumulated over the many years of interaction with Taiwanese Han in normal life, contemporary ritual seemed to serve as an appropriate context to give people the opportunity to compensate for some of these feelings. Scenes of subversion of Han authority and Han culture were no rarity,

---

[35] Though the man playing the big chief was by no means a real chief (he was a hunter who earned his living with making traditional Taroko-knifes for the tourist industry), he surely had some traditional wisdom.

[36] For a detailed description of *slbuxan* see Gariyi Jihong 2001a. In traditional Taroko society, only those women who were able to weave the complicated red pattern of the *slbuxan* were qualified to obtain their full facial tattoo.

[37] In his notion of *communitas*, Victor Turner (1969) suggests that ritual is a medium that negotiates and mediates social relations. In this context, Turner also refers to "rituals of status reversal".

and there were even occurrences of "reversed symbolic violence" as discussed in Part I.

One concrete example of this kind of subversion was an incident that happened during the ritualized food-sharing in one of the events. After the slaughtering of the prey, pieces of the raw liver of the animal are generally distributed to the hunters and their relatives and are eaten as prescribed by tradition. This is also the case in the private ancestor-spirits-rituals conducted within families today. In one of the public performances, however, raw liver was also given to two attending Han school directors who first reacted with great embarrassment, but who finally pretended to eat it. The attending crowd rewarded the spectacle with delighted whispering and giggling. In order to fully understand the meaning behind this scene, which was not mentioned in the script, one has to know that Taiwan's Taroko, who, like their Atayal neighbors, were formerly known as 'tattooed barbarians', had once been despised explicitly because of their extreme wildness. In the decades following the reacquisition of the island by the Han Chinese after Japanese colonial rule, the Taroko endured heavier discrimination by the Han than all other aboriginal groups in Taiwan. This was not only because of their former head-hunting habits, which were still tattooed on the faces of the older people, but also because of their uncivilized manners, including their custom of eating raw intestines and drinking blood. In large scale re-education programs during the authoritarian period, the Han government had tried to transform the Taroko into "civilized" beings and to eradicate these habits. In the scene mentioned above, the cultural violence the Taroko had endured for decades was now turned against the Han – now they were forced to accept the cultural values of the Taroko in the same way that they had formerly forced the Taroko to accept Han values. Because of the alleged sacredness of the ritual in which the school directors were invited to take part, they could not refuse the offering. The exertion of reversed cultural violence here very obviously had the function of a rejection of the deep seated cultural stigma imposed on the Taroko by the "bringers of civilization". Nevertheless, the very ambiguity which is so characteristic of ritual also hindered any subsequent uncovering of alleged viciousness or ulterior motives behind the act. It is interesting to have a short look at the explanations, provided by the ritual actors themselves, of the scene. One of the actors stated that it was normal for the Taroko to share everything with their guests, so the raw liver had to be shared as well – this expressed the Taroko's hospitality and warm-heartedness. A second actor, however, declared that there existed no custom of sharing ritual items like raw liver with guests. Nevertheless, the proceeding might be an adequate treatment vis à vis the chiefs of other tribes – the school directors were obviously treated like the chiefs of other tribes. That this was also not an ultimate explanation could be seen from the reaction of the man who had ordered the raw liver brought to the Han – the head of the Taroko village where the festival took place. He argued that he had not had any specific intention at all. He had simply wanted to let the people on the tribune have some of the ritual meat.[38]

Another improvisation in the ancestor-spirits-ritual that highlighted the conflict between Aborigines and Han was an allusion to the Han-made land and hunting rights made every time the prey (pigs that looked like wild pigs) was carried in. This was a very sensitive moment, as everyone knew that hunting was actually prohibited in the *Taroko National Park*. However, at the first ancestor-spirits-ritual in 1999, the moderator ironically stated that "the pigs had not had to be hunted but had voluntarily come down from the mountains." And – grossly ridiculing reality – he then added: "Actually, the *National Park Office* now allows us to hunt wild pigs." In the Xiulin festival 2000, the interdiction of hunting rights was ridiculed again. Here, the moderator proclaimed: "Though we have a *Taroko National Park* now, we still succeed in eating the meat of wild animals". The interdiction of hunting and gathering on their own traditional land was intolerable for most Taroko; however, the conflict seemed to be defused simply by ridiculing it.

An important characteristic of contemporary reinvented Taroko ritual was the use of body signs from the traditional repertoire in a way that gave them a catalyzing function in terms of role- and identity construction. An example already mentioned was the emblematic use of traditional cloth in the course of status mediations between elites and ordinary

---

[38] Gariyi 2004: 162-64.

people.[39] A prominent body sign that was emblematically used with respect to the latent conflict between Aborigines and Han was reproduc-
tions of the traditional facial tattoos. As I stated above, the unveiled contempt of the Han for the "tattooed barbarians" had haunted the Taroko
for many decades, and most middle-aged people still remembered how
they were once despised for their tattooed grandparents. What had once
been considered to be of the highest cultural value in one's own cultural
group had been treated with utmost contempt by the Han people.

**Figure 18: Children with fake tattoos at a head-hunting ritual organized by
the Church elites in 2002.**

In order to remedy the deep feeling of cultural inferiority caused by an
uncomprehending environment in the past, Taroko intellectuals insisted
that this sign of former ethnic pride and superiority should be worn once
again during cultural events. Therefore, the younger people now, after

---

[39] "Emblematic" here means those body signs and gestures that are consciously and
intentionally used to communicate certain messages.

decades of painful discrimination, began to apply tattoos again to tell the Han that they had discarded their feelings of cultural inferiority and come to feel like "real Taroko" again. Representative for this kind of new pride is the 2002 music recording "Head-Hunting" by Pideru Wuga introduced in Part I above.[40] Because of its alleged destigmatizing and liberating psychological effects, the practice of applying fake tattoos was also continued in the rituals of the Church that replaced the ancestor-spirits-rituals after 2001.

To what extent animal sacrifices were themselves attempts to demonstrate subversiveness becomes clear in two incidences that happened in 2002, about one year after the last official ancestor-spirits-ritual had taken place. In this year, educational elites organized two performances of animal sacrifices in the Taroko village of Fushi.[41] While the first event took place at a car race organized by the Han, the second occurred at an international marathon. In both incidences, the performers urged ancestor-spirits to let the events happen smoothly. The implicit provocation can hardly be overlooked. Although the original meaning of the sacrifice may have been to implore the ancestor-spirits to equip the sacrificer and his people with supernatural powers (*bhring*) in order to lead them unharmed to success,[42] the ritual's observation in these particular situations could be understood differently. The ritual also emphasized the powerlessness of the Han on the lands that originally belonged to the Taroko, where the Han could only be protected through rituals conducted by the Taroko. The fact that animal sacrifices had already taken on the additional meaning of "protest", "subversion", and "re-empowerment" in Taroko intellectual circles was also demonstrated by young Taroko intel-

---

[40] Not only the melody, but also the comments on the head-hunting-ritual were inspired by the head-hunting-ritual organized by PCT-elites. However, as Pideru does not refer to "Taroko", but only to "Sedek" in his CD's title, this caused some annoyance to Imi, the re-inventor of the ritual. Pideru justifies himself by saying that he does not ideologically support the Taroko-independence-movement of the Church (Pideru 14.4.2003, personal interview).

[41] Fushi, which is located at the entrance to the *Taroko National Park,* was also the place where the first demonstration against the national park took place in 1994.

[42] Gariy Jihong 2001b.

lectuals in 1999 when they used an animal sacrifice to accentuate their protest against the occupation of their land by the cement industry.[43]

1.5 Concluding Remarks: Conversion, the status of traditional relig-ion, and the development of contemporary ritual

The analysis above has shown that reinvented Taroko ritual played a crucial role in the reorganization of values and cultural attitudes in Taroko society – values and attitudes that were proposed, defended and assimilated by young ethnic elites who were also the initiators of the ritu-als. Although the content of the new performances drew only loosely on fragments from the traditional repertoire and seemed, at first glance, not to have much in common with reality, underlying psychological and so-cial tensions were not only reflected, but also renegotiated, and cultural and religious traditions were reconsidered and newly assessed in respect to their significance for the Taroko's adequate representation in contem-porary Taiwan. Interesting is the way in which this renegotiation took place. It involved a dynamic that Stanley Tambiah (1979) has correctly identified as "ritual's duplex existence" – in each of the examples listed above, symbols and actions that were connected to the Taroko's tradi-tional cosmology were "re-contextualized" or "reframed" so that they could also be understood differently.[44] This special effect was achieved through the strategic synthesis of the cosmological specifications with certain aspects of the real life world of the Taroko, either by the use of speech, or, more often, by the mere juxtaposition of ritual roles and sym-bols with real roles, experiences and memories of the participants. In order to express their messages, various elites additionally enhanced the suggestive power and ambivalence of ritual symbols; however, the sym-bols could, in each case, also be interpreted purely cosmologically and without any political or social implications. In this way, the rituals re-

---

[43] See the documentary of Pan Chaocheng 2003.

[44] However, the application of Tambiah's theory to contemporary Taroko ritual is asymmetrical in so far as Tambiah, in his account of ritual involution, does not dis-cuss the interrelation of social life and a traditional cosmology from the past, but the interrelation of social life and the current cosmology of a people.

mained socially acceptable within the performances and were able to proceed uninterrupted in spite of the sensitive issues upon which they touched. This would not have been the case had the elites addressed their interests openly in other contexts. I have referred to this advantage of ritual ambiguity in Part I.

If we look for the reasons for the failure of the ancestor-spirits-ritual to become the Taroko's "standard-ritual", the most important one seems to be the ritual's incompatibility with this people's contemporary belief system. Although only few people in Taroko society openly admitted that the new collective performances were efficacious in a traditional sense, most of them were deeply involved with the question of which cultural symbols should be adopted and which should be discarded in favor of a positive representation of contemporary Taroko culture. "Christian religion and culture should be one thing and should not be separated", ordinary people often told me. For them, this meant that the Taroko as good Christians were supposed to live exclusively and unmistakably according to Christian values. This attitude contrasted with the conviction of non-Church elites, who believed indigenous and foreign culture should be dealt with as two different things: "Western religion belongs to Western religion, Taroko culture to Taroko culture", they said, "We ought not to forget our *gaya*" – "*gaya*" being a concept that for them was equal to "discipline and solidarity". Ordinary people, however, generally understood "*gaya*" differently when the term was used in reference to the traditional religion. For them, disastrous fates such as alcoholism, handicaps and miscarriages were *gaya*[45] that were caused by the sins and misdoings of the head-hunting ancestors. In order to escape further misfortune, they secretly conducted animal sacrifices after wrongdoings or before important undertakings. On the other hand, they regarded the public ancestor-spirits-rituals conducted by the intellectuals with some unease and discomfort because the spirits – no matter whether it was the Christian God

---

[45] Within the Christian religion, the term "*gaya*" continued to exist as "*kyokai gaya*" for the "ten commandments".

or the ancestor-spirits – should not be provoked nor joked with, as this could have bad consequences.[46]

This shows that people were actually still deeply involved in their traditional belief system. Qiu Yunfang (2004), a Taiwanese anthropologist who conducted extensive fieldwork in Taroko villages and whose research focused on the reinvented rituals, makes it clear that it was exactly this involvement resulting from the continuing vitality of the traditional religion that caused the rejection of the ancestor-spirits-ritual. The Taroko's ambivalent spiritual condition was connected to their specific mode of conversion, which was characterized by "complementary coexistence" (*bingcun hubu*). Qiu argues that the way in which traditional religion could "coexist" with Christianity primarily depended on the character of the religion.[47] If it proclaimed universal validity in the same way as Christianity, and if it insisted on its right of existence, it often developed a rival relationship vis-à-vis Christianity, such as the Kwara'ae of the Solomon Islands (Burt 1984). Such rivalry could, in the end, produce syncretism (*zongshexing de zongjiao yundong*) as a way to cope with the tensions and conflicts that developed between the religions. For Qiu, the Kwara'ae case is an example for "rival coexistence" (*bingcun jingzheng*) of two "strongly institutionalized religions". If the traditional religion on the other hand was only "weakly institutionalized" and did not defend its symbols with too much exclusivity, there was a good chance that it could keep on existing unmolested at the outer edge of society, taking over functions that were neglected by Christianity. For a long time, the Taroko's relation to Christianity had been "complementary existence" in exactly this sense. The *Presbyterian Church of Taiwan* paid no more attention to the traditional religion after it had, by defining the old deities and spirits as "Satan", forced it into a niche where it stagnated almost invisibly. In this way, traditional Taroko religion had survived beside Christianity and fulfilled functions not provided by Christianity. While the Christian God was deemed responsible for the remission of

---

[46] Minyou 13.4.03, personal interview.

[47] As indicated above, two other prominent modes of conversion were the total abandonment of traditional religion as well as syncretism.

sins and good luck, the traditional gods were, as in the past, feared and worshipped as generators of worldly misfortune, which could haunt even the children and grandchildren of the original wrongdoer. Only when, motivated by nativist traditionalism, the ancestor-spirits-rituals were seeming to imply a thorough revitalization of traditional religion and its original significance, did the PCT begin to fight back.[48] Because the Church had, however, its own nativist interests and considerations (considerations that were partly instigated by an internal process of reflection), it did not simply prohibit the reinventions, but rather strongly attempted to establish alternative representations of Taroko culture.

The question now is why Taroko traditionalists did not refer to key concepts of their culture somewhat more cautiously in order not to challenge underlying sensitivities. A stereotypical answer from the traditionalists themselves was that it was necessary to challenge the conservative thinking of their people, which was so greatly affected by mental colonialization carried out by the Han and the Church.[49] Another answer is given by the Taiwanese anthropologist, Qiu Yunfang. She contends that the process of revitalization (*fuzhen*) actually had two directions. It was not only directed towards Aborigines, but also towards the Han, who had to be convinced of the significance of aboriginal culture. The intellectuals, who were the main initiators of the revitalization process, studied the concepts like researchers from the outside and translated them in a way that they could be understood by the Han, thereby changing the original meaning so much that ordinary people in the communities could no longer grasp it.[50]

---

[48] In her study, Qiu (2004) still lists further reasons why Taiwan's Aborigines did not develop nativist and syncretic religious movements. Christianity was always able to convincingly offer consolation because it did not come from the oppressors. Even if, in the early days of Christianity, missionaries were Han, this was during Japanese colonial rule when the Han were themselves colonized. A further reason for the successful adoption of Christianity was the organizational structure of the PCT, i.e. the practice of spreading the Gospel in the various mother languages, the employment of aboriginal ministers, as well as the practice of making the tribe the center of the parish so that people with a common language flocked together.

[49] Lodi 28.10.2002, personal interview.

[50] Qiu Yunfang 2002: 16-17; Qiu Yunfang 2004.

For Richard Schechner, theatre is created when an audience emerges as a separate group, when it is accidental rather than integral.[51] In the case of reinvented Taroko ritual, the audience is clearly integral:[52] nearly all members of this society participate in ritual criticism. And nearly all of them react very positively when they see the Han being forced to eat raw liver or see their own children wearing the fake tattoos. Even though nearly all of the participants are paid and refunded for their time, preparatory work and materials, and although local politicians very obviously instrumentalize the activities for their individual aims, the rituals are actually much more than stiff theatrical performances with the main function of entertainment or the manifestation of political power. At least in terms of its social role, reinvented Taroko ritual thus is highly efficacious:[53] The performances contribute to the renegotiation, the reevaluation and the modification of the participants' relationship to themselves, to other Taroko and to the Han. Rather than, as generally in theatre, simply representing social structure, these activities have the power to create, change and subvert social reality, which is clearly a characteristic of ritual.[54] Despite Taroko society's constant disintegration, "integral" here of course comes close to Giddens' (1994) "traditional society" or to Tambiah's (1979: 158) "ritually involuted society", in which "the domains of religion, polity, and economy fuse into a single total phenomenon". The issues enacted not only directly affect (or may affect) the villagers' living conditions (at least in a negative sense if a god gets angry), but also real social status and relationships.

---

[51] Richard Schechner 1985: 117 and 1977: 63ff.

[52] The audiences of Taroko rituals consist mainly of the members of the respective villages. Han spectators were present in some of the ancestor-spirits-rituals, but not in the other rituals I watched. Although the *Hualian County Government* has promoted the development of tourism for many years, hardly any tourists are seen in Taroko villages today.

[53] Both for Pierre Bourdieu (1977) and Catherine Bell (1997), the "true efficacy" of the rite lies in its contribution to social structure.

[54] See for instance Jean Comaroff (1985) who emphasizes that "ritual provides an appropriate medium through which the values and structures of a contradictory world may be addressed and manipulated." (Comaroff 1985:196).

The initiative of the traditionalists in "revitalizing" collective rituals has thus been very effective. What had started out as a measure of authentication in order to obtain governmental resources,[55] had finally become an identity-instilling activity with a life of its own. In the course of the revival of the Taroko's non-Christian traditions, the traditionalists, however, had underestimated or even disregarded the Taroko's peculiar form of Christianity and the Church's specific role in the control of Taroko traditions. As long as the "old superstitions" were only practiced privately and were not put on the stage publicly, the inherent inconsistencies and ambivalence in the people's religious and cultural attitudes were not problematized. Only after the appearance of the collective rituals, did people begin to visualize their own cultural positions. It was exactly this effect that also caused the resistance and recriminations by the Church.

---

[55] As primary school director Unang-Kasaw, one of the two main initiators of the ancestor-spirits-ritual, describes, at least the establishment of the Taroko-Culture-Association in 1992 had the aim of preventing that financial resources were completely used up by the Ami who already had an Ami-Culture-Association (Gariyi Jihong 2003: 11). In a personal interview, Gariyi Jihong makes clear that the funds raised by such organizations for administrational work and for activities were seldom only used for these declared purposes, but were rather spent in election campaigns (28.11.2002, personal interview).

2. Competing Ritual Traditions of Taiwan's Ami

2.1 The Ami's "harvest-festival"

In the previous chapter, we saw that contemporary Taroko ritual bears many of the traits that characterize the representation rituals discussed in the first part of the book, especially its control and domination by elites, the reference of these elites to supernatural powers in order to legitimate themselves, as well as subtle attempts at subversion and transgression accompanying the rituals. In both cases, ritual not only served identity exigencies, but also the authentication of elites. What is different from aboriginal elite's representation rituals is that actors and audiences in contemporary Taroko rituals are, despite the religious and political partitions dividing this society, still very much "integral" to the events in a way that these rituals serve as forums of negotiation of social relations and statuses of the members of the community.

In this chapter, I will look at the role contemporary ritual plays in Ami society. As I stated above, the positive re-evaluation and re-assessment of aboriginal traditions in Taiwan occurred at a time when there was hardly any traditional life style remaining in aboriginal villages. Since Ami society was, similar to Taroko society, also very much Christianized, the question arises how people here dealt with the (now officially prescribed) task of protecting and handing on traditional culture. I will center my attention on the annual "harvest-festival" of the Ami of Taibalang, the largest Ami tribe on Taiwan's east coast.[1] One of the main characteristics of the festival – a five-day-event that consists of a number of smaller rites and ritualized actions[2] – is its thorough blending of Christian and tradi-

---

[1] Taibalang is also one of the oldest Ami tribes. Mabuchi (1935) confirmed in 1931 that people in Taibalang are able to trace back at least 40 generations, a time span of approximately 1000 years.

[2] As the Chinese word *ji* today denotes both festival and ritual, the Chinese expression *fengnian ji* can also be translated as "harvest worship-ritual". Actually, the whole

tional elements.[3] This becomes clear from the fact that its officially recognized opening ceremony is dominated by Christian elements, while the symbolism of many sequences and actions within the festival (for instance dietary taboos: no fish or vegetables are to be eaten during the whole festival; only meat is permitted) refer to beliefs in traditional Ami religion. Another main characteristic of the festival is the competition among various elites who strive for predominance in one of these traditions. While the two main competing positions are a Christian and a traditionalist one, as we have seen in contemporary Taroko ritual, these two currents also ally themselves with other social interest groups such as political parties, cultural associations, genders etc.. The fact that everybody in Taibalang is connected to at least one of these interest groups (or identities) predetermines his or her active engagement in ritual criticism.

I will address the following two issues in the course of the chapter. In addition to assessing the main social functions of the festival and their modification over time, I will show how societal elites today actively structure and modify ritual symbols and actions during the event in order to enhance their authority. In order to do this, I will also take a closer look at the social embeddedness and historical trajectories of both the Ami mainstream tradition which is today represented by a Catholic power alliance, and of the traditionalist challenge represented by rivaling societal forces.

In spite of the relatively small number of Malayo-Polynesian Aborigines in Taiwan (less than two percent), Taiwan's Han have all heard or read of the harvest-festivals of the matrilinear Ami, an aboriginal group

---

festival can without a problem be defined as a ritual, as it has a clear cut ritual frame (Christian prayers / worship) within which certain, especially dietary, taboos are still cautiously observed. Nevertheless, as the whole activity lasts more than five days during which different rituals as well as different ritualized actions take place, I usually refer to it as a "festival".

[3] I intentionally avoid using the term "syncretism" here. As I made clear earlier, "syncretism" today denotes a pattern that may develop as a way to cope with the tensions and conflicts that exist between the religions. In the Ami case, it seems – similar to the Taroko case discussed in the previous chapter – more appropriate to speak of a "pattern of coexistence" with respect to the contemporary religion (Qiu 2004).

with approximately 130.000 individuals, most of whom live on the island's east coast. Every year from July to August, newspapers, journals and TV programs provide special reports on these joyful and colorful festivals that include square dancing, wild singing, and the liberal consumption of alcohol. Since the festivals are also officially announced by the *Bureau of Tourism,* which is trying to develop the tourist resources on the east coast, hundreds of Han tourists come down from the cities to participate in the joyful dancing and Ami singing. These customs gained in popularity in Taiwan in the 90s, a popularity that must partly be attributed to Taiwanese nativism, but also to the international success of the 1996 Olympic song "Return to Innocence" by the French pop-group Enigma.[4] Journalists writing about these festivals have often focused on the fact that the Ami – with their archaic dances and with men wearing feathers in their hair – very strongly resemble Native Americans.

However, media reports reveal little about the historical and cultural background of the festivals, which today last between three to five days in rural Ami villages and only one day in urban communities.[5] It is rarely mentioned that they originally were an equivalent to the Chinese and Western "New Year". The aim of these festivals, which in Ami language are called *Ilisin,* was, at one time, to ring out the old year in the appropriate way and to introduce the New Year auspiciously. What is also not mentioned by the media reports is the fact that ritual in traditional matrilineal Ami society was almost exclusively the domain of the men,

---

[4] Without applying for permission, Enigma blended voices of Ami Singers – originally recorded by music anthropologists – into this song. The case aroused a fierce debate on cultural and intellectual property and copy rights in Taiwan.

[5] According to the guidebook of Taibalang's harvest-festival as well as to the Japanese-language records of an Ami chief who ruled Taibalang during the Japanese colonial period, the harvest-festival was once celebrated for up to twelve days. While the activities from the first to the seventh day were mainly dedicated to the disciplining of the young men as well as to the worship of supernatural beings like gods and ancestors, many activities from the ninth to the twelfth day were similar to those of today's festivals.

women being mainly excluded.[6] This means that in former days the observer would rarely have had the opportunity to observe the colorfully dressed Ami woman and their dances,[7] let alone the red costumes, which were an invention of the late sixties when the Ami tried to satisfy the aesthetic requirements of Japanese tourists. Another fact not known by the Taiwanese public is that these festivals were once linked to head-hunting rites. Ethnographic sources from the Japanese period describe how the ancestor-spirits were not only worshiped with millet wine, millet cakes and meat during the first days of the ritual, but also with the heads of slain enemies. At least until the beginning of Japanese colonial rule, there existed the notion that abundant offerings of humans and big game (such as wild boar, bears and deer) made to the ancestor-spirits at the beginning of the twelve days of the harvest-festival could assure and even increase the future harvest.[8] By observing these and other rules, for instance by participating in the collective dancing and singing and by drinking the formerly rare millet wine, members of the group could get closer to the ancestor-spirits who ruled the world as well as heaven, and who provided protection and shelter to those who pleased them by submitting to their rules.

The festivals thus originated out of an intense communication and interaction with supernatural powers. In the past, festival organization and moderation was carried out exclusively by male members of Ami society, who were organized in so called age-ranks and who were headed by the

---

[6] This does not apply to shamans who were almost exclusively female in Ami society and who – apart from their role in healing – at one time also played an important role in the harvest-festivals.

[7] Ming Liguo 1991: 152f. Ming points out that in Taibalang women were formerly excluded from the dances because "this would have annoyed the ancestor-spirits". However, he also mentions that the harvest-festivals had an important function for the attending women in so far as it was a good occasion to chose one's spouse (i.e., by listening to the criticism of the old men who evaluated the conduct of the young men) (Ming 1991: 155).

[8] Furuno Kiyoto 2000: 81. Tian Zheyi 2001: 149, 159. The linkage of the former harvest-festival to head-hunting is also documented in the Japanese-language records of a chief who ruled Taibalang during Japanese colonization in Taiwan (1895-1945).

ritual leader.[9] If we take the Ami tribe of Taibalang as an example, the ritual underwent little change until the end of Japanese colonial rule. Neither the artificial replacement of the former headman, the ritual leader, with a chief selected by the Japanese in order to exert more effective control, nor the obligation to adhere to Shintoism could really disrupt the foundation of Ami ritual.[10] A profound transformation started only after the end of Japanese rule in the fifties with the arrival of Christianity and its discrimination against animism and polytheism. While members of the Protestant Church[11] now found themselves completely banned from participation in the traditional festival, Catholics were at least allowed to maintain the outer appearance of the festival. Such elements as collective ancestor-worship in the first days of the festival, ritualized sports competition in the central part, and the ritual singing, dancing and drinking that dominates most sequences of the festival were allowed to continue to be practiced. As for the worship itself, the people were now instructed to concentrate on a single Christian God, in a way that corresponded to the logic of western Harvest and Thanksgiving festivals.[12] The traditional

---

[9] All men in Taibalang are organized in so-called "age-ranks", each of which includes people of the same age (+/- 2.5 years), and over which two men of the age-rank above exert strict control. Altogether there exist fourteen age-ranks in Taibalang today. However, the formerly very hierarchichal system is exposed to rapid erosion today. As the young men return more and more seldom from the big cities where they work, initiation into the first age-rank is often postponed, which is causing a growing delay in the establishment of the lowest age-ranks – a reason why initiation ceremonies that are to be arranged at the harvest festivals every five years can often not be held anymore.

[10] Though steady modifications must have occurred as a result of repetition, the ritual did not change its identity as an act of worshiping supernatural beings.

[11] In aboriginal society, the *Protestant Church* is mostly represented through the *Presbyterian Church of Taiwan* (PCT), which usually completely prohibited the observance of traditional rituals.

[12] Up to today, the majority of Catholic priests in Ami society are foreigners, in contrast to the protestant ministers of the *Aboriginal Presbyterian Church of Taiwan,* who are mostly Aborigines themselves. In comparison to the very conservative Protestant Ami ministers, the Catholic priests generally regard local traditions much more liberally and pragmatically, and try to achieve a synthesis between Christianity and indigenous religion. As I pointed out above, the situation in Taroko society was

mediums that had formerly assisted the ritual leader during this sequence were now banned from the festivals. Another fundamental change occurred with respect to the institution responsible for the festival's organization. For reasons of better control in times of authoritarian rule, the KMT government established the so called *Great Assembly* – an association headed by local politicians, in which the tribe's elders, the chief, and the ritual leader had voting rights.[13] Besides using the festival to increase their own popularity, the local politicians, loyal to the state, now adapted the festival to the nationalist requirements of the authoritarian state. The singing of the anthem, the raising of the national flag and very popular performances like the "frogmen-dance" all belonged to the set of rites displayed, while collective dancing in the evenings was for a long time not possible as a consequence of martial law. Due to the multitude of restrictions on religion and politics, the outer appearance of the festival in times of authoritarian rule was described as "much more monotonous" than it is today. As the enthusiasm of the nineties for aboriginal culture had not yet begun and the Han still despised Aborigines, Han tourists were hardly ever seen at and never participated in the festival.[14]

With the arrival of nativism in the nineties, the government changed the original time of celebration, in order to facilitate the attendance of politicians and tourists, to Taiwan's summer vacation, the hottest time of the year. The different tribes were now assigned to celebrate their festivals on different weekends in July and August.[15] If we take the festival in

---

slightly different because Taroko rituals had, at least on the surface, already "died out" when the PCT arrived, so there was no need to oppose them.

[13] From the 1950s to the 1970s, 'Great Assemblies' (*dahui*) were established not only in Taibalang, but in most other Ami tribes as well.

[14] Zhang Weiqi 2003. Ami dancing as a tourist attraction, however, had been popular long before this time. Thorne (1997) points to the fact that the Ami's custom of dancing to entertain important guests had been a regular feature of the hospitality extended to Japanese visitors since the 1920s. It is because of this history, linking aboriginal dance with tourism, that dance has come to symbolize aboriginal culture for most Taiwanese, and to symbolize the Ami's culture in particular (Thorne 1997: 216).

[15] Another factor made responsible for the change in the date of the celebration was the change from millet to rice cultivation in times of Japanese rule (1895-1945). The

Taibalang, the once "earnest and solemn character" of the festival[16] now changed dramatically, at least in all those sequences of the event now open to the public. On three evenings of the festival, busloads of tourists come to watch and to participate in the Ami dances that take place on Taibalang's sports field. The opening ceremony at the tribe's presumed place of origin, which until, end of the eighties, mainly consisted of Christian prayers by Catholic elders, was now increasingly enriched with traditional elements, such as the integration of the tribe's chief as well as a sub-chief (a role that in later years was again replaced by that of the "ritual leader"). Much less change occurred in those parts of the festival that were solely reserved for activities within the age-ranks, such as collective gathering and hunting on the day before the official beginning of the festival, collective dancing of each age-rank in private households on the second and third day,[17] or the collective meal of each age-rank, with the participation of the women, on the fifth day. In all of these activities, tourists and other outsiders were rarely invited to participate. However, as the subsequent account of the 2003 harvest-festival shows, even these sequences have become more and more affected by party politics and economic considerations in recent years. Before I start with the description of the political implications of the festival, however, I will sketch a ritual event that happened shortly before Taibalang's harvest-festival of 2003 and that in subsequent years not only exerted an increasing impact on the festival itself, but also on the cultural and political life of the tribe as a whole, developing very similar dynamics to those I described in the case of the Taroko's ancestor-spirits-festivals.

---

rice in this region, however, was harvested several months before and after the festival.

[16] See the 2003 version of the guidebook that is distributed at each harvest-festival. Here, the once "earnest and solemn character" of the festival is particularly emphasized.

[17] Most impressive for me were the consolation-dances conducted by each age-rank at the households of those of its members who had died within the previous year.

2.2 Unexpected resurgence from the pre-Christian past: the procession of Taibalang's shamans

In March 2003, the inhabitants of Taibalang witnessed an extraordinary ceremony: invited by a well known local parliamentarian, a number of traditional Ami mediums from the area assembled at Taibalang's activity center and held a procession, in which the spirits of the ancestors were transferred to the tribe's new commemoration site. As the local politician put it, this procedure was long overdue. Since the new site had been established eighteen years ago at the tribe's presumed place of origin in close proximity to Taibalang, the ancestor-spirits had been ignored at the old worship site, today's activity center. No wonder this caused the spirits to be unhappy – everybody in the village knew the stories about the mischief they caused to people who harmed the bodhi-trees under which the ancestor-spirits had rested for so many years without being honored[18]

The site to which the ancestor souls were now transferred was, however, exactly where the official opening ceremony of Taibalang's "traditional harvest-festival" used to take place – a yearly ceremony that was to a large degree dominated by Christian influences and that in the last few years had been held in cooperation with politicians from the *Chinese National Party* (KMT), the political mainstream in Taibalang.[19] Although the parliamentarian who had arranged the procession of the mediums did not belong to this political mainstream but to the small *People First Party* (PFP),[20] he was very much respected by villagers for his commit-

---

[18] I was told that most of these victims had been Han, who constitute a very small percentage of the population in Taibalang.

[19] This local political "mainstream" is not identical with the Taiwanese political mainstream on a national scale. Since May 2000, Taiwan has been governed by the *Democratic Progress Party* (DPP) whose adherents are mainly Taiwan-born Chinese. The DPP was officially acknowledged after the end of authoritarian KMT-rule in 1987 and functioned as Taiwan's main political opposition until 2000.

[20] The *People First Party* is also often labeled a "mainlander's party", as most of its voters are people who fled to Taiwan from the Communists after 1945 or their offspring. Both the *Chinese National Party* (KMT) and the *People First Party* oppose independence from China.

ment to traditional culture, especially as he was the founder of a number of cultural projects that engaged many unemployed Ami. As a result of the procession, the tribe's traditional mediums, who decades before had been scattered and displaced and had officially ceased to exist, finally had, once again, a common place to conduct their worship. Thus, it was quite natural that they appeared at the stele at dawn on the first day of the harvest-festival of 2003, wisely choosing a time when the official ancestor-reverence had not yet started. As prescribed by tradition, they presented their offerings to the gods of heaven, the gods of the underworld, and to the ancestors, spat rice-wine on the stele and then left the site again before the eyes of the surprised crowd that was already gathering for the celebration of the official harvest-festival.[21] The only documenters of the event were a couple of young supporters of the rivaling parliamentarian mentioned above, who had been informed before the event took place.[22] As was usual on such occasions, the shamans were given red envelopes to pay for their services.[23]

This short description suggests that Ami ritual is highly politicized today: matters of religious and cultural identity seem to be very much tied to local politics. Let us see below how ordinary people deal with this

---

[21] In contrast to the spitting of rice wine in the closing scenes of Taroko rituals, where the gesture means "to chase the spirits away: you have already eaten, now be satisfied and go" (Gariyi 14.9.2003, personal interview), the spitting of rice wine in Ami ritual stands for the cleansing and purifying of the air, the place or the body from disturbing spirits or influences in order to communicate more efficiently with the spirits. In Taiwanese folk religion, the spitting of rice wine into an possessed person's face has the function of driving the spirit out of the person in order to let her/his own spirit come back so that he/she can wake up again. As Ami shamans in recent times practice both traditions, the spitting of rice wine into the person's face in Ami ritual can also have this latter meaning (Zeng Jinlan 19.9.2004, and Wan Chengwen 16.9.2004, personal interviews).

[22] Since they invited me to join them, I was able to observe the ceremony.

[23] Muli 15.03.2006, personal interview. "Red envelopes" were also given in all further performances by the shamans. It is extremely hard to find out about the sums paid. As the rituals were supposed to look authentic, organizers sometimes even told me that no money had been given at all. This, however, was extremely unlikely, as shamans in Taiwan were used to receiving money for their services.

situation and what it means for the organization and reorganization of power relations in contemporary Ami society.

2.3 Party politics and ritual modifications in Taibalang's official harvest-festival

Before the festival of 2003 started, all Taibalang-Ami I talked to asserted that their harvest-festival was an "unbroken tradition" with two main aims: to honor the ancestors, and to maintain the solidarity and discipline of the tribe's members. In theory, these aims were successfully accomplished by way of activities such as the worship of ancestors in the official opening ceremony, collective dancing and singing for the ancestors, and the ritualized sports competition, as well as through the training activities of the young men before and during the festival. In all these sequences, the most important virtues of Ami society – discipline and solidarity – were particularly emphasized and could testify to the exclusiveness of Taibalang's Ami vis-à-vis "morally degenerating" Han-society [24] as well as vis-à-vis the Ami of the neighboring tribe of Matai'an, who have been the Taibalang Amis' rivals for many centuries.[25]

In the course of the festival however, many people, especially members of the age-rank who had provisionally "adopted" me and who became more and more outspoken during my five-day participation in this institution, gradually revealed one major concern. With obvious grief they pointed out the negative impact of party politics – a phenomenon that in their opinion was the main reason why discipline and solidarity were deteriorating. A rising number of delinquencies and deviant behavior among youngsters, more and more adults who did not care for their elderly parents, and the decreasing number of the festival's participants were all signs of this deterioration. The strongest criticism was directed

---

[24] There was a wide consensus in Taibalang that morals in Taibalang were in a better condition than in the cities of the Han where "the people did not care about each other anymore".

[25] Zhang Weiqi 1998: 38-40.

against the actions and decisions of this year's *Great Assembly* leader, a KMT parliamentarian who planned to campaign for the office of aboriginal legislator in the following year.[26] A major misfortune was that the traditional young men's training-excursion, which normally took place the day before the official opening, had been skipped – for the first time in the festival's history, as people told me. Needing an opportunity to convince the tribe's male members of his power and his political agenda, the *Great Assembly* leader had replaced this very popular activity with a collective billiard competition in his own house, emphasizing that billiards was also a reputable sport and that the ritual tradition was thus not violated.[27] As a consequence, only very few of the young men were able to participate in the ancestor worship the next morning, since most of them had not recovered from their hangovers by daybreak. People also commented with much suspicion on the open campaigning of the *Great Assembly* leader and his party colleagues during the private dances of the age-ranks. Even more annoyance, however, was caused by the appearance of Diaspora-Ami dancing groups, who had been invited from faraway cities by the politician and who performed their dances on the common celebration place, the sports field of the *Taibalang Elementary School*. As Taibalang had at least three of their own dancing ensembles, who all would have liked to earn the money paid for such performances, the act was unmasked as a further tactic of the politician to enlarge his electoral base – everyone knew that he wanted to campaign as aboriginal legislator the next year. Another ritual infelicity that was indirectly linked to the *Great Assembly* leader's influence was the intrusion of the women

---

[26] This man's appointment as the *Great Assembly* leader in 2003, one month before the festival, was due to the fact that the KMT in Hualian County had just defeated the *People First Party* (PFP) in recent elections. In spite of the pro-independence and nativist currents that, in Taiwan's urban areas, had started about one-and-a-half decades ago, Taiwan's mountain regions are under firm control of Taiwan's "conservative political influences". This is due to the very effective KMT organizational system, which the party established during forty years of authoritarian rule and which effectively infiltrated people with pro-China nationalist-values.

[27] The activity was skipped with the argument that the ground on the mountains was too slippery due to some rain in the days before.

of the Catholic choir during ancestor worship. As stated before, the participation of women was originally taboo in Ami ritual. Though women were generally tolerated in collective dancing and even in the dancing activities of the age-ranks, they were not supposed to enter sacred places like Taibalang's commemoration site. An exception to this rule had gradually started approximately five years ago as a result of Church pressure which was trying to overcome old beliefs.[28] This year, however, the women not only entered the sacred site, but also participated in the dancing directly after the worship.

Unmistakably, the greatest dissatisfaction of the ordinary people concerned how non-traditional authorities influenced and manipulated the festival according to their own interests, thus threatening the community's social control and inner cohesion. However, people also submitted to these pressures or at least were not able to oppose them effectively. They admitted that excessive politicization had also existed in the harvest-festivals of previous years, but that they could not really change it. After all, the harvest-festival was Taibalang's most important yearly event and had to be continued at all costs.

2.4 Ritual and authority in contemporary Ami society

In the following, I will take a closer look at power structures and relations in Taibalang and their manifestation in contemporary Ami ritual. What were the reasons for the tolerant attitude of the participants in the face of elite manipulations? And how did the elites legitimate their actions? In performance theory, several authors have paid special attention to the ways and methods of leaders, elites and authorities in manipulating

---

[28] Church people argued that if things really were celebrated "in the name of god", as the introductory prayer of the ancestor-reverence suggested, there should be no problem in letting the mixed choir of the *Catholic Church* enter the sacred site. They also pointed to the constant degradation of the "former superior status" of women in traditional matrilineal Ami society, a problem that needed to be faced in order to fit the requirements of an egalitarian, democratic society. This view was supported by Taibalang's more liberal political representatives who hoped that such a procedure might also convince the Protestants of the harmless nature of the event.

peoples' perceptions through ritual. Stanley Tambiah (1979), for instance, shows how ritual symbols and actions with a certain cosmological meaning may be deliberately used, modulated or even modified in a way that they indexically emphasize, legitimate and realize social hierarchies.[29] Tambiah refers to the example of Thailand's historical King Mongkut, who showed his courage and reformist zeal to the public by performing the tonsure ritual for his son personally and unprotected in an outdoor event. Since a king's life at that time was considered to be too precious and too endangered, the ritual was usually carried out by the king's ministers. The King's innovation, however, helped the royal family to increase their prestige. In a study of "the nature of the communication mediums of ritual", Maurice Bloch (1989) shows how in ritualized speech, music, body movements and even material symbols, formalization or "reduction of choice" drastically decreases creativity and the potential for communication, while at the same time increasing the authority of the ritual and the potential for social control. Bloch characterizes this phenomenon as a feature of "traditional authority".[30] For instance, a tribe's elder may, in the perception of participants who accept the code, merge with a mythical ancestor merely by way of his formalized ritual rhetoric, thus gaining authority which can not be contested.[31] In an article entitled "Borrowed Authority", Klaus-Peter Köpping (2004a) extends Bloch's argument, showing how leaders may achieve special effects with symbolic ritual actions by way of "borrowing" or referring to the authority of others (often transcendental powers), and that this borrowing may in turn also enlarge the counterpart's authority, similar to citation processes in academic writing. One example Köpping refers to are the "pri-

---

[29] Tambiah 1979: 153. In this outstanding article, Tambiah argues that ritual symbols in general have this "duplex" nature, but that their indexical effect may be increased with the help of certain measures.

[30] In traditional authority, the power of an individual or an office is understood to come from sources beyond the control of the community, as the power of a king who rules by "divine right" differs from the power of an elected official (Bell 1997: 70).

[31] Bloch 1989. According to Bloch, this effect is due to the fact that people who belong to the group and who accept the code (Bloch 1989: 28; 38) often see no other choice than to adhere to the protocol.

vate" pilgrimages of Japanese Prime Ministers to the Yasukuni Shrine, a Shinto shrine from the Meiji-period where not only victims, but also World War II war criminals are enshrined. By way of symbolically linking their actions to the former Meiji cosmology, they subtly invoke the perception of a restoration of the past or make such a restoration seem legitimated.[32]

**Figure 19: Official ancestor worship in front of Taibalang's ancestor stele
with representatives of the Church (left), political elites (middle), traditional elites (right)**

Intertwining authorities

We will now see how authority is gained and borrowed, consolidated and challenged in the course of Taibalang's harvest-festival. A sequence of the 2003 festival, in which these dynamics became abundantly visible, was the festival's official opening ceremony, i.e. the ancestor worship

---

[32] Köpping 2004a: 70f.

that took place on the first day shortly after the shamans' ritual mentioned above. During the ancestor worship, which was, as usual, moderated by Taibalang's *Catholic Church* on the tribe's new commemoration site, no allusions were made to any traditional deities.[33] In addition to the ritual leader and tribal chief, the main actors in this activity were the *Great Assembly*'s political members, who were welcomed by the chief in a lengthy hand-shaking ceremony according to their political importance and who then formed a line in front of the tribe's ancestor stele. (When one of the village heads [34] tried to be the first hand-shaker, he was brusquely dispatched by the chief). After a Christian prayer by one of the tribe's Catholic elders, the tribal chief and the ritual leader stepped one after the other up to the stele, remembered and prayed for the tribe's ancestors in long formalized recitations, spat rice-wine on the stele in the traditional way and finally began to speak to the ancestors, a climax that was, in each case, introduced by a long, throaty scream. In between, the mixed choir of the *Catholic Church* chanted chorales in the Ami language, all of them blended with traditional melodies. During the whole scene, the members of the *Great Assembly* stood in a row, their hands folded as in prayer, some of them, including the *Great Assembly* leader, reportedly a non-Christian, even making the sign of the cross. The end of the commemoration ceremony was again marked by a Christian prayer, after which the *Great Assembly*'s members, political as well as traditional leaders, all stepped on to the lawn next to the ancestor stele and, one after the other, joined the male representatives from the age-ranks who had now started to dance the traditional *malikuda* – a kind of square-dance with a highly repetitive alternating chant that can only be moderated and interpreted by a few people with traditional wisdom. After each of the leaders had been welcomed and hailed by the representatives of the age-ranks, the red-clad women of the Catholic choir appeared in a line at the

---

[33] The site had been established in the late 1980s at a place with ruins and remnants of an old settlement. It is surrounded by betel nut palms and situated at the foot of the hills behind the village.

[34] Taibalang has four village heads, as Futian (the official name of the tribe's location) is divided into the North-, the South-, the West-, and the East-village.

outer edge of the lawn, and – after a failed attempt to dance around the circle of men – participated in the dancing and singing from the side.

This short sequence from the five-day-event exemplifies the correlation and intertwining of religious, traditional and modern political authorities in contemporary Ami society. As we saw, Catholic, traditional and political elites were directly involved in the event. At least virtually present in the minds of the participants, however, were also the competing counterparts of each of these social forces, i.e., the Protestants as well as the rivaling traditional and political elites who, as I described in the beginning of this chapter, had demonstrated their existence directly before the event. In the following, I will take a closer look at each of these elites with respect to authority.

"Traditional" elites

The ritual leader and the tribal chief clearly represent "traditional authority" in contemporary Ami society in the sense pointed out by Bloch. This is remarkable in so far as the chief is an invention from the Japanese colonial period, and the ritual leader, whose role had once been that of the genuine tribal leader, no longer comes from the traditional *Kakitaan* – ,an aristocrat family.[35] Further, neither the chief nor the ritual leader worship any of the ancient Ami gods during the whole ceremony, but rather address the gods as "ancestors".[36] Today, their competence is seen in their skill in leading and interpreting the traditional songs as well as in

---

[35] Li Jingchong 1998: 101f. Until the late 19th century, it was the head of the *Kakitaan* who executed both the role of ritual leader and that of the tribal chief. To diminish his burden (as the head of the *Kakitaan*, he had to participate in all collective ritual events in addition to his political and administrative work), the office of the tribal administrator (*shezhang*) was established in 1887. During Japanese colonial rule, however, the role of the tribal administrator was redefined as that of the tribal chief. The former ruling institution – the *Kakitaan* – ceased to exert any influence after the death of the last official *Kakitaan* head in 1930.

[36] An exception is the reference to Maladao, an Ami god who, as the "master of heaven", once dwelt on top of the Ami pantheon and who was also worshipped by the shamans (Li, Wu, Huang 1992), but whose name has today become a synonym for the Christian God.

their ability to speak to the ancestors in the described manner. In modern times, however, these "traditional" elites also have to confirm their worldly competence. In order to be appointed, both leaders must have occupied important political positions such as village head man or parliamentarian.[37] In most cases, they belong to the KMT, the party that controlled Taiwan from the mid-forties until the end of the nineties.

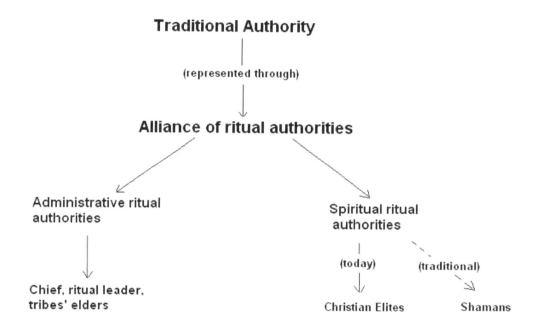

Figure 20: Alliance of ritual elites who represent traditional authority in Taibalang

Equally important is their good relationship with the *Catholic Church*. If all these preconditions are fulfilled, no one dares to challenge or undermine their authority. No matter how bad their reputation, they are treated like kings – a fact that could be observed in almost all sequences of the 2003 festival. Wherever they appeared – always closely followed

---

[37] Beginning in 1989, the chief of Taibalang is elected for 2-4 years. In addition to the qualities mentioned above, he must also have an outstanding reputation within his age-rank (Zhang Weiqi 1998: 62-64).

by the political elites – they were passionately revered and honored by the people.[38]

Christian elites

Traditional elites, however, are not the only ones who are perceived as linked to "traditional authority" in Taibalang today. After five decades of missionary activity, Christianity and especially Catholicism has become a well-established social force in Ami society, almost entirely replacing traditional shamanism. This means that, although "traditional authority" is, as in former times, represented by an alliance of ritual authorities (see Figure), the composition of the elements that constitute this alliance has today changed. While the traditional elites mentioned above, i.e. the ritual leader, the chief as well as the leaders of the age-ranks, continue to care for the administrative aspects of collective ritual including the proper attendance upon the ancestors, it is the representatives of Christianity who now serve as their spiritual complements, being responsible for the efficient communication with supernatural powers.[39] This explains why the official ceremony of 2003 was "framed" with Christian prayers. The members of this alliance of ritual authorities support each other in any aspect that is supportive to their mutual agency. Since the ritual leader and the chief of the 2003 festival were good Christians, they could not tolerate the presence of the mediums during the official harvest-festival. In addition, as the chief was on good terms with the female members of the Catholic choir – they had once supported him in his election campaign – the women were allowed to enter the sacred site, a privilege that could help to convince Protestants that Catholicism had genu-

---

[38] Although people accused the current chief of being corrupt and hopelessly caught up in party politics, they never showed anything but respect in his presence.

[39] The ideological fragility of this new alliance becomes clear if one considers that most people clandestinely see their ancestors as tied to the spiritual pantheon under the power of which the former had once lived, i.e. the traditional deities and spirits. The alliance can persist, however, because of the ambiguous and often shameful feelings attached to the old beliefs.

inely defeated sinister and backward traditions and thus was one of the more progressive forces in Taibalang.

Political elites

A similar mutual interdependence becomes apparent if we look at the role of the participating political elites. Without their and their party's financial support, the festival could hardly take place. Huge sums are spent in preparing for the festival (e.g. costumes) as well as for dinners, actors and dancers. Local politicians openly make monetary "donations" during the events in order to convince the people of their power vis-à-vis other competitors. In return, these politicians are allowed to participate as actors in the event, where they profit from the atmosphere of "heightened sensitivity" that is produced by the presence of "traditional authority" as well as by the singing and dancing. Clearly visible to all participants, authority is transferred to them during the initial lengthy hand-shaking ceremony. In such a situation, making the sign of the cross in front of the representatives of traditional authority and the public was a very clear statement: as long as the present coalition was in power, there would be no harm from sinister forces (traditional spirits) or from their supporters (shamans and rivaling politicians), who were waiting for their opportunity to interfere.

2.5 The traditionalist offensive

Rivaling political elites

We now understand the helplessness of the common people in face of the increasing "politicization" of their collective ritual and the manipulations of political elites. The complex power constellation that was exposed and reconfirmed by way of the ritual had more or less a paralyzing effect on them. As a consequence of his obvious closeness to "traditional authority", the *Great Assembly* leader enjoyed almost a kind of political immunity in Taibalang.

Nativism, as well as new economic constraints, had however already begun to introduce a new parameter into the power network described above. The appearance of the mediums at the ancestor stele as well as the politicians ostentatiously crossing themselves during the ancestor worship can be interpreted as clear signs that alternative visions of tradition were on the advance in Taibalang. While the first years of Taiwanese nativism mainly contributed to an increase in the financial resources available to the festival, more and more voices could be now heard calling for a paradigm shift with respect to the culture exposed to the outside world. Also among these voices was the rivaling parliamentarian who had organized the procession of the mediums.[40] In recent years, this parliamentarian had, with the help of *Hualian's Environmental Protection Association* and a couple of young Ami intellectuals, established a *Taibalang Culture and Art Development Association* (*Shequ wenhua yishu fazhan xiehui*) in charge of the restoration of the tribe's culture. Generously funded by the Taiwanese government, the association was able to employ many of Taibalang's inhabitants to build traditional straw huts, carve traditional totem poles etc.. In personal interviews, this politician made it clear that the most wide-ranging cultural preservation and revitalization was the best solution for the maintenance of social well-being and social peace in the village, especially in times of capitalist globalization and the massive influx of South Asian guest workers that caused thousands of urban Aborigines to return to their tribal villages. In order to make Taibalang more attractive for tourism and develop tourism as a source of income for the people, there was a need not only to highlight ethnic differences, but also to demonstrate tribal uniqueness with special

---

[40] The parliamentarian harbored a relatively skeptical attitude towards Christianity, not an uncommon trait in the more intellectual circles of post-colonial aboriginal society, as Taiwanese nativism had stirred up a certain sensitivity and reflexivity vis-à-vis established power structures. Being a member of a party that, since its establishment in the late nineties, had much experience with the instrumentalization of ethnic differences in Taiwan, this man also had close contacts with vanguard circles including *Taiwan's Environmental Protection Association,* which, as an offspring of the pro-independence-movement, promoted the protection and promotion of local ethnic culture.

emphasis on authentic tradition. He pointed to the neighboring tribe of Matai'an that was situated next to the North-South-Highway and that had succeeded in attracting large numbers of tourists in recent years by presenting a rather hybrid culture mixed with a multitude of modern elements. In order to explore new tourist sources in Taibalang, there was no choice but to work out a different cultural strategy, e.g. to cling to authentic Ami culture.[41] As an example, the politician named the planned restoration of the *Kakitaan*, the former ritual center of the tribe. Another cultural consideration of this rivaling parliamentarian was connected to the re-establishment of traditional discipline and order in Ami society, which was being more and more affected by the negative effects of the loss of culture and globalization. He was convinced that only by way of the revitalization of some crucial elements of the once hierarchically organized Ami society, would it be possible to re-establish a system of social control in Taibalang.[42]

This attitude actually strongly appealed to Taibalang's age-ranks, whose influence and authority had decreased in recent years. The more devoted members and young intellectuals especially held this traditionalist perspective and felt a strong need to revive some of the former virtues. In diverse internal roundtables conducted within these hierarchically

---

[41] Tourism in Taibalang was (similar to the situation in Taroko villages) actually much less developed than I had originally expected. Even during the annual harvest-festivals, tourists only entered the village on two or three evenings and did not stay there overnight – the rest of the five-day festival was entirely reserved for the Ami and their politicians.

[42] However, it will be difficult to convince Taiwan's non-intellectual domestic tourists of the value of aboriginal "authentic" culture, since their taste is more oriented towards mass amusement culture in the style of "Disneyland culture". This tendency is highlighted by Xie Shizhong in several studies, published since the beginning of the 1990s (see for instance Xie Shizhong 1992b), on Aborigines and tourism, and there seems to have been no change yet. Taiwan's six-year national development strategy, which commenced in 2000, targeted domestic tourism. A highlight of this was the 2000 opening of the US$180 million aboriginal-themed Mala Bay Water Park near Taichung in the style of a Disney Park: sacred hundred-step snakes twistingly soaring above an ancestor's head decorate a waterslide named the "A-Chu Slide". Paiwan Ancestors appear in relief around the "Big Wave" pool (Munsterhjelm 2002: 10).

structured groups on each day of the festival, the incidents and items mentioned above were discussed and evaluated. A broad consensus was reached that the two main functions of the festival (viz., an appropriate form of ancestor-worship and the re-enforcement of solidarity and of social control in Taibalang) could not be maintained under the present conditions of rampant politicization. On the last official day of the 2003 festival,[43] the *Great Assembly* suddenly announced that organizational tasks concerning the harvest-festival would no longer be executed by local politicians, but should be returned to the age-ranks. And so it was done: in the afternoon of the same day, just before the whole tribe carried out their big final dancing, singing and drinking ceremony on the Taibalang sports field, the *Great Assembly* solemnly surrendered the flag of Taibalang, which only some years ago had replaced the ROC's national flag, to the representatives of the age-ranks.[44]

Rivaling "traditional" elites

At this point, I want to take a closer look at those forces in Taibalang that represented "traditional authority" and that had disappeared from the official canon of tradition over the course of modernization and Christianization – i.e., the shamans as well as the members of the once so influential *Kakitaan* family. How had their authority changed over the course of time, and what measures did they and their supporters take to regain some of their former influence? We will see that the borrowing of and the

---

[43] The fourth day is the last official day of Taibalang's harvest-festival. On the fifth day, the members of each age-rank including their families gather at different places at the riverside, where, after a final round of self-criticism and mutual discipline, all supernatural beings are sent back to where they come from. Symbolically, this is generally accomplished by returning to the usual diet (fish). During the festival itself, participants were only allowed to eat meat and millet that was prepared daily by special teams within the age-ranks.

[44] The age-rank entrusted with the organization of the harvest-festival of the following year was the rank with the most experienced middle-aged men from 55 to 60 years old. All age-ranks of men older than 60 were traditionally exempted from organizational tasks.

endowment with authority as it has been described with respect to traditional and political elites above is a recurrent interaction pattern in Ami society.

Figure 21: Taibalang's shamans at unofficial ancestor worship in front of Taibalang's ancestor-stele (photo taken from video-file provided by *Taibalang Zhanwang xiehui*)

As we learn from earlier sources on the Ami's harvest-festival, the ritual actions of the *Kakitaan* head (once ritual leader and tribal chief in one person) were formerly complemented by the mediums or shamans (*chikawasay*), who had the task of communicating with the good and the evil spirits of the Ami pantheon. In major ritual events like the harvest-festival, the shamans, who were mostly female, and the ritual leader gathered in front of the *Kakitaan* building, the ancestral hall (*zongci*) of the tribe's leading family, where they jointly conducted the sacrifices.[45] Lin Qingsheng (1998), an aboriginal minister who grew up in Taibalang, states in a research report on Ami shamanism that the power of the traditional mediums had actually already began to decline before and during the Japanese period. In order to make their rituals more efficacious, the Ami had continuously integrated elements of Han folk religion into their traditional shamanism (as an example, Lin mentions the shamans' beating their backs with swords during the performances).

By the end of Japanese rule, large numbers of Ami had adopted Han shamanism because it addressed diseases much more concretely than Ami shamanism did and because the medium's contact with patients was more intensive. However, Ami patients generally only had very superficial knowledge of the complex pantheon of Taiwanese folk religion and of the Han shaman's gods such as Guanyin, Matsu or Qigong. Therefore, they were easily convinced of the usefulness of Christianity when this religion arrived in combination with Western medicine, economic help, and healing rituals that suggested cure through praying and fasting.[46] While many people became followers of Protestantism when it arrived in Taibalang in the mid-forties, the majority of Ami later converted to Catholicism, which was more compatible with their hierarchical social system.

---

[45] For this division of labor see Zhang Weiqi 2003; also see Li Laiwang, Wu Mingyi, Huang Dongqiu 1992. Both these sources emphasize that the *chikawasay* also performed rites at the end of past harvest-festivals. In her report, Zhang relies heavily on the Japanese language account of Kati'Lata, a Taibalang chief who was in power at the end of Japanese colonial rule. The account of Kati'Lata does not make it very clear whether the "female" spirit mediums who assisted the ritual leader in his work were really *chikawasay*. This however was the discourse put forward by Taibalang's traditionalist elites as well as by the shamans themselves (Zeng Jinlan 19.9.2004, personal interview).

[46] According to Lin Qingsheng, the phenomenon of Christian prayer healings had begun in the 1950s when groups of Ami Christians went to hospitals and private homes and prayed with the patients. Lin tells the conversion story of a man from Taibalang who was treated by fasting Christians in hospital and who began to promote Christianity in Taibalang after his recovery in 1944 (Lin Qingsheng 1998: 37-39).

In the charismatic movement that developed out of the Protestant *Presbyterian Church* (PCT) during the mid-seventies and that absorbed elements of Japan's Christian *Ashiram* movement as well as of Korean Pentacostism, the majority of mediums who became possessed by the Holy Spirit were, similar to traditional Ami shamanism, also women.[47] In ecstatic prayer/fasting sessions led by these female shamans, participants "spoke in tongues" and beseeched God to forgive them their sins in order to have their souls purified. Lin states that these events, with respect to their functions and inner logic, were strongly reminiscent of the traditional shamanist healing rituals in which the attempt was made to cure the patients also through intensive psychological care.[48] Similar to the shamans, the Christian healers relied on the authorization of supernatural forces before the actual healing ritual could begin. While the shamans implored the spirits to assist them and to give them the necessary power, the Christian healers appealed to the Christian God. Instead of the dietary taboos of the traditional shamans, the Christian shamans had the custom of fasting and in some cases began this as early as seven days before the event. Lin sees only one major difference in the religious attitudes of the two groups – in shamanist healing rituals, the patients had to rely entirely on the skills of the *chikawasay* (lit.: those who are obsessed by the spirits)[49] and good fate, the latter being also very much emphasized by the healers.[50] In Christian healing rituals, on the other hand, the patient had more possibilities for individual agency, as the individual was more in-

---

[47] Protestants in Taiwan refer to the movement as the "spiritual" (*ling'en*) movement or the "Prayer Mountain" (*qidaoshan*) movement.

[48] Since people had officially already relinquished non-Christian idols and polytheism, the Christian prayer healings were, according to Lin, not a conscious practice of tradition. Instead, the practice was more like a compensation for that feeling of social isolation that modernity had brought to aboriginal society. The experience of common prayers, speaking in tongues etc. created a psychological hold in Taiwan's larger society where many people were no longer able to cope with the pressure of individual decision-making (Lin 1998: 55-62). Si Xiong (2002) tells us that the practice of speaking in tongues started no earlier than the 1980s. During the 1970s, people predominantly concentrated on healing rituals.

[49] Lin 1998: 29.

[50] Lin 1998: 35.

volved in acting, dancing, and singing. While the first form of healing was more dependent on charms, the second was dependent on the patient's self-confidence. In the traditional healing ritual, the patient hoped for cure through the expulsion of harmful *kawas* (spirits); the Pentecostal rituals focused on the unloading of guilt that, if successful, would bring with it the cure of the body.[51]

Figure 22: Ami shaman Zeng as San Taizi at a Taiwanese folk religious Pudu (annual festival for the hungry ghosts) 2004

The phenomenon of female Christian shamanism and charismatic evangelism, however, seems to have evolved exclusively from a Protestant Christian tradition. At a time when Ami matrilineal societal traditions (including female authority) were crumbling, those Ami who had converted to Protestantism and who were now confronted with a single

---

[51] see Lin 1998: 61 for a comparison of the functions of the shamanist and the Christian healing rituals in Taibalang.

male authority in their congregations felt particularly attracted by the newly arising female spiritual authorities, who competed with the pastors. As Thorne (1997) explains, this kind of attraction was less significant in Catholicism, in which foreign priests advanced an interpretation of monotheism in which the spiritual figure of the female Virgin was enthroned beside that of the male figure of Christ. More importantly, the *Catholic Church* was characterized by a higher degree of elaboration of "mystical" events and, last but not least, a greater degree of accommodation of "traditional" Ami cultural practices. In contrast to the Protestant churches[52], which completely prohibited the participation in traditional events such as the harvest-festival because it considered them to be inherently anti-Christian, Catholic Ami believers negotiated with Church authorities to retain the festival, and the priests, most of whom were Europeans, found ways to reinterpret and bless the activities and bring the Church into the festival as a participant and supporter. In this way, the *Catholic Church* on the one hand adapted the existing rituals to their needs. On the other hand, the high degree of formal categorical elaboration of this church and its clearer subordination to an international, systemically-integrated, power-driven bureaucracy left less space for individual religious experimentation with life-world structures than did Protestant churches (Thorne 1997). This does not mean, however, that the PCT tolerated or supported the Pentecostal movement or shamanism among its followers. It actually strictly opposed the trend, but was not able to suppress it.[53]

---

[52] Although Presbyterians, who had had missionary experience in Taiwan since 1865, had the advantage over other Protestants in missionary efforts (Rudolph 2003), missionaries from various other denominations, chiefly from the US, also arrived following the KMT's establishment on Taiwan. The Protestant sects missionizing in aboriginal society included the *Mennonites*, the Pentecostal *Holiness* and *True Jesus* churches, the *Free Methodists*, the *Baptist Evangelical Society*, the *7th-Day Adventists*, *Jehovah's Witnesses*, and *World Vision*.

[53] Thorne (1997) describes that "the activities of the female shamans grew and spread. They traveled around holding sessions in East Taiwan villages in homes or in open areas at night (the Ami's Presbytery had refused to allow them to make use of churches for their sessions) and began to add healing to their ministries, praying over water to make it "holy water" which was then rubbed on the body of the sup-

We now realize that shamanism – albeit not necessarily the Ami's "traditional" shamanism – has had a long history in Ami society. As I discovered during my own field work, however, contemporary Ami shamanism is less strongly represented today through Christian healers than through female healers connected to Taiwanese folk religion. In their own temples established near Ami villages, these female healers held so called *"Pudu"* (annual festival for hungry ghosts) and other kinds of folk religious rituals in Ami language. In addition, they conducted, in individual households, healing rituals that were carried out in the manner of Taiwanese religion, i.e, without banana-leaves, as my informants always told me, because banana-leaves were one of the most visible characteristics of Ami traditional shamanism.[54] Today, there are also Christians from different denominations among their followers. Zeng Jinlan, the leader of the temple in Taibalang, is a prominent example of this kind of hybrid spirit medium. Like her colleague Huang, a woman who after her marriage moved to Hualian and established a Buddhist/Daoist temple there, she had originally been Christian. During their childhood, both women were brought to a traditional Ami shaman because of an incurable illness They were cured there and then stayed on as apprentices, as was prescribed by traditional religion. Since traditional shamanism, however, was not well enough respected at that time to allow them to make a living, they decided to practice Taiwanese folk religion, which in terms of philosophy, Zeng contended, was very close to Ami traditional shamanism. In both religions, the healer had to be able to receive intuitions in order to establish communication (*tong*) with the spirits. Many gestures were also almost identical, such as the spitting of rice wine in order to cleanse the atmosphere, or falling into a trance. All in all, Zeng only saw one major difference, i.e., that the medium in Han shamanism (the *jitong*) was truly possessed by the spirit, while the medium in Ami shamanism (the *chikawasay*) only communicated with the spirits, a commu-

---

plicant; or sometimes the supplicant was instructed in self-healing practices such as praying over cold water to make it warm and then bathing in it or drinking it, the water then acting as medicine".

[54] Zeng Jinlan (19.9.2004, personal interview) confirmed that in contemporary Ami shamanist performances, banana-leaves are no longer used.

nication that often involved long journeys in which the medium sometimes also appeared to be possessed.[55]

**Figure 23: Ami shaman Zeng in her role as traditional Ami medium in front of
Taibalang's ancestor stele 2003**

Until the arrival of Christianity, about 25 partly traditional, partly folk
religious mediums must have existed in and around Taibalang. After
1955, however, their number was reduced dramatically, as the churches
did not allow them to practice their skills openly.[56] Though not officially
tolerated, these mediums were actually still in charge of several tasks
concerning the annual harvest-festival. If, for instance, one of the age-
ranks was at risk of disappearing because of the death of too many of its
members, a medium was engaged to change the name of the age-rank.
The same procedure was undertaken when a person was deemed incura-

---

[55] Zeng Jinlan 19.9.2004, personal interview.
[56] Lin Qingsheng 1998; John F. Thorne 1997.

bly ill by Western medicine. In the course of the festival, people usually did not miss any opportunity to offer libations (*mifetik*) to the spirits: Whenever one intended to drink some wine, one first sprinkled some drops of the wine on the ground: "A sip for the gods above, a sip for the gods below, and a sip for the ancestors", I was told. Aside from this, a couple of taboos were still cautiously observed by most people. If, for instance, a person's close relatives had died since the last harvest-festival, that person was neither allowed to get too close to other people's meals, nor was he or she allowed to participate in the harvest-festival. This shows that pre-Christian beliefs had by no means died out in Taibalang, but rather, despite the ambiguous and often shameful feelings connected to these beliefs (they were referred to as "superstition"), they continued to exist in the people's minds.

Exactly these two folk religious healers mentioned above, Zeng and Huang, were invited in spring 2003 by the traditionalists to revitalize Taibalang's shamanism. As we have seen, their procession and their appearance in front of the ancestor stele had considerable consequences for the interpretation of the official harvest-festival in the fall of that year. However, this was only been the beginning. In 2004, the number of mediums appearing in front of the ancestor stele before the festival rose to over fifteen. Since the *Great Assembly* had explicitly prohibited the mediums' appearance on the first day of Taibalang's harvest-festival, they simply staged their performance one day before the official opening, claiming that this was in fact the "true" beginning of the festival. Waving banana-leaves and spitting rice wine, they solemnly marched to the ancestor stele, delivered their sacrifices (betelnut, pork, millet, and rice-wine), and helped several members to fall into trances and communicate with the spirits. No one dared to interfere, neither the *Great Assembly,* which had officially entrusted the age-ranks with the organization of this year's festival, nor the age-ranks themselves, which had often emphasized the necessity of the preservation of traditional culture.[57]

---

[57] Aside from this, the fact that this year's festival was organized by the representatives of the age-ranks had almost no visible effect. Just as in the year before, it was again

Again, the traditionalist forces in Taibalang had succeeded in "reframing" the ritual, and, as the numbers show, their power had grown compared to 2003. In 2004, however, the appearance of the mediums was not initiated by the rivaling politician (who had advocated the restoration of the *Kakitaan* for tourism purposes, but who strongly opposed the re-empowerment of the *Kakitaan* family because of the concomitant land issue). This time, Taibalang's young intellectual elites who had witnessed the medium's performance the year before were responsible for the summoning of these representatives of alternative traditional authority. Arguing that they wanted to avoid any further politicization of Ami ritual, they had split from the politician and were now relying on more direct channels of governmental cultural subsidies.[58]

The reshaping of Taibalang's harvest-festival with the help of the mediums, they were convinced, could be a starting point for the "revitalization" of Taibalang's traditional culture in general.[59] In order to prepare the mediums for this task, they had organized at least five medium events over the course of the year, in which the mediums had the opportunity to practice and to demonstrate their skills and their power. In addition, they had laid the foundation for a new alliance that they considered to be crucial for the restoration of the original harvest-festival – the alliance of the

---

the politicians who, after the demonstration of their alliance with traditional authority, moderated and controlled the whole event.

[58] After the foundation of the *Prospect Association* (*Zhanwang xiehui*) in Taibalang, the young traditionalists were eligible to receive money fom the *Republic of China Integrated Community Construction Study Association* (*Zhonghua minguo shequ yingzao xuehui)*, which had been established by the Han in Hualian County and which coordinated different initiatives of *Integrated Community Construction* in the area.

[59] As the above account has shown, the revitalist endeavors of aboriginal traditionalists draw heavily on values and cultural attitudes popular in Taiwan's Han-society today. The outcome of these endeavors is of course not less "hybrid" or "syncretic" than contemporary Christianized aboriginal culture. I discussed a similar question in my doctoral dissertation "Taiwan's Multi-Ethnic Society and the Movement of Aborigines – Assimilation or Cultural Revitalization?" (Rudolph 2003, in German), in which I argued that the cultural revitalization work pursued by aboriginal elites since the beginning of the nineties is in a fact another form of assimilation to Taiwan's modern Han-society.

mediums with the members of the *Kakitaan* family. After the Japanese establishment of a tribal chief, the *Kakitaan*'s authority had become obsolete; therefore, the family had not continued its tradition after the death of the last ruling *Kakitaan* head in 1931. In 1957, the *Kakitaan* building, the tribe's former center, was demolished by a typhoon. The land on which the building once stood was now officially classified as public land; however, the family was desperately trying to keep hold of this piece of traditional land. The *Kakitaan's* remaining artefacts were brought to the *Academia Sinica* in Taipei, Taiwan's leading research institution, to serve as research items.

Figure 24: Ami shamans at Academia Sinica, Taipei, 2003 (Photo: Zhang Yaling)

This incident was taken by the young traditionalists as a starting point to unfold their initiative in favor of the restoration of the harvest-festival. Arguing that the spirits were still lingering within the pillars of the former ancestral hall and had to be brought back to Taibalang, they arranged several journeys to the *Academia Sinica*, together with the shamans, the

Kakitaan family, and Taibalang's "traditional elites". While the first journey had to be made without the *Kakitaan* family members, as they were afraid that the whole action might be a clever attempt to take away their precious piece of traditional land, the second and the third trips, in which the *Kakitaan* family participated, were more successful. Not only were they able to inform Taipei's anthropologists about the crucial significance of the *Kakitaan*, the shamans also, during the third trip, succeeded in retrieving Taibalang's spirits in eight rice wine bottles and transferring them to Taibalang.[60]

Figure 25: Ami shamans making a pig drunk before divination (Photo: Zhang Yaling)

Before this was achieved, however, a divination ritual was arranged at the *Academia Sinica* in order to discover the spirit's inclinations. In this ritual, the participants of the excursion stepped, one after another, onto a living pig that had previously been made drunk with rice wine. The sha-

---

[60] Jinnslim 2005/06.

mans then stood in front of each person and began to communicate with the spirits, requesting that the person move back and forth on the screaming animal to the sounds of their mystic chants, while they waved their arms back and forth in front of him or her.[61] Even the "traditional elites" were successfully convinced to take part in the rite. At the end, the pig was killed and eaten. It is crucial to add here that the same kind of ceremony had been conducted in Taibalang some months before, exclusively together with the members of the *Kakitaan* family. In this process, the direct successor of the *Kakitaan* – a woman – was identified, confirmed, and installed. Furthermore, it was decided that the ancestral hall was to be rebuilt as the tribe's authentic ritual center using the family's own assets. This was a courageous decision, since the establishment of the building on public land with financial resources from the Kakitaan family not only touched on the question of the future legitimacy of the present "traditional elites", but also on the unresolved land problem that meanwhile had become a sensitive political issue in the tribe. From this perspective, it is quite remarkable that the young traditionalists had been able to convince the "traditional elites" to take part in the journeys to the *Academia Sinica* and especially in the divination ritual that was performed there. The "traditional elites", however, firmly refused to involve themselves in any of the shaman's rituals conducted at the ancestor stele before the harvest-festivals of 2003, 2004, and 2005.

Since, in 2005, the reconstruction of the Kakitaan building was almost finished, the mediums that year held their ritual (now called ancestor-spirits-ritual) not only at the ancestor stele, but also at the new *Kakitaan* building. As was to be expected, the tensions between Taibalang's traditionalist forces and the official "traditional elites" had now risen to a cli-

---

[61] The shamans argued that the pig served as a tool for more efficient communication. Although they emphasized that they had learnt this method from their master, I have found no evidence of such a rite in Taibalang's history, nor did any of the people in Taibalang know about such a rite. The only precedents for such pig-treading rites can be found in the ritual traditions of the Mosuo – a national minority in Mainland China – in their initiation rites for young people (see the website "Lugu Lake Institute of Matriarchal Culture of Mosuo People", retrieved on 5.5.2007 from http://www.lugu-lake.com/cn/cdly.htm).

max. The tribal chief even threatened to have the building torn down again – an understandable measure, as his authority was gradually being undermined and dismantled.

Figure 26: Ami shamans dancing on living pig before divination in 2004 (Photo: Zhang Yaling)

The same threat was made by the local politician who had initiated the shaman's revival in 2003, but who had been left out of the re-empowerment of the *Kakitaan* family, since he, although willing to re-build the *Kakitaan* for tourism purposes, opposed a privatization of the institution and the territory in question.

Figure 27: Taibalang's new Kakitaan with stone stele and inauguration text for the new Kakitaan head 2005

Nonetheless, in January 2006, the new building was inaugurated in front of a huge crowd; among the invited guests were not only repre-sentatives of the *Council for Indigenous Peoples* (CIP), but also anthro-pologists from the *Academia Sinica*. In an extravagant ritual, the ritual leader, who did not dare to be absent at such an important event, took up the eight bottles holding the spirits that had been salvaged two years be-fore at the *Academia Sinica* and, after the shamans had entered into communication with them, finally released them at the new site.[62] From

---

[62] In spite of the tensions, the young traditionalists had succeeded in convincing the
ritual leader to take part in the inauguration. This is remarkable because after the

now on, the shamans solemnly announced, the harvest-festival as well as the preceding ancestor-spirits-ritual should be held at the reestablished *Kakitaan*.

Several precautions were taken in order to cement the newly revitalized history. A stone stele at the entrance of the new *Kakitaan* building gave the name of the newly inaugurated head, He Yulan, with explicit reference to her aristocratic ancestry and the 58 generations of *Kakitaan* heads which preceded her. A further stone plate, which was set up directly in front of the *Kakitaan* building, mentioned the names of the new building's supporters (including references to the *Academia Sinica*) as well as the names of those who had participated in the ancestor-gods worship ceremony that had been held shortly before the official ancestor worship ceremony of the 2005-harvest-festival.[63] The first line read:

> Below are listed the names of those members of the *Kakitaan* family who respectfully listened to the ancestor god's admonitions at the worship ceremony on the 16.08.2005 (harvest-festival): ...

By adding the word "harvest-festival" in brackets, it was made clear that the "authentic" harvest-festival started with the activities at the *Kakitaan* building under the guidance of the traditional tribal head – i.e., the *Kakitaan* head – as well as the shamans. In a further step, a text with a description of the occurrences depicted above was published in a blog on the internet.[64] In this way, the traditionalist forces in Taibalang had consolidated their vision of historical facts in exactly the way one of their representatives had explained to me in an interview the year before. Annoyed at the non-acceptance of the shaman's activities that had recently been revitalized, this young intellectual stated:

Kakitaan head's installation, his status was as endangered as the status of the tribal chief.
[63] i.e., on the 16.08.2005, five days before the official beginning of the harvest-festival.
[64] Jinnslim 2005/06.

The minds of the tribes-people are simply too colonized by the church. If the tribe's inhabitants don't want to face their cultural traditions now, they will have to do it later when they face the questions of Taiwan's Han-Chinese. The Han will ask them why the tribal rituals are different from those representations and descriptions that can be seen on the internet … and that are given by Han scholars like those of the *Academia Sinica*. [65]

2.6 Concluding Remarks

The analysis of Taibalang's harvest-festival has shown that despite profound changes in religious meaning and social function, contemporary Ami ritual nevertheless has strong society-shaping efficacy in so far as it supports the structuring of status and power relations in this society as well as the reorganization of identity. As we saw, this efficacy must largely be attributed to the fact that the audiences of Ami rituals are, as in Taroko society, still very much integral: people know each other very well and even interact with each other in daily life in church organizations, political parties etc.. The festival's efficacy, however, also relies on such catalyzing forces as Taiwan's current nativism (that not only brings in new resources, but also confronts people with their non-Christian traditions), as well as the competition among elites. Within the highly creolized cosmology of Ami society today, various political, clerical and traditional leaders select and employ cultural symbols in specific ways in order to reinforce or to gain legitimacy and to bring common people in line with their power ambitions. Essential to the performances is the elites' demonstration of their connection to traditional authority, which in today's hybrid cultural setting has become manifold and multiple – a phenomenon that enables rivaling elites to restore and instrumentalize alternative forms of traditional authority. Although supporters of the creolized status quo who rely on well-established corporate traditional authority (i.e., traditional leaders and Christian representatives) are still predominant today, rapid changes in the ethnic group's exogenous political and economical environment are enhancing the popularity of tradi-

---

[65] Lin Hengzhi 1.9.2004, personal interview.

tionalist forces who underline their legitimacy by clinging to traditional authorities different from that of Christianized aboriginal religion. Until quite recently, most Aborigines considered Christianity in combination with steady modernization to be the appropriate cultural strategy, since the former could compensate for one's feelings of inferiority resulting from years of discrimination in Han-society, while modernization promised future prosperity.[66] After a thorough disillusionment caused by rising unemployment, however, Taiwan's present culturalism seems to offer new solutions at least for some members in Ami society. On one hand, by emphasizing traditional values that are superior to those of "degenerating" Han society, people do not necessarily need the Christian religion anymore to strengthen their self-respect and self-pride. On the other hand, an increasing number of people believe that participation in Taiwan's search for "authenticity" and the re-adjustment of the aboriginal tourism strategy to this ideology might eventually also lead to a better economic situation.[67] The official handover of ritual authority to the age-ranks at the end of the 2003 harvest-festival was an expression of the formation of this kind of vision (see the section on "rivaling political elites" above). As a forum of constant renegotiation and reassessment of cultural values and attitudes, contemporary collective ritual is thus an important identity-shaping force in Ami society today. The modifications resulting from the dynamic interplay of different elites as well as their mutual criticism during and after ritual practice cause ordinary people to

---

[66] Stainton (1995: 210-211) argues that Christianity provided Aborigines with an alternative path to modernity, one which allowed them to claim both equality and difference simultaneously. However, as mentioned above, there was a more immediate incentive as well, which was the provision of food and medical supplies by the missionaries to regions that had been hard hit by the war. Many aboriginal families would send one child to the Protestants and one to the Catholics in order to maximize their returns (Thorne, 1997: 171-172; Friedman 2005: Chapter 6).

[67] Xie Shizhong (1994c) analyzes two kinds of ethnic tourism in Taiwan: the tourism of adventures and those who are looking for the exotic (*yiguo qingdiao*) - a style of tourism which is rather uncritical and which will inevitably also involve amusement and leisure activities. The other kind is the tourism of those who are in search of native culture (*bentu wenhua*), who would rather visit activities where aboriginal culture is exhibited on a more elaborate level.

look at their own cultures with heightened sensitivity and reflexivity, which will eventually also lead to changes in future cultural practices.

Still today, however, the harvest-festival mainly follows a Christian logic. Contrary to the expectations of Taibalang's traditionalists, the festival of 2006 was neither opened nor conducted at the reconstructed *Kakitaan*.[68] As a substantial and legitimate part of a well established traditional authority in Ami society, the church has, against the traditionalists' reframing endeavors, successfully reinforced its vision of a Christianized Ami tradition. Although the confrontation of the Church and the traditionalists occurred in a less extreme and less direct manner than we saw in the Taroko ritual in the previous chapter, the failure of the harvest-festival's traditionalist interpretation to be canonized seems to have very similar reasons to those described in the Taroko case. The main cause is not so much the Ami's deep-rooted commitment to Christianity, but rather Catholicism's successful adaptation to Ami patterns of hierarchy and authority, which enables the representatives of this religion to exert an effective control on the tribe's members.[69] Very similar to the case of the mainly protestant Taroko, complementary coexistence rather than rivaling coexistence of Ami religion with Catholicism had been the prevailing conversion pattern in Ami society, at least up to the traditionalist's offensive. This can be seen from the fact that diseases that can not be cured by Western medicine are still treated by Ami shamans who practice with the methods of Taiwanese folk religion in private homes or in Taoist temples established by them. On such occasions, the shamans always remind their patients of their obligations towards their ancestors.[70]

---

[68] At the 2006 harvest-festival, the mediums did not appear at all, claiming that the death of one of their dear-ones forbade them to hold the ceremony (Muli 28.09.2006, personal interview). However, as my informants in the tribe foresaw this outcome several months before the festival because of the rising criticism towards the actions of the mediums, it may well be concluded that the mediums' non-appearance in 2006 was connected to this latter reason.

[69] See Huang Yinggui (1992: 295f; 2001: 35f) for a discussion of the strongly hierarchical organization of the *Roman Catholic Church* in comparison to the democratically structured organization of the *Presbyterian Church of Taiwan* (PCT).

[70] Yasuko 17.3.2006, personal interview.

Consequently, many of the graves of Catholic followers in Taibalang's cemetery are decorated with betel nut, bottles of rice wine, and incense. Very obviously, Ami traditional religion continues to exist inside the "skin" of Han-religion, a state of affairs that does not really trouble the *Catholic Church*, since its followers do not worship the former ancestor-spirits (*zuling*), but merely dead ancestors (*zuxian*). One of the main characteristics of the *Catholic Church*'s approach to traditional ritual is that it is much less skeptical of the worship of ancestors (*ji zuxian*) than the Protestant churches. As one Catholic priest told me, the *Catholic Church* principally tolerates ancestor worship as long as the Christian God remains at the center of veneration.[71] On the other hand, an official recognition of the traditional "ancestor gods" and of "polytheism" is, very similar to the Protestant attitude, intolerable. This is why traditional elites, who have formed a symbiotic power alliance with Catholicism in the last decades, did not dare to modify the yearly opening ritual of the harvest-festival moderated by the *Catholic Church*, although they did occasionally take part in traditionalist events that had less representative function, like the journeys to the *Academia Sinica* or the inauguration of the reconstructed *Kakitaan* as described above.

As we have seen, the sometimes subversive challenges that came from the traditionalist forces in Taibalang were not only ideologically, but also financially backed by external supporters. The main support came from those Han intellectuals and Han institutions that were devoted to the government's *Integrated Community Construction* and who worked in foundations and associations that helped to administrate and to implement the government policy.[72] The concern and interest for the preservation and revitalization of Taibalang's old culture had actually started as early as 1995, when the first projects connected to the *Integrated Community Construction Plan* were granted to the village. What must be said here is

---

[71] Jiro Ubus 17.3.2006, personal interview.

[72] Above, I have named some of these organizations led by Han intellectuals, like the *Republic of China Integrated Community Construction Study Association* (*Zhonghua minguo shequ yingzao xuehui*) as well as Hualian's *Environmental Protection Alliance* (*Huanbao lianmeng*).

that the whole process of the revitalization of shamanism and the restoration of the *Kakitaan* described above was supervised and coordinated by young Han intellectuals – cultural workers, students and idealistic scholars who knew how to apply for government funding and who in some cases even lived in the tribe. This, however, does not mean that the traditions highlighted were completely invented, since these Han worked closely together with the tribe's traditionalist elites;[73] it would be more accurate to say that some relinquished traditions were newly reinforced, as most of them still latently existed in people's minds and memories or still coexisted with major cultural patterns at the edge of society, only waiting for an opportunity to regain influence. On the other hand, their revitalization was anachronistic in so far as it did not mirror or match the majority of the tribe's longing for progress and sense of aesthetics: very similar to my Taroko interviewees, common people tried to look as "civilized" and "modern" as possible. In some cases, even the traditionalist tribal elites themselves admitted that certain symbols or designs might have been revived in order to satisfy aesthetic needs and preferences within Han society, as for instance the sensational pig-treading ceremony of the shamans.[74] The fact that Taibalang's shamans and their intellectual supporters tried to gain and increase their legitimacy through repeated visits at the *Academia Sinica*, Taiwan's most renowned research institution, was of course related to a phenomenon that Roberte Nicole Hamayon, (2001) has referred to as "the revaluation of shamanism in the present context of cultural globalization". Nowhere else in Taiwan could traditionalists expect more support than at the *Academia Sinica*, where scholars not only principally supported cultural restoration, but had also gotten into contact with these concepts. Hamayon writes:

> "Due to the recent reversal of ascribed values, shamanism is now claimed to support modernization and praised as a representative of

---

[73] When I started my research in Taibalang in 2003, it had already become a common conviction of Han intellectuals and the traditionalist tribal elites that the restoration of the *Kakitaan*'s earlier significance was a necessary condition for the authentic rectification of the harvest-festival.

[74] Lin Hengzhi 21.07.2006, personal interview.

a genuinely *natural* philosophy particularly useful in our modern Technocratic World. Primitive is turned to primordial, wild into ecological, magic into mystic, makeshift into artistic. This revaluation has entailed a more or less genuine revitalization of related practices all over the world."[75]

Figure 28: New building housing Taibalang's activity center 2005

Another example in which aesthetic patterns and designs were evidently imported by external forces was Taibalang's activity center, the place that had once not only been the tribe's man's house (*sulaladan*), but also the place were the ancestor spirits had been worshipped in pre-Christian times. After the successful application for funding by a cultural foundation led by Han, the centre was rebuilt in a fancy *Disney Park* style (figure), to the great annoyance of the village people, for whom the new building had no representational value at all. As the architect and

---

[75] Hamayon 2001: 5.

construction company engaged had also been appointed by the foundation in earlier projects in other villages, the village people soon expressed their suspicion that the foundation only wanted to earn the provisions for the arrangement of working opportunities and did not care for the interests of aboriginal society at all.[76]

Some final words must be said about the similarities and differences in contemporary Taroko and Ami ritual. As has become clear, the main factor that distinguished the way that performances were carried out was not so much the socio-cultural system, but the denomination that the respective group belonged to. In this respect, the socio-cultural systems were only indirectly involved.[77] Although the religious questions that were negotiated in both societies were the same (i.e., principally the question of how much polytheism could be tolerated), the degree of rigorousness was different, since the *Presbyterian Church*'s stance against polytheism was so firm that it was hard for it to tolerate any "traditional" rituals at all, while the *Catholic Church* allowed more syncretic solutions.

A phenomenon more directly connected to the difference of socio-cultural systems was the different way of dealing with authority in ritual. In Ami ritual, dissent or conflict never surfaced in the rituals themselves, but rather in counter rituals or modest ritual criticism. Ritual authority seemed to be rather homogeneous, the statuses of the leaders much more respected. Taroko ritual, on the contrary, was characterized by the involvement of different heterogeneous forces in the performances who all tried to take the lead and to exert their authority – i.e., church elites, individual church intellectuals, traditionalist politicians, and educational el-

---

[76] Muli 15.03.2006, personal interview. I mention this point because corruption is a frequent problem within Taiwan's cultural foundations and associations. It is also one of the reasons why real societal needs have often come up short despite the government's well-meant multiculturalist endeavors in the last decade (see Zhang Weiqi 1998 and 1999, in which the author not only refers to Taiwan's *Integrated Community Construction* policy of the last years as a "failure", but in which she also cites Aborigines who identify this policy with "contracting" (*bao gongcheng*).

[77] As I have remarked in my introduction, denominations were chosen according to their compatibility with the socio-cultural system.

ites. Ritual criticism in Taroko society was always fierce and often ended in furious cursing. On the one hand, this phenomenon can be explained by the fact that in Taroko ritual the actors were merely actors, while in Ami ritual people embodied the status and the authority they had in real life. On the other hand, the phenomenon observed here can also be attributed to socio-culturally determined differences in reaction patterns. As early as the beginning of the 1980s, concerned Taiwanese anthropologists had begun to examine the reasons for remarkable differences between the Atayal's and the Ami's abilities in psycho-social adaptation to Han society (Li 1982; Huang 1984; Xu 1987; Hsu 1991). While the Atayal (until 2004, these also included the Taroko) manifested a high degree of anomie behavior, the Ami's behavior in Taiwanese society was rather unremarkable. As the scholars found out, this divergence was, on one hand, due to the different degree of acculturation of both groups. On the other hand, however, the two groups had very different social systems. The Ami, who were characterized by a high degree of impunitivity and readiness to adjust, were able to gradually adapt to the social system of the Han without rapid loss of their social structures, because their strongly hierarchical system did not hold any severe contradictions to the hierarchical social system of the Han. In some points, the Han system was even fully compatible. This was different in the cases of the Atayal and the Taroko, whose social systems were completely incompatible with Han society and who (due to socialization) have rather extrapunitive reaction patterns (this means that guilt and blame are not turned on the individual itself but rather to the outside).[78] The social systems of the Atayal as well as of the Taroko traditionally were akephal (led only by one "Big Man"), where social status and authority had to be incessantly le-

---

[78] Xu Muzhu 1987: 59. Xu works with the three concepts extrapunitive (*waize fanying*), intrapunitive (*neize fanying*), and impunitive (*wuze fanying*) reaction patterns. According to Xu, extrapunitive denotes when aggression that results from frustration is turned to the outside: the individual does not put the blame on himself, but on others. In the case of an intrapunitive reaction pattern, the individual puts the blame and the guilt for sth. on himself; aggressions are not turned to the outside. In the case of an impunitive reaction pattern, aggression is neither turned to the outside nor on oneself; emotional reactions are suppressed.

gitimated through the testification of individual courage and demonstration of abilities. The incompatibility of the social systems led to a fast collapse of the cultures of the Atayal and Taroko at the moment of their integration into modern Taiwanese Han society after Japanese colonial rule. Some main psychological traits, however, such as the difficulty to adapt oneself to hierarchical conditions, persisted. The Atayal and the Taroko therefore showed a rather high readiness for conflict not only in Han society, but in their own societies as well.

CONCLUSION

Conclusion

1. Retraditionalizing rituals: sacred events, folklorization, or politics?

Reflecting on what they call the "modern crisis of authority" in many Asian states, the editors of the volume *Asian Visions of Authority: Religion and the Modern States of East and Southeast Asia* (Keyes, Kendall, Hardacre 1994) make the following statement:

> Nation building requires a very different stance toward the past than does modernization. While commitment to modernization entails rejection of those aspects of a society's past deemed impediments to a rationalized bureaucratic order, nation building depends on the very opposite move. (…) The process of creating modern nation states has, thus, entailed two rather contradictory stances towards religion: While the modernizing stance leads to a de-emphasis of ritual practices, the nation building one leads to the promotion of selected practices and even the invention of new rites. Modernization emphasizes rational action; nation building insists on a commitment of faith.[1]

The contradiction described here and its consequences can currently be very well observed in China's "renegade province" Taiwan. Quite differently from the argument of the study mentioned above, however, it is not the repression of indigenous religious traditions that leads to tensions in this case, but the overemphasis of difference and cultural traditions in multiculturalism. While the Taiwanese government on one hand is pushing technical, social and political modernization (such as the consolidation of the island's young liberal democracy), it is, on the other hand, encouraging the development of a multicultural national identity that is independent from China and free from the quasi-colonial pressures of the recent past. It is during this process that ancient and at times al-

---

[1] Keyes, Kendall, Hardacre 1994: 5.

ready extinct religious traditions are again dug up and thematized. Although the new state-supported traditionalism is often praised for effectively contributing to halting the irreversible loss of many unique traditions and practices, the development simultaneously has far-reaching effects on and implications for society. While political and societal elites in general seem to profit from the official endeavors of cultural reconstruction and consciously adapt them to their own needs, common people often face new dilemmas. This seems to be particularly true for the trend of ritual reconstruction and revitalization going on in Taiwan today.

All the ritual performances referred to by me in this volume appear somehow politically motivated: the matters that are negotiated are connected either to national, local, or tribal politics. This may seem unfamiliar in the light of the conventional assumption that ritual is mainly a religious or cultural phenomenon in which cultural values are communicated to the members of a society – an assumption that is even stronger when indigenous people are involved. We find similar attitudes in Taiwan. Anthropologist Zhang Weiqi remarked in 1998 that

> research on Aborigines generally avoids touching political issues. When it however does so, it always deals with "antique politics" that are detached from real life, such as the "traditional" age rank system, or the tribal chief system. It seems as if – as soon as one begins to talk about politics – this might pollute "the noble Aborigine" or "the pure Aborigine".[2]

Indeed, this book could have been written very differently if I had focused more on the cosmological meanings of ritual symbols in aboriginal rituals and on the function these symbols and rituals previously had. A famous Taiwanese anthropologist who does just this extensively in her works on contemporary aboriginal rituals is Hu Taili from the Academia Sinica. As an example, I will cite here some episodes from her book *Tai-*

---

[2] Zhang 1998: 135.

wan's Aborigines and Cultural Performances (Hu 2003).[3] Throughout
the book, Hu speaks of the "sacredness of the holy dances and songs" of
Taiwan's Aborigines and requests that this sacredness be respected and
not disturbed. Hu is particularly concerned with this problem in the chapter entitled "Cultural authenticity and performance: the experience from
the Saixiat and the Paiwan" in which she discusses the question of what
happens to authenticity when sacred rituals and sacred ritual elements are
put on the stage.[4] As an anthropologist who trained a pan-aboriginal
dancing ensemble (*Yuanwuzhe*) and who made a number of documentary
films on aboriginal ritual, Hu is personally involved in this question.
Comparing the Saixiat's and the Paiwan's reactions towards *Yuanwuzhe's* dancing activities, she found that the Saixiat treated representations of their rituals by non-Saixiat very differently than the Paiwan.[5]
While the Saixiat believed that any kind of ritual representation was efficacious or even harmful if it was merely performed correctly, no matter
whether by strangers or by Saixiat, the Paiwan were convinced that
solely those rituals that were enacted by Paiwan themselves had efficacy:

> The Paiwan were always very cautious with performances of au-
> thentic and sacred ancestor spirits songs. But we observed that
> when people from their village gave performances outside, they
> considered this to be a very serious matter, in any case there needed
> be made a ritual to report the situation to the spirits (*shenling*) and
> to the ancestors (*zuxian*).[6]

---

[3] Most of the chapters in this book have been published previously as research papers.

[4] Hu 2003: 423-58; ix-x. The title of the chapter in Chinese is "Wenhua zhenzhi yu
zhanyan: Saixia, Paiwan jingyan". Hu holds that the different behaviours towards
outsiders are in fact expressions of reflexivity in ritual. This reflexivity went so far
that at least the Saixiat, who had mostly forgotten the traditional songs and texts,
were influenced by the endeavours of Hu and her dance ensemble such that they
learned these things again, which "helped the maintenance of the sacred song and
dance traditions" of the respective ritual.

[5] In her studies, Hu mainly concentrates on the rituals of the Saixiat in Taiwan's North-
west and the Paiwan in the Southwest where she has done most of her fieldwork.

[6] Hu 2003: 449.

If however, Hu continues, the ritual was performed outside the village by non-Paiwan, the Paiwan did not worry at all, because they believed that this had nothing to do with them.

In other chapters, Hu gives meticulous descriptions of diverse rituals. In long elaborations, she introduces the original meanings of every sacred symbol and action, thereby obviously making statements about the natives' contemporary worldview and religion.

On the other hand, there are episodes in the same book that make it quite clear that Hu Taili also knows the other side of the coin. This not only pertains to a chapter in which she discusses the influx of Christianity and its immense consequences for aboriginal rituals,[7] but also to interviews like the following that was conducted with one of the performers of Hu's documentaries during a workshop. Asked about the impact of foreign cultural influences like Christianity, he answered in Paiwan language (in the book, the episode is translated into Chinese):

> At the moment when our traditional culture had declined to its lowest point, the new religion came into the aboriginal tribes. This means that these Christian denominations have been here for a very long time. In the years after 1951, they missionized the people in each of our aboriginal tribes. I can only say that this is the reason why a new representative character has emerged. By now, all people in all of our aboriginal tribes have converted to Christianity; there is almost no one who is not Christian. ...The problem is that there is no one left in our aboriginal tribes who can carry out a real traditional ritual: there are just no people who are able to recover our traditional rituals. For this reason, we all think that it is very difficult to recover our original traditional rituals. Actually, we all feel very sorry about this; however, we console ourselves by saying that the essence of these religions is the same.

---

[7] Hu 2003: 279-313. The title of the chapter is "Taiwan Yuanzhumin de jidian yihi: xiankuang pinggu" [The rituals of Taiwan's Aborigines: an evaluation of the present situation].

At this point in the interview, a Paiwan cultural worker chimed in in Chinese:

> I would also like to answer a part of the question. What has just been said is actually the biggest problem I face. Let me give an example: today, all the Paiwan harvest festivals that we can observe are in reality fake; there is not a single one which is real. I would very much like to let the past real harvest festivals – some of them lasted seven days, some of them ten days – I would very much like to help them reappear in order to let everybody see them. But I face a very big problem; I think every honest Paiwan cultural worker has come upon this problem – the problem is that it is not possible to overcome the power of religion.[8]

Another inconsistency where even Hu herself seems to be sceptical about her approach to alleged sacred traditions is an episode in which she discusses her documentary film "Perspectives from Orchid Island". With respect to the Tao's ancestor spirits belief, the *anito* belief, she admits that during her filming on Orchid Island, she finally discovered that the *anito* were (contrary to the arguments of previous sources) actually not just "evil spirits", but that they were in fact "the nearest relatives" of the people who became ill – relatives who were for some reason upset and who had no other way to let people know. Since the *anito* belief had, however, been adapted to the anti-nuclear-waste movement, she also took up this point in her documentary's explorations of the nuclear waste problem; a problem that deeply concerned her when she was on Orchid Island, as she herself writes. She therefore justifies her adoption of the sequence in which angry Tao men symbolically chase away the nuclear waste invaders with the following words ... only to show doubts in the next moment:

> When the natives wore their armour, seized their weapons, and made the gesture of chasing away the bad *anito* spirits, this atmos-

---

[8] Hu 2003: 126-28.

phere of defending one's people's life and cultural dignity was full
of shaking power. (...)

However, in the ritual song and dance activities, in this case the
traditional boat launching ceremony, they arranged for the tourists
in exchange for a filming fee we witnessed that the gesture of chasing away the bad *anito* spirits was made up on purpose. After all
what was it that they wanted to chase away?[9]

Quite obviously, Hu had involuntarily collaborated here in the
Tao's intellectuals' endeavours to make the "chasing away the bad spirits" ritual appear to be an authentic, traditional action that was supposed
to move Han society. As a matter of fact, however, the action had been
strongly influenced by modern Christian perspectives, as I have tried to
show in the beginning of Part I.

The point I want to make here is the following: if one has already
realized that cosmological symbols enacted today no longer have their
earlier semantic meanings, what sense does it make to describe them as if
they still carried these former meanings?[10] Would it not be more useful
to write about the ambivalent meaning these symbols have in the contemporary context or, if they no longer have any earlier semantic meaning, to write about the indexical meanings that are attached to them today? This is what I have tried to do in the present study. After reading
many books and articles in which earlier meanings of traditional symbols
were explained, I simply could not understand why people should make
anthropologists believe that they enacted all these things for their ancestor spirits and traditional gods as if Christianization or Sinisization had

---

[9] Hu 2003: 52-54. Hu wonders whether the gestures in this case were made towards the
invading tourists, but she admits that she is not sure and "puzzled".

[10] From the perspective of salvation anthropology, however, the collecting of such data
seems to make much sense. With the crumbling aboriginal cultures before their eyes
and no reliable source available, many people in Taiwan have the impression that
the multifarious cultural possibilities that die with the different traditional cultures
have to be thoroughly saved before being left to oblivion.

never taken place.[11] Either the accounts really neglected these influences
– and then it would have to be asked why (and what kind of) informants
neglected them –, or anthropologists just did not want to understand what
they were told, as Zhang Weiqi (1998) intimates in her study on *Integrated Community Construction* in aboriginal communities cited in Part
I.[12] In order to come to a more thorough understanding of the dynamics
of aboriginal contemporary rituals, I therefore decided to focus on those
components of rituals or festivals whose representational value was particularly emphasized by the organizers, usually those parts where sacrifices were made or worship was carried out. I found that ritual criticism
towards these parts was most intense, which gave me a good position to
look for changed semantic meanings and contemporary indexical functions behind certain symbols or actions. One of my results was that
"pragmatic indexical functions" prevail in retraditionalizing rituals: most
symbols point to concrete political and power interests. This is not to say
that these performances are totally devoid of semantic meaning. Because
of the contemporary socially and culturally hybrid setting, however, these
meanings never match with earlier, "traditional" meanings.[13]

---

[11] My criticism that it is often not clear whether an ancient or a present worldview is
portrayed not only applies to the work by Hu cited above, but also to books by Han
scholars and authors such as Ming Liguo (1991), Lin Jiancheng (2002), or Liu
Huanyue (2001), as well as to books by aboriginal researchers such as Wu Mingyi
(2002; Li Laiwang, Wu Mingyi, Huang Dongqiu eds 1992) or Tian Zheyi (2001).
The most astonishing description with regard to Taiwan's Aborigines' contemporary
religions and rituals can be found in Wang Chongshan's book *Society and Culture of
Taiwan's Aborigines'* (2001). In a chapter entitled "Religion and ritual", he describes rituals and ritual symbols exclusively from the perspective of the respective
traditional religions (Wang 2001: 81-98), claiming that Aborigines' contemporary
value and moral system is determined by these religious values (there is no reference
to the impact of Christianity). On the other hand, he also straightforwardly states
that these religious representations are used today as instruments in order to obtain
political advantages and to push through political demands (Wang 2001: 188; 98).

[12] On page 138 of her study, Zhang contends: "The majority of the tribes-people (...)
understand better than the tribes' elites and the scholars with their wishful thinking
that straw huts, old cultural relics, and traditional cloth are things that in reality no
longer "exist". But they also understand that this is exactly what the government and
the scholars want to see. ..."

[13] I also do not intend to deny that retraditionalizing rituals may in some cases have
"sacred" elements: at least in those cases where they are blended with Christian be-

A study that reveals that very different results can be obtained by concentrating on less exposed components of ritual activities where politics play a minor role is the research of Futuru Tsai Cheng-liang (2005), who examined the plays and dancing competitions following the enactment of the main rituals of the harvest festival of Dulan village. Here, Futuru is particularly concerned with the socializing and solidarity endowing aspects of ritual innovation – in this case Hip Hop style dances that in recent years have gradually replaced the more traditional dance styles. The dances, in which different age grade groups compete, combine local traditional dance moves, which embody connection to the land and harvest activities, along with dance movements and music from other Taiwanese Aborigines, and other indigenous groups such as Maori, American Indian, and African, with even some Korean pop and Slavonic dance interspersed. Futuru, who himself participates in these activities, states that even the Discovery Channel has been the source for many of these dances,.[14] However, while outsiders often bemoan the so-called "loss of culture," the innovative Hip Hop styles of young men's dance performances actually accomplish their traditional role of entertaining the elders. Transgressive behaviour in these dances is – as in the past – the rule, a finding that suggests that despite thorough symbolical innovation and integration of global trends, certain structural features and functions of the former activity persist.

Since activities like those examined by Futuru are not arranged by politicians and have no central status, political questions only seem to play a marginal role. However, we can clearly see ritual's potential regarding the constitution and restructuring of society and identity. This is a characteristic which undoubtedly surpasses the role Émile Durkheim

---

liefs, this is certainly sometimes the case. However, this sacredness is very complex and loaded and therefore needs deep analysis. In addition, there are some aboriginal groups – including the Pingpu and the Saixiat (one of Hu Taili's research themes) who are very much sinizized and less Christianized. The Paiwan and the Tao, however, have strongly been influenced by Christianity.

[14] Most of the Ami youth work outside villages, so the harvest festival and its dance competitions are a chance to reinvigorate local ties, by participating in the traditional social structure of age grades. The innovation of the young men's age grades contrasts with the traditionalism of the middle-aged and older members.

(1915) once attributed to ritual. For Durkheim, ritual played a key role in maintaining and producing social solidarity and cohesion. At the same time, however, he also considered it a force that supported the conservation of culture and the maintenance of the status quo. This view was challenged by a new understanding that emerged during the 1960s. Following Victor Turner and his study on *liminality* and *communitas* in ritual, researchers of ritual at that time increasingly discovered the transformative and even subversive potential of rituals.[15] Although ritual was not denied its solidarity-engendering potential nor its psychological functions,[16] scholars now particularly emphasized ritual's power in temporarily dissolving existing social hierarchies, remaking personal identity, and engendering cultural and social creativity. This formed a sharp contrast to the earlier view that had considered rituals to be staunch conservators of culture and consolidators of power relationships.[17] Exactly because of this restructuring potential, David I. Kertzer (1988) has shown, ritual also plays a very prominent role in politics, as it not only serves the interests of power holders, but of rebels and revolutionaries as well. In this study, I assumed this latter perspective on ritual, but also went a step further. I argued that under certain political conditions, such as Taiwan's nativist context, ritual fulfils, in the first place, authenticating functions particularly for elites, while efficacy often comes as a side-effect. Consciously and reflexively designed and arranged by societal elites, retraditionalizing rituals are highly interactive mediums that are characterized by a strong provocative potential. Since they serve as authenticating mediums, that is performances through which elites try to prove their identification with certain discourses and attitudes, they touch upon matters that are of great relevance for the respective social, cultural or political community before which they are enacted – matters of status, power, and authority, but also matters of cultural identity, religion, as well as historical and

---

[15] In a *liminal* state, Turner (1969) contended, a peculiarly important kind of temporary community emerges, i.e., the state of *communitas* which was not only extremely creative, but which was also the origin of social structure.

[16] Apart from the notion that ritual provided social cohesion (Durkheim), another widespread assumption in the beginning of the 20th century was that it also provided personal consolation (Freud).

[17] Grimes 2001: 229.

ethnic status. For this reason, audiences are all to some degree personally or psychologically involved, no matter whether they are integral as in Part II or non-integral as in most of the performances described in Part I.[18] It is this involvement that entails dissent, controversies, and negotiation. Particularly the aspect of negotiation marks contemporary aboriginal rituals clearly off from theatre, which aims first at entertainment.[19] The fact that they are forums for negotiation also marks these rituals off from mere folklorization, in which a selected cultural heritage serves the members of a culture as a rationalization of their own worldview. Although negotiation does not always become apparent in individual performances, it becomes evident when we look at series of events and performances in their cultural and political context. In this sense, even the theatrical rituals of the Presbyterian Church, which were enacted as a reaction to the traditionalist ancestor-spirits-rituals can not be considered to be mere folklorizations. They not only re-emphasized the Christian belief of the people, but also tried to enhance the participants' positive identification with their own Taroko past, for instance by proudly wearing artificially applied tattoos that had the function of sublimating wounds of previous discrimination, or by theatrically presenting the former headhunting habits as almost altruistic acts in the highly sophisticated social system of the past. By means of performance, cultural memory was regenerated in such a way that it could serve as a basis for an unstigmatised and uninhibited Taroko identity.

What I intend to do in the remainder of this volume is to recapitulate the main characteristics of retraditionalizing rituals that serve as au-

---

[18] The involvement of audiences in the case of the rituals performed for Han audiences is of course more abstract than in the case of the rituals performed for tribal audiences where everybody knows each other. However, even here involvement is unavoidable, since the ritual designers take advantage of the Han's psychological complexes and cultural idiosyncrasies in order to influence their thinking and their actions.

[19] Richard Schechner argued that both ritualistic and theatrical activity have effect and entertain, but ritual emphasizes efficacy and theatre entertainment (Schechner 1985: 117ff and 1977: 63ff). Negotiation, however, appears to be a feature that exclusively pertains to ritual and not to theatre.

thenticating practices in Taiwan's political realm. To do this, I will first discuss elites' involvement in contemporary aboriginal ritual; second, I will summarize how and with which means different elites try to enhance their legitimacy and authority through ritual; and, third, I will review the main impacts retraditionalizing rituals have on the state and on society. In a final section, I will then try to assess the role retraditionalizing rituals play in the context of Taiwanese nativism and ongoing acculturation.

2. Elites' involvement in contemporary aboriginal ritual

One of the most illuminating analyses of the political dynamics concerning cultural restoration and revitalization in contemporary Taiwan comes from Zhang Weiqi (1998). Zhang clearly describes here the different levels on which elites use rituals as instruments of authentication. As she puts it, Taiwan's government, Han scholars, aboriginal intellectuals, tribal politicians, and traditional elites formed an alliance that "re-colonized" aboriginal society.

Zhang's criticism actually points to the extension of a problem which, in the beginning of the 1990s, Taiwanese anthropologist Xie Shizhong (1992) had called the "elites without people" phenomenon. At that time, aboriginal intellectual elites who were distanced from the tribal population with regard to culture and ideology fought for the official recognition of their peoples. They generated and emphasized a couple of ethnic symbols with which they hoped to win their struggle against the Han government. These symbols included new ethnonyms such as "Aborigines" and "Austronesians", but also idealizations of an authentic aboriginal culture, such as distinct indigenous vernaculars, non-Han family names, and distinct pre-Christian religious traditions which were to be respected and protected. Despite strong support from Han intellectuals, it turned out that the aboriginal movement was incapable of obtaining much support from the ranks of the common people, since they usually wanted rather to integrate imperceptibly into Han society.

As Taiwanese nativism gained momentum, however, many aboriginal intellectuals returned to the local areas where they communicated their traditionalist concepts to such local elites as political, educational, traditional, and Church elites. Since the advocating and the implementation of these concepts was linked to official funding and financial support from government institutions such as the *Council for Cultural Affairs* or the *Council for Indigenous Peoples*, local elites soon realized the value of traditional culture for the enhancement of their own authority and legitimacy. The promotion of authentic tradition therefore gradually became, despite the reserved attitude of the common people, a new embattled resource for local elites in their competition with other aboriginal elites. Even if they were not always able to convince people of their cultural interpretations, they could still point to their own influence and effectiveness and win supporters. As Kertzer (1988) has shown, it is not only the way in which ritual alludes to ancient truths, ancient belonging, and pure identities that makes it an effective instrument for authentication and authorization (of the state, political and cultural collectives, or individual politicians), but also the concomitant glamorizing effects.

On the other hand, scholars of ritual show that ritual must not be necessarily convincing in terms of ideology or world view in order to be popular or even socially effective. In *The Rites of Rulers*, for instance, Christel Lane (1981) describes how national and local political leaders (especially from the party and the youth organizations) in the former Soviet Union deliberately created a set of socialist life-style, wedding, and birth rituals in order to re-educate the public. As Lane's study shows, however, mass participation in this kind of ritual was clearly aided by the fact that these ideologically cumbersome rites were addressing real human and emotional needs. In addition, they were financially supported by the state. Having no alternatives available, many Soviet citizens actually managed to use these rituals to add "color, beauty, heightened significance and dignity" to their lives.[20] As Catherine Bell (1997) adds in her comments to this type of state-ordained ritual,

"it is far from clear … that these rites were very effective in socializing anybody to embody particular ideological attitudes and dispositions. […] Researchers point to the stubborn selectivity with which Soviet citizens accepted and participated in the civic activities of the state, and both Soviet and Western scholars have remarked in surprise at the degree to which people can differentiate what they do and what they believe."[21]

A similar dynamic seems to be at work with respect to contemporary retraditionalizing rituals in Taiwan. As we have seen, common people do attend and participate in these events. And – even if they are instrumentalized by traditionalist elites, and even if people's true religious identifications may be misrepresented – these rituals often prove to be efficacious, since they enhance the dialogue in questions concerning religion and ethnic identity and help people to compensate for psychological tensions.[22] The performances contribute to the renegotiation, the re-evaluation and the modification of the participants' relationship to themselves, to other Aborigines and to the Han. In this respect, the provocations of the elites may eventually even have a positive effect on common people's identities. Further, local inhabitants also obtain some financial benefits from the rituals in which they act as actors and supernumeraries. Ordinary people today always request "red envelopes" (a metonymy for the money enveloped within these) for their assistance in collective ritual – a convention which is often called a "bad habit" by the responsible elites. Zhang Weiqi (1998: 138) explains this practice with the people's realization that they themselves do not benefit in any other way from the public performances, which are arranged by elites for the needs of elites.

---

[20] Lane 1981: 33-34, cited from Bell 1997: 225-229.

[21] Bell 1997: 225.

[22] Exactly this kind of efficacy is also confirmed by Gariyi Jihong's in his work on the ancestor spirits rituals of the Taroko (Gariyi Jihong 2004: 177-78). Gariyi – himself a Taroko – argues that this efficacy very much exceeds the effects envisaged in the ritual script and thus has "transcending" force.

This may serve as an indication that people in no way merely slavishly follow what the elites tell them, but look for their own coping strategies in each specific situation and only follow the elites as far as it serves their interests.

In spite of the social efficacy which is manifested here, however, retraditionalizing rituals in Taiwan seem to confirm the basic theory of Brass (1991) who contends that in modern societies, ethnic culture is very much the result of the activity of competing elites who – in their quest for power and authority – design, invent or manipulate identity symbols. In the cases of local rituals that I studied, the two main competing positions were a traditionalist one and a Christian one. Each of these positions, however, was represented and defended by coalitions of political parties, cultural associations and civil organizations within the respective society. While the Christian interpretation, which today generally tolerates any cultural restoration except for the revitalization of the belief in the ancestor-spirits, has a much broader basis in aboriginal society, the traditionalist interpretation has found more and more adherents in recent years. This is not only due to the fact that political elites can make use of government subsidies, which are offered for the restoration of tradition, in their competition with other elites; another reason is that there is a new hope for the development of cultural tourism, which can become a new job opportunity for thousands of unemployed young men who are returning from the construction sites in the big cities where they have lost their jobs after the influx of large numbers of guest workers from Southeast Asia. In the case of Ami ritual, we have further seen that those traditional elites who had been ostracized have instrumentalized traditionalist interpretations in the process of modernisation and Christianization in order to gain relegitimation.

3. Strategies of authentication in ritual

To some degree, the situation that Taiwanese Han face with regard to legitimating their existence on the island vis-à-vis the mainland's property claims can be compared to the authentication problem of settler societies of the New World. As Bill Ashcroft (1989) remarks:

> White European settlers in the Americas, Australia, and New Zealand faced the problem of establishing their "indigeneity" and distinguishing it from their continuing sense of their European inheritance. In this respect their situation differs from that of Indians or Africans whose problem was to retrieve or reconstruct their culture at the end of a period of foreign rule. The colonial settlers had to create the indigenous, to discover what they perceived to be, in Emerson's phrase, their "original relation with the universe." [23]

Therefore, it is not astonishing that the Government of Australia in 2006 states in its Culture and Recreation Portal:

> Aboriginal art has come to the forefront of Australia's national identity in recent years, celebrated by Australians and the world in the opening ceremony of the 2000 Olympic Games. [24]

Very similar statements also come from the Government of New Zealand. On the website of the Ministry of Social Development, we can read:

> Maori culture may form one aspect of national identity, since it is unique to New Zealand and forms part of our identity in the outside world. [25]

---

[23] Ashcroft 1989: 135.

[24] Australian Government, Culture and Recreation Portal. Retrieved on 22.11.2006 from http://www.cultureandrecreation.gov.au/articles/indigenousart/.

In the case of Taiwan, I have described how the "indigenous" became a strong point of reference for a distinctive Taiwanese identity during the 1990s. It gradually developed as a figurehead in Taiwan's democratic multiculturalism, not only for independence-orientated Han intellectuals, but also for the ruling KMT government. Democratic multiculturalism, politicians believed, was on one hand apt to neutralize inter-ethnic animosities and increase the inner stability in a multi-ethnic state; on the other hand, this policy should help Taiwan not only to become visible and acceptable, but also distinctive in a world of nations.[26] Taiwan's distinctiveness and "subjectivity" (*Taiwan zhutixing*) could best be demonstrated by reference to the island's diverse cultural heritages, in which Aborigines and their interaction with the Han played an important role. As an effective form of cultural representation in which messages could be transported with few words and which, in addition, had a strongly solidarizing function because of its performativity, ritual received a privileged place in the wide variety of cultural traditions that were now particularly supported by the government. Well documented by specially trained journalists, the survival and the revival of traditions deemed representative for Taiwan's culture was also extensively displayed on the internet and made accessible to the whole Chinese- speaking world.

Meta-communicative cues

While the initial impetus for cultural revitalisation and identity search thus came from Taiwan's Han, this impulse soon also reached the elite strata in aboriginal society: i.e., the pan-ethnic aboriginal intellectuals in the centre of Han society and those elites who still lived in the local communities at the periphery of Taiwan's society. Although the main

---

[25] The Ministry of Social Development of New Zealand. Retrieved on 22.11.2006 from http://www.socialreport.msd.govt.nz/2004/cultural-identity/index.html

[26] Wallerstein argues that the nationalisms of the modern world are in fact the ambivalent expression of the desire for assimilation to the universal and the attachment to the particular, the rediscovery of differences. For him, it is a universalism through particularism and a particularism through universalism (Wallerstein 1984: 166).

logic of cultural representation remained the same here – i.e., the abundant display of particularities that demonstrated Taiwan's non-Han roots –, there can be also found some remarkable differences regarding the way in which elites tried to use these opportunities of state-supported cultural representation for their own authentication.

A decisive feature in rituals designed and arranged by aboriginal intellectuals, no matter whether in the case of pan-ethnic elites or local elites, is the reference to unimpeachable transcendent authorities, i.e., the ancestor spirits that had represented an all-encompassing authority in traditional aboriginal religions. The fact that this pattern was not always so popular, we can clearly see in the example of the Tao's chasing away of the polluting "evil spirits" shortly after the lifting of martial law (I referred to this ritual in Part I). At that time, no one dared to challenge the main contemporary religious authority of Taiwan's aboriginal society, i.e., the Christian God; "borrowing" the authority of the ancestor-spirits (for instance by invoking them to chase away the Han invaders) did not seem to be an option yet. In order to impress the Han, aboriginal intellectuals instead aimed at the feelings of guilt that many Han harbored with respect to the unjust treatment Aborigines endured in Taiwan's democratizing society.

Nativism, however, brought with it a rising awareness on the part of aboriginal elites that Christianity was in fact also an external and non-indigenous force. During the 1990s, this awareness increasingly affected how spiritual authorities were invoked in ritual. Calling on the ancestor spirits, on one hand, satisfied the Han's call for authentic aboriginal religion, while, on the other hand, it gave aboriginal elites a certain kind of fool's license and invulnerable authority. By claiming that the respective rituals were unavoidable measures in the face of the ancestors, the rituals as well as their organizers themselves became unassailable. This was not only because leaders seemed to act in the name of their ethnic collectives, but also because of a special sense of political correctness popular in Taiwan since the beginning of multiculturalism. However, as I have shown in the case of local rituals, the reference to the ancestor spirits not only had indexical functions as those outlined above, but was also often connected to a process I referred to as "framing" and "reframing". Repre-

sentatives of Christianity or elites allying with them "framed" their rituals with Christian prayers, with the sign of the cross, or the singing of
Christian anthems, while traditionalist elites, on the other hand, "reframed" the performances by invoking the ancestor spirits, performing
shamanic rituals and making blood sacrifices. Since frames instruct participants to perceive what occurs within the frame as a different sort of
acting and thinking, this kind of ritual technique is also often referred to
as a kind of meta-communication (Handelman 1977). In the case of Taiwan, it is remarkable that meta-communicative elements of rituals are
intentionally manipulated by elites, while non-elites seem not to take part
in active ritual construction and are also not always willing to accept
these meta-communicative messages. Another sort of intentional meta-
communication in the contemporary rituals is the frequent use of symbols
that refer to certain post-colonial discourses in Taiwan, for instance to the
suppression of aboriginal hunting rights, the eradication of aboriginal
traditions, or the long period of discrimination. As I have shown, the
meta-communicative messages mentioned here were often used in a
transgressive or even subversive way, helping people to compensate for
postcolonial wounds in their collective and individual psychologies.[27] On
the other hand, these references also boosted, by way of diminishing or
ridiculing the authority of the Han as the superior counterpart, the authority of the one who made these references, even if there were no Han-
Chinese around.

        In some spectacular cases, the authority-endowing effect of the
performances was additionally enhanced with animal and blood sacrifices. Blood sacrifices are not unknown in Taiwanese Han society, although they are not widely practiced today. Paul Katz (2004), for instance, examines the practice, during the Japanese occupation of Taiwan
(1895–1945), of beheading chickens (*zhan jitou*) as blood oaths, which
constituted part of a ritual system aimed at attaining divine justice. And
Taiwan's Hakka ethnic group holds an annual festival during the seventh
lunar month, with a unique custom of sacrificing "spirit pigs" (*shenzhu*)

---

[27] In line with the traditional functionalist view, one can argue that ritual in such cases
     fulfils the function of a safety valve which allows opposition to be dissipated in a
     harmless way, leaving the system and its leaders intact (Kertzer 1988: 128-30).

which are traditionally grown to a huge size before being ritually killed. The pigs that are sacrificed in honour of the *Yimin* martyrs[28] are considered to be lucky beasts, raised in the lap of luxury with air-conditioning in the summer and an unlimited supply of food such as rice, potatoes and fruit. Affluent families buy huge pigs to show off their wealth. Promoters of Taiwanese identity hold that the *Yimin* belief is a representation of the Hakka people's strong recognition of Taiwan,[29] an interpretation that led President Chen Shuibian to offer a divine pig to the *Yimin* spirits in 2003, in line with "the promises given to the *Yimin* spirits". The controversial ceremony was well-covered by the media, as it was heavily criticized by animal conservationists.[30]

The last example shows how the spectacularity of blood sacrifices can help leaders to gain attention and to boost their authority.[31] This effect seems to even be enhanced in an environment that takes a critical stance towards such sacrifices since the sacrificer now can now even more effectively emphasize that his actions are "in the name of the gods" who have a reality beyond his own. Maurice Bloch (1977) contends that power holders need rituals in order for their actions to lose the appearance of a creation of the speaker. As an act performed according to acknowledgably archetypical prescriptions, ritual has a strong taste of indisputable genuineness, selflessness and non-intentionality and is therefore less disputable and attackable. The chicken beheading rituals of the Taroko and the shamanic pig treading ceremonies of the Ami seem to follow a similar logic. The fact that the performers could even kill real animals in the name of their respective gods gave them some sort of

---

[28] The *Yimin* belief is a controversial issue in Taiwan. Most sources state that the *Yimin* (righteous people) were Hakka who defended their families and their land against invading insurrectors who tried to restore the Ming dynasty in 1786. Although the Hakka martyrs who died in this insurrection were later honoured by the Qing emperor, people with a Taiwanese consciousness emphasize the aspect that the Hakka had died for their homeland Taiwan.

[29] See for instance Government Information Office, 2006, *The Taiwan Yearbook*.

[30] See "Protest too late to save 'President Pig'". In: Peacetime Foundation of Taiwan 11.8.2003, retrieved on 11.11.2006 from http://www.peace.org.tw/english/aboutus/english_press_onnews_20030811_01.htm.

[31] See also Kertzer who describes this effect by referring to human sacrifices (1988: 33; 85) and to animal sacrifices (1988: 35, 171).

genuine authority and a quality of being "chosen". In addition, the performers in each case were real mediums, making the case even more complicated for the audiences, who were no longer capable of separating cosmological icons and indexical meanings, which made performances look real to them. Although the authority of the respective performers was undoubtedly enhanced through the rituals, the rituals could not be tolerated, since their authentic appearance was considered to be a kind of blasphemy by the common people which could lead to the retaliation of the gods. However, because of the skilful involution of cosmological icons and indexical meanings, retraditionalizing performances were charged with an ambivalence that made it difficult to oppose them directly. As we have seen in the case of the local rituals, innovations were generally enacted at least several times until they succumbed, if deemed to be infelicitous or inadequate, to ritual criticism.

While this latter effect caused by ritual's characteristic of ambivalence is quite familiar and often discussed in performance theory (Tambiah 1979; Kertzer 1988; Bell 1997), the observation that rituals may also be vested with an undue religious efficacy seems to be a rather unnoticed phenomenon. In general, performers have to work hard – and this may even be the case in theatrical performances – to convince their audiences of their ability to evoke divinities, fictional characters, the dead or their ghosts. Theorists of performance therefore hold that both ritual and theatre performances always involve risk for performers (Koepping 2003; Schieffelin 1996). In *Failure of Performance*, for instance, Schieffelin (1996) discusses the case of the Kaluli of New Guinea who judge performative failure or success according to theatrical elements of stagecraft and acting ability. This also includes the performers' talent to respond intuitively to the requirements of the audience and the situation. Shamans may even be "thrown out of the séance" if they are not able to evoke resonance about the divine presence in their audience. In the cases discussed in this study, however, religious efficacy seems to disturb local audiences. What they expect to watch are folkloristic, theatrical performances in which the "playacting" mode is obvious, since this mode seems to reduce the risk that any transcendent authorities of one's different religions can come into conflict with each other. Using the (problematic) categorization of "liturgical" vs. "performative" rituals mentioned in section 3.3 of the introduction, one might also say that these audiences prefer the liturgical Christian or Christianized rituals of the Church in which they only have to care that things are done correctly in the eyes of the Christian god.[32] The new rituals of traditionalist elites, on the other hand, are strongly performative in character, even in spite of the scripts which have been written for most of them. It must be expected that in comparable hybrid contexts where the Christian religion is well established alongside complementarily coexisting elements of indigenous religions (as it has been described in sections II.1.5 and II.2.6), expectations of local non-elite audiences will be quite similar.

Socio-cultural differences

As I have shown in Part II, the way in which rituals were used for authentication was also affected by certain socio-cultural characteristics of the respective groups. As for the Taroko, a formerly acephalic society, social authority traditionally had to be constantly earned and re-earned by the individual. In the contemporary rituals, this trait was manifested by a large degree of improvisation. On the other hand, in the case of the Ami (a traditionally strongly hierarchical society with a frequently still existing age rank system), the willingness to recognize super-ordinate authorities still persisted structurally. Despite considerable changes in the way these authorities were constituted today, this readiness to submit oneself to what people perceived as "traditional authority" entailed a strong acceptance of formalized ritual blueprints, even if these blueprints were constantly transformed by the traditional authorities. For this reason, local politicians must, if they want to authenticate themselves, form alliances with elites who represent "traditional authorities". Consequently, the most efficient way for rivalling politicians to challenge these alliances is to mobilize those groups that were traditionally also equipped

---

[32] The categorization "liturgical – performative" is problematic because liturgical rituals may also be performative. It proves useful, however, to point to certain tendencies.

with traditional authority, but that have been rejected in the course of modernization and Christianization.

However, I have also pointed out that the main variations in the way in which ritual restoration is pursued in different ethnic groups today are only indirectly linked to socio-cultural differences; instead, they are more directly dependent on divergences in the respective ethnic group's conversion process and the respective denominational choice, which was itself dependent on certain socio-cultural conditions. Ami converted to Catholicism because of its hierarchical structures, Taroko to Protestantism because of the looser and more democratic structure of this denomination. Partly because of the scarce presence of the priest in the parishes, partly because of the more liberal and tolerant stance of the mostly foreign priests towards local religions, the Catholic Church's control over traditional elements within the rituals today is less rigid than that of the PCT, to the extent that it even tolerates ancestor worship to a moderate degree. Contrary to this, the local ministers of the Protestant Church monitor ritual practices incessantly and usually forbid all symbols that are deemed a challenge to the Church's monotheist ideology, including ancestor worship. They do so partly because of the conviction that the Christian way is the better way for Aborigines, partly, however, also because of their competition with political elites, with whom they (different from the power coalitions in Ami society) rarely form alliances.

In spite of these differences in the choice of denominations, however, the main form of conversion in Taiwan's aboriginal society seems to have been complementary coexistence. After traditional religions were successfully forced into the underground by the Church, these traditions were able to survive as so-called "superstitions", and took on functions that Christianity did not fulfill. However, they could not have survived on their own, as their existence had become merely complementary. When traditionalism was on the rise, the churches felt particularly menaced and showed strong reactions, as they knew about the continuing, latent existence of indigenous religions. There was no support for traditionalism from the common people either, since most of them were satisfied with the *status quo*.

Different reflexivities

My account of the collective rituals on the local level has shown how representatives of rivaling social groups use meta-communicative clues (allusions to meta discourses, reframing) in order to charge ritual performances with additional messages and in order to influence the perception of audiences and participants. The constructivity which ritual manifests here seems to be particularly enhanced in times of thorough socio-cultural change, but also through the conditions of modernization and globalization, both of which have a strong impact on human reflexivity. The reflexive turn on one's own doings, however, is not accomplished by all ritual audiences and participants in the same way. This is mainly due to the different experiences of members of hybrid cultures and the pre-selections made by them during the performances. For the common people, this could be most clearly observed in their attitude towards traditionalist rituals. On one hand, they were often unable to understand the cultural symbols integrated into the rituals by traditionalists because connotations of these symbols were in fact more complicated (hybridized) than anticipated by the designers of these performances. One example was the traditionalists' frequent reference to the traditional concept *gaya* in the Taroko's ancestor-spirits-rituals – a concept that had, however, in reality already thoroughly changed in meaning because common people today look at it from a Christianized perspective. In the case of the common people, these synthesized mind-sets determined their attitudes towards retraditionalizing rituals in general. Based on concrete cultural and historical experiences, these mind-sets are today part of the common people's habitus, which has pre-reflexive rather than reflexive dimensions. Reflexively controlled, however, are the concomitant ritual criticism and the rejection of rituals that are under suspicion of being religiously efficacious.[33] For instance, theatrical performances of actors who just play shamans during the Ami harvest festivals are not unusual and absolutely accepted. However, the shamanist performances that I

---

[33] As I have shown elsewhere (Rudolph forthcoming 3), "religious" efficacy is not to be confused with "social" efficacy.

dealt with in Part II were unacceptable for the majority of the people, not only because they were performed outside of the official Christian frame, but also because they were enacted by ambiguous performers, that is folk-religious priestesses who were reputed for their interaction with non-Christian supernatural powers.[34] In such a scenario, common people who were – despite Japanization, Sinification, and Christianization – latently still attached to their traditional religions and who still carried this stance with them when watching the performances, could not but fear that the rituals might still in some way be effective and might result in the retaliation of the gods. Similar reasons also led to the rejection of the ancestor-spirits-rituals in Taroko society. Thus, the most decisive reason for the failure of the canonisation of the traditionalist rituals in the villages was their undue religious efficacy: in a society whose members harboured an ambivalent belief system, religious efficacy seemed not to fit into collective rituals that were supposed to enhance solidarity and a common identity.[35]

Modern and cosmopolitan aboriginal elites, however, look back on different socio-cultural experiences and thus also have another perception regarding contemporary ritual. First, since their socialisation mostly occurred in Han society, their cultural perspective is strongly influenced by that of Han elites, in whose cultural and political context mottos such as "de-colonialization" and "search for subjectivity" have a different current relevance than in rural communities. Because they live in a Han environment, most aboriginal intellectuals have the common experience of a loss of culture and a feeling of crisis concerning their native languages, which can explain a nostalgic, romanticizing, or sometimes even fundamentalist stance ("now or never more") regarding their native cultures. However, they also have the experience of stigmatisation and discrimination, especially because of their thorough participation in the Han's school and academic system, in which they were often discriminated against because they (as citizens from remote areas) benefited from the

---

[34] Mother of Garao 19.9.2004, personal interview.
[35] In the chapters on contemporary Taroko and Ami ritual, I pointed out that non-Christian religious beliefs actually "coexist" in both groups with the Christian mainstream.

bonus system (*jiafen zhidu*). Thus, sudden outbursts of "reverse symbolic violence" must not necessarily be strategic, but may also have this psychological background.

Second, aboriginal elites have a profound knowledge of certain "weak points" in the consciousness of Taiwanese Han. Taiwan wants to be recognized as a nation in a world of nations. In order to reach this goal, however, it not only has to constantly prove its commitment to universal human rights, but also to emphasize "difference" – "difference" from Communist China or other countries with which it might otherwise be confused. This paradox is susceptible to instrumentalization. Every non-recognition of the Aborigines' evocation of their ancestor-spirits can be not only interpreted as harmful to the establishment of national culture, but can also easily be charged with being politically incorrect, with demonstrating "Han-chauvinism", or with revealing a lack of respect towards minorities. The promotion of "difference" thus develops its own dynamics and may have immeasurable consequences, which however have to be tolerated. From this perspective, Taiwan's Han have made themselves susceptible to pressure from the outside. When aboriginal elites in their ritualized protests call on their traditional ancestor-spirits, their rules, and their legacy, they seem to deliver their individual agency into the hands of the gods. Simultaneously, however, they „borrow" the ancestor-spirits' authority, which can hardly be counteracted by secular arguments. In this situation, Taiwan's Han do not have much leeway to act, although such performances as those of legislator Gao Jin Sumei can send dangerous signals to those observers who carefully are watching the development of democracy and human rights in Taiwan (such as the KMT, China, and the UN). From this perspective, aboriginal intellectuals seem to "borrow" even other additional authorities in their "rituals of resistance".

Third, aboriginal intellectuals and politicians often do not have much contact with Christianity or their own traditional cultures. They primarily live in a polytheist environment, because for Taiwan's Han, polytheism is the most normal thing in the world and well-accepted. Many of their reconstructions of traditional rituals are based on the accounts of Japanese anthropologists of the colonial period – accounts which convey the essentialisms, romanticizations, mystifications, and fetishizations of the scholars and which are themselves often based on the interpretations and authenticating endeavours of the ruling elites of the past (Keesing 1989). From this perspective, the traditionalist's frequent proclamation that traditionalist rituals can liberate their people from the colonial conditioning caused by Japanization, Sinicization, and Christianization often seems absurd. On the other hand, however, such claims can be easily understood by Taiwan's Han who see the need for profound mental "decolonialization" in their own society. This may serve as an explanation of why aboriginal intellectuals and politicians often fail to adjust certain ideas and concepts surfacing in retraditionalizing rituals to the situation within aboriginal communities. As Qiu Yunfang (2004) contends in her analysis of the new ancestor-spirits-rituals in Taroko society and the failure of canonization of these rituals, aboriginal elites' main addressees in these representations were Taiwan's Han. The intellectuals studied the concepts like researchers from the outside and translated them in a way that could be understood by the Han, thereby changing the original meaning so much that ordinary people in the communities could no longer grasp it. According to my own observations, instead of searching for traditional authenticity, a more successful way to promote aboriginal subjectivity would probably have been to recognize the Aborigines' hybridised *status quo* in which every aboriginal group has formed its own, very distinct Christian culture with its own art styles, music styles, ritual performances, bible language etc..

Fourth, a certain level of education and intercultural competence also seem to play a decisive role regarding the readiness for re-interpretation und re-composition of rituals. The *Presbyterian Church of Taiwan* (PCT) has had experience with the "contextualization" of religion since the early 1970s. Due to their work as mediators between different religious orientations, Church elites more intensively than other members of their groups have experienced the relativity of boundaries. As for aboriginal politicians, their clientele generally comes from a multitude of different denominations and religions. Due to their close interaction with Han enterprises and politicians, they also have to look far outside of their own religious and cultural community. The same can be said for the situation of aboriginal intellectuals and cultural workers who constantly interacted with Han intellectuals. We can assume that such an environment supports the detachment of formerly compelling patterns of action and religious practices from their normative foundations in the sense pointed out by Giddens (1994) in his reflections on the increase of reflexivity in post-traditional societies, so that they become free for pragmatic re-contextualizations. From this perspective, retraditionalization of aboriginal rituals as we can observe it today rather seems to be the expression of a particular state of elitist reflexivity, a particular state of "disembeded-ment". It is, on one hand, rooted in the attempt of the state to prevent (actually unavoidable) alienation[36] for the sake of national identity search and solidarization; on the other hand, it reflects the attempt of ethnic el-ites to authorize themselves through "authentic traditions" under the con-ditions of nativism and multiculturalism. As we have seen, this process also entailed an increasing incorporation of elements from concepts and ideas not only from contemporary Han-society, but also from other parts of the world in the sense pointed out by Ardener (1989) in his notion of the parameter collapse. From Taiwan's ethnologists and Church mission-aries, Aborigines gained knowledge about the meaning and the tactics of the Fourth World Movement. Taiwan's oppositional Han intellectuals (at that time opposed to the KMT) broadly discussed concepts like post-colonialism and nationalism. Since the early nineties, regular programs with information on the traditional cultures of indigenous people in America and Asia and of Austronesians all over the Pacific have ap-peared on TV, where especially rituals like shamanic practices, initiation rites or animal sacrifices were introduced to the public. Similar interest for indigenous populations and Austronesian peoples could be observed in the print media including daily newspapers. Even though no particular foreign elements had to have been appropriated in aboriginal rituals, it can be assumed that at least the expectations, ideas, and phantasies of

---

[36] Modern social philosophy regards alienation as a normality in modern societies: it is not only unavoidable, but is also basic condition of modern societies (see Jürgen Habermas 1981, who defines this process as the "colonialization of the life world through the systems").

Han and Aborigines have been influenced in this process.[37] I pointed out this possibility when I discussed the newly growing Ami shamanism which seems to build on inspirations not only coming from traditional Ami religion, but also from Christian charismatic religions, from Taiwanese folk religion as well as – as in the spectacular pig-treading ceremony – folk religious elements from Mainland China.[38] Most evident was the incorporation of medially mediated global impulses in the case of the new Hip Hop style dances in the harvest festival of the Ami of Dulan described by Futuru (Tsai Cheng-Liang 2005), which fuse music and dance styles from all over the world. The fact that the internet is abundantly employed in Taiwan in the process of dissemination of different global and local cultures (as for instance in the case of the pig-treading rituals and the Hip Hop rites) contributes to further diffusion of new concepts into the local traditions.

This brings us back to the question of whether the pragmatic use and the reflexive recontextualization that can be observed with respect to retraditionalizing aboriginal rituals in contemporary Taiwan point to an "ossification" of ritual in the sense expected by Tambiah (1979). It seems to be safe to say that – not only because of the steady influx of vibrant new elements as described above, but predominantly because of the meeting of different reflexivities in these rituals – such an "ossification" with respect to cosmological content has in fact not taken place yet. At least from the perspective of common people, retraditionalizing rituals instead have the effect of reminding them instantly of their essential cosmological ideas and convictions. In the process of close inspection of

---

[37] In 1996, the successful artist Saguliu from the Paiwan ethnic group showed me a couple of books on art works of indigenous populations in Melanesia and Indonesia from which he took his inspirations (personal interview with Saguliu 25.3.2006).

[38] There is a high probability that inspirations from Mainland folk traditions have an influence on aboriginal traditions in Taiwan. Yiyong, a local aboriginal parliamentarian who is in charge of the cultural reconstruction work in the Taroko village of Hongye, told me in 2006 that he had already participated in more than twenty delegations to the autonomous zones of Mainland China's national minorities in the past ten years. The invitations are part of the ideological battle between the People's Republic of China and the Republic of China (Taiwan) about adequate minority politics.

the rituals with respect to the adequate relationship between contemporary religious and representational exigencies, people revise and readapt their own beliefs more than in any other activity. In other words, although these rituals may start out as practices with primarily indexical intentions, they gain – due to the expectations of the audiences – a strongly cosmological plane in the course of performance and ritual criticism. This can not be said for the theatrical, Christianized rituals of the churches in which church elites have in advance ostentatiously skipped those parts deemed as blasphemy and which therefore lack such stimulations. If this result differs from Tambiah's (1979) assumption that functional indexical uses may prevail in the case of an ossification of rituals, a possible explanation for this divergence is that Tambiah's research focused on a different context. He was concerned with traditional societies within a rather homogeneous religious and cultural setting. The present research, however, focuses on an extremely hybrid setting in which the coexistence and interaction of different religions is not only officially approved and propagated, but in which people with different religious backgrounds and worldviews take part, organize, and watch the rituals in question. It is for this reason that the aspect of negotiation and renegotiation of the right form of representation becomes particularly strong within these rituals.

4. Implications for state and society

However, the phenomenon of a diverging reflexivity of different societal groups also seems to pose new challenges in a multicultural, democratic nation. By the mid-nineties, Taiwan's national political elites had largely agreed that in a multi-ethnic Taiwan, the claim of equal rights, equal respect and non-discrimination of all citizens could no longer be satisfied merely by a politics of "recognition of universal human dignity". Instead, cultural difference would have to be more thoroughly recognized and even to be taken as the basis for differential practice. In an era in which erstwhile reciprocity-based social bonds had waned and in which the satisfaction of individuals' basic need for recognition was hence no longer a foregone conclusion, the recognition of the unique, unmistakable identity of any individual was necessary. This entailed the recognition of his/her difference and of the variable cultural contexts and collectives from which an individual came and to which he/she bound his/her identity. The main aim of this new policy was to give non-mainstream members of the "life (or fate) community" Taiwan the feeling of a more respected existence and thereby to reduce the chances for conflict.[39]

If we look at the situation of contemporary rituals, however, we can see quite clearly that those societal groups that were particularly meant to be supported by Taiwan's multi-culturalist policy, are often neglected in their cultural needs and excluded from the process of cultural production. Proposals that apply for the sponsorship of cultural projects and activities are written exclusively by modern Han or aboriginal elites, even if it is stated otherwise in the proposals. If put aside those disagreements that develop when elites redirect money for election campaigns, divergences in reflexivity such as those mentioned above often cause considerable dissonance within the communities. Indeed, new intra-ethnic inequalities seem to develop between elite and non-elite-members of aboriginal society, as the former increasingly impose a new hegemony on those segments of society which do not want their (Christianized) cultural *status quo* to change or which want to keep in step with Taiwan's modernization process. It would be especially problematic if traditionalist groups were successful in their attempts to convince the Taiwanese Han of their own "traditional legitimacy" or "traditional rights" by way of their biased cultural representations before the island's academic community, on the internet or in other media, thus causing a redefinition of aboriginal culture not desired by the common people. Such redefinitions would inevitably bear the risk that the expectations and inclinations of large population groups within aboriginal society are

---

[39] Rudolph 2003b.

ignored or not represented.[40] In some cases, they might even cause economical harm, as became clear in the case of Taibalang where traditionalist elites organized shamanist rituals in order to be re-legitimated in
certain "traditional rights" and "traditional land rights". Traditionalists in
this case hoped that the enactment of cultural representations that seemed
more authentic and archetypical than those of their tribal rivals would
eventually re-legitimate them and their alleged primordial rights in the
eyes of the Han public. As a result, so they calculated, these rights would,
on the grounds of the new policy stating that the distinct cultural traditions of Aborigines had to be protected and enhanced, have to be conceded to them. A similar tactic or "play" with the new sense for political
correctness in Taiwan's public (as well as in the international community) could be observed in the case of May Jin's performances in Japan.
Here, ethnic elites publicly, though indirectly, criticized Taiwan's government and anticipated that the ostentatious demonstration of close affiliation to religious traditions and the ancestor spirits would eventually
let them seem legitimized through their cultural collectives. For Taiwan's
leaders, however, not only social conflict and social misrepresentation
seem to be at stake in the case of such provocations, but also Taiwan's
international image in a more comprehensive perspective. In the above
case, the action very effectively focussed attention on the inappropriate
conduct of the Taiwanese government and its pan-green allies who, by
sending their own delegations to the Yaskuni shrine, not only revealed an
undue Japan-friendly attitude, but also showed disrespect towards the
sensibilities of other Asian countries. The implicit suggestion of fascist
tendencies and continued suppression of political attitudes within Taiwan

---

[40] I have mentioned this problem in earlier writings, in which I have pointed to the risks
inherent to the (planned but yet unrealised) stipulation of the forced rehabilitation of
aboriginal first and last names. My research in communities of the Paiwan and Ru-
kai, for instance, has shown that non-aristocrat members of these societies are usually not unsatisfied with their Han-Chinese names which no longer reveal differences in status as the traditional names had done (Rudolph 2003a; b). The rehabilitation of aboriginal names is possible since 1995. Until 2007, only 6000 people (1,3%
of Taiwan's aboriginal population) had changed their names (China Times
30.1.2007).

seemed to denounce the sincerity of the democratisation efforts of the present Taiwanese government.

To summarize, one can say that retraditionalizing rituals fulfill important functions in the constitution of society and identity, since they negotiate current social, cultural, and religious questions. However, certain problems also developed under the auspices of Taiwanese multiculturalism and nation building. Thus, we saw that tradition is often monopolized and instrumentalized by members of political parties and other interest groups for their own authentication in a way that challenges the authority of the state and its original democratic ideals. This kind of challenge does not necessarily have to be negative or harmful. Answered in the right way, it may strengthen and confirm a democracy, since only through constant negotiation and readjustment can totalizing, hegemonizing, or monopolizing developments be contained. As the present study has shown, however, the contemporary, state-supported traditionalism of some intellectual and political elites does not equally satisfy all societal segments within aboriginal society. It not only collides with the religious (Christianized) identity developed by common people in the last decades, but also supports the artificial empowerment of social forces that are not necessarily legitimised by the majority of the people. Although the people – that is the cultural collectives – are remunerated for their performances and are given the opportunity for self contemplation, those who truly profit are the socially privileged ethnic elites with a range of experience that is compatible with Han society and Han idealizations and that enables them to convert economic capital into other forms of capital.[41] Further, one essential function of ritual once envisaged by Taiwan's national political elites, the re-enforcement of community solidarity, seems to be no longer guaranteed.

However, due to the divergence of ethnic groups and extreme regional variations within these groups – depending on matters such as the

---

[41] This difference between Aboriginal non-elites and elites reminds of Sahlins' notion of "develop-man vs development". Non-Western develop-man uses his encounter with the world capitalist system to develop / perpetuate his own culture in its own terms. He does not – as in the case of "development" – remake his social relations along Western lines what would have opened up to him at least the possibility of reinvesting what the market brings into the capitalist system. The cultural logics governing social relations remain recognizably indigenous (Sahlins 2005).

degree of assimilation into Han society, conversion experiences, geographical location (climate, proximity to the big cities) etc. – the results of this study should not be generalized. I have attempted only to point to a trend that I have discovered in those societies that I have closely examined. For instance, Christianity is not as deeply-rooted everywhere in aboriginal society as it is in the villages I studied: the number of Christians in the Saixait villages on the west side of Taiwan's Central Mountain Range has diminished to less than 30% in recent years; in the case of the reappearing Pingpu population which today is increasingly recognized as a part of Taiwan's aboriginal population, the percentage is even lower.[42] Such dispositions can have considerable impact on ritual performances, ritual criticism, and the way these performances are used for authentication, and will have to be taken into account in future research.

5. Retraditionalizing rituals in the context of Taiwanese nativism

When I made my initial remarks and definitions about Taiwanese nativism and aboriginal retraditionalization efforts in the introduction of this volume, I also pointed to the possibility that these two movements might differ from each other in nature and in quality. Can the process of cultural reconstruction and retraditionalization observed in Taiwan's contemporary aboriginal society today be referred to as a nativist, revitalist movement in the sense indicated by theorists like Wallace (1956) and Linton (1963), or does it have to be considered as a different phenomenon with different consequences and outcomes? While there is no doubt that those cultural and political endeavors of Taiwan's Han that try to underscore and to manifest the island's "subjectivity" can really be identified as "nativism" in the classical sense, many of the traditionalist endeavors of aboriginal elites rather seem to be a mere reflection of – or an adaptation to – this larger context.

---

[42] Jian Hongmo 2003. Lin Suzhen 1992: 115.

According to my own observations, this phenomenon is mainly due to the special form of acculturation Taiwan's Aborigines have undergone in the past five decades. By the time that China's nationalist army entered Taiwan and proclaimed martial law, fierce resistance on the part of the island's indigenous population had – after half a century of very effective taming- and subjugation policy of the Japanese – already come to an end. Where traditional religious beliefs and convictions still existed, they were more or less eliminated by the modernization and assimilation policy of the Chinese Nationalist government as well as by the new religious beliefs imported by the Christian churches. However, rather than being considered as invaders, both institutions stood for the possibility and the opportunity to catch up with modernity after other values had been thoroughly disencouraged and stigmatized. Under such conditions, the majority of Taiwan's aboriginal population never underwent a genuine postcolonial situation in the sense that a demarcation from former or alleged oppressors occurred or seemed necessary. Identity did not become a critical issue - a phenomenon that was largely due to the mediating role Christianity took over in this process. As Huang Shiun-Wey (2003) emphasizes, Christianity, which did not come to the island as part of a colonial project, even helped to "avert an identity crisis."[43] It not only effectively compensated for many of the hardships people were confronted with in the national assimilation process by practical support (saving unions, mass in aboriginal languages etc.), it also helped Aborigines to build up a positive identity within their current living environment. As members of a modern, monotheist religion, Aborigines could differentiate themselves positively from Taiwan's Han people in general. However, this borrowed religion at the same time also linked them to their country's most well-known and most capable representatives. This multivalent function of Christianity is expressed by the fact

---

[43] Huang Shiun-Wey 2003: 277. As Huang makes clear, the situation of Christianity in Taiwan was very different from the situation in Melanesia or Latin-America. Coming from the West, though not with colonial powers, it is usually believed to be the most advanced religion of the world, which helps Aborigines to feel – at least in terms of religion – more advanced than Chinese Han who are mostly members of Taiwanese Folk Religion.

that people like to remind outsiders that many of the highest leaders of the ROC were all Christians, among them the ROC's national father Sun Yat-sen, late president Chiang Kai-shek, as well as president Li Denghui.[44] Huang explains this integrative attitude as a result of Taiwanese Aborigines' specific, eclectic (Huang uses "diffuse") concept of power. For them, not only their traditional supernatural beings have power (or cosmic potency) when rituals are properly conducted, but other people's religions can produce power as well. As I described it in the case of the Ami, people are even (although only covertly) ready to accept elements from Taiwanese folk religion if this seems helpful. This perception of power is quite different from – as for instance – that of the Chambri in Melanesia who perceive religious borrowing as providing a new way of getting old power.[45]

In terms of acculturation theory, I would therefore describe the main form of reaction of Taiwan's indigenous peoples to acculturative contact as a combination of acceptance and adaptation:[46] acceptance of the contact cultures' traits and eventual assimilation into them, as well as adaptation by fusing the different cultures into a "meaningful whole", as I have described in the case of "complementary coexistence" of rudimentary traditional beliefs with Christianity under Taiwan's specific environmental circumstances.

For aboriginal intellectuals, however, the situation was different because of their close cultural contact with Han society. In the course of Taiwan's ethnification process of the 1990s in which oppositional Han redefined Aborigines as a distinct ethnic group, identity became a problem for aboriginal elites. This new situation entailed the development of a stronger reflexivity with respect to one's own cultural conditions and a process of an "objectification of culture" (Handler 1984, Norton 1993), as we have witnessed in the very selective use of traditional religion in

---

[44] Huang Shiun-Wey 2003: 276.

[45] Huang 2003: 275. Huang here cites the research of Errington, F., & D. Gewertz, 1986, "The Confluence of Power: Entropy and Importation among the Chambri". In: Oceania 57: 99-113.

[46] Redfield, Linton, Herskovits 1936: 152.

the authentication endeavors of aboriginal elites.[47] However, similar to the case of the relationship between aboriginal common people and the Han, there never developed a real postcolonial situation between these elites and Taiwan's Han, since the latter anticipated and defined the Aborigines' possible psychological problems and their necessary coping methods in such a convincing way that there was basically no opportunity for Aborigines to demarcate oneself from them. In the case of aboriginal elites, it was thus (the borrowing of) Taiwan's Han's new nativist and multiculturalist ideology that not only averted a severe identity crisis, but that also dissolved the possibility for any real conflict. The mediating function of the Han's nativism and multiculturalism even led to the phenomenon that cultural objectifications did not need to be the Aborigine's own ones, but could be borrowed from Taiwan's Han who found themselves under imminent pressure to bring about such objectifications in their quest for "subjectivity". These objectivations not only included idealizations like that of twelve aboriginal groups with neatly separated cultural features and with religious traditions like head-hunting, shamanism, and the veneration of the ancestor-gods, but also such perceptions as that of the "noble savage" truthful to his traditions, thus totally ignoring the possibility of new, contemporary forms of aboriginal subjectivity (as for instance Christianized aboriginal culture). Another mediating factor besides nativism and multiculturalism was of course the Han's substantial economic power. This dilemma is confirmed by anthropologist Zhang Weiqi (1998) who contends that as a result of the Han's economic power, aboriginal culture was thoroughly reconstructed through the eyes of the dominant ethnic group of the island, the Han:[48]

> The closer a tribe is to the national [nativist] policy, the more resources it can obtain. This is not because of national welfare. In-

---

[47] In his monograph on nationalism and cultural objectification in Quebec, Richard Handler describes the cultural reconstruction process of Franco-Canadians in Canada. Norton (1993: 742) refers to "objectification" as a reflexive stance where "people may come to talk about, exaggerate or modify certain beliefs and practices as signifiers of their identity, as distinct from simply routinely living their culture."
[48] Zhang Weiqi 1998: 137.

stead, the better a tribe can echo the nation, that is the better it can extract cultural elements and transform them into refined perform-ance styles, the more resources it will obtain in comparison to other tribes (...).

In sum, we may conclude that aboriginal elites as well as non-elites have strong inclinations to acculturate successfully into Taiwan's main society. The fact that this is manifested in different ways today is not only because of different reflexivities and religiosities, but also be-cause of the different groups of reference both societal segments have in Han society. Common people have to interact with Taiwan's lower mid-dle classes where discrimination against Aborigines still prevails and where the perception of the "noble savage" is not yet deeply rooted. Therefore, the intellectuals' quest for authenticity and 'subjectivity' often seems absurd and strange to them. Elites identify instead with the ideals of intellectual circles within Han society where "the recognition of dif-ference" and "multiculturalism" have become core values over the course of political paradigm change. These processes of identification, of course, do not occur without crisis and psychic conflict. In section IV of their *Memorandum on the study of acculturation* entitled "Psychological mechanisms of selection and integration of traits under acculturation", Redfield, Linton, and Herskovits (1936) contend that psychic conflict results from attempts to reconcile different social behaviours and norms, and hence should be greatest for individuals engaged in bicultural adapta-tion and should be least for those who reject acculturative change.[49] In the case of Aborigines in Taiwan, psychic conflict resulting from accul-turative stress is most obviously expressed in the form of frequent alco-hol abuse as well as in "passing" behaviour (De Vos 1975).[50] In the case of the elites, it takes the shape of recurrent jokes and allusions to the Han's weaknesses as well as attempts at transgression and subversion, as I have indicated it in the case of retraditionalizing rituals.

---

[49] Redfield, Linton, and Herskovits 1936: 152.
[50] By passing behaviour, George De Vos means the denial of one's own cultural or ethnic identity (De Vos 1975: 26).

However, it would be misleading to consider processes of cultural exchange as one-dimensional. Redfield, Linton, and Herskovits (1936) remind us that „Acculturation comprehends those phenomena which result when groups of individuals having different cultures come into continuous first-hand contact, with subsequent changes in the original cultural patterns of either or both groups."[51] In the case of Taiwan, we have seen that the development of the island's nativism and multiculturalism was largely dependent on the existence of Aborigines as a group that was considered as ethnically different. Further, many objectifications made by Taiwanese Han – even if they were romanticizations or idealizations – were definitely inspired by contact with these groups. Finally, the analysis of retraditionalizing rituals has shown that the negotiations and authenticating practices characterizing these rituals effectively affected and restructured social reality. They not only reinforced pre-existing romanticizations and idealizations, but also had visible effects on the power relations of Han and Non-Han and on the identity formation of the two groups.

Despite this constant interaction and exchange – or perhaps because of it – the relationship between Han and Aborigines remains problematic and ambiguous. Boundaries increasingly overlap, making it even more difficult for people in "Taiwan's pluralist and multi-ethnic society" to define themselves.[52] In an earlier study, I described how, in times of authoritarian rule, the despised "savage" (i.e., native women) was taken to satisfy the sexual needs of lower middle-class Han individuals, despite or because of the difference they felt between themselves and these people (Rudolph 1993). I referred to this phenomenon as a kind of fetishization, a kind of "anthrophagic incorporation" of the object of one's own fantasies. Numerous scholars have pointed to the dynamics of exotism, where the "othering" of the other, for instance of indigenous people, is in fact a kind of appropriation – the "most subtle" form of appropriation, as Waldenfels (1997) has pointed out. Today, the former "savage" has become a "noble savage", and difference is no longer negatively connoted. In

---

[51] Redfield, Linton, and Herskovits 1936: 149.
[52] By the middle of the 1990s, "*Taiwan duoyuan / duo zuqun shehui*" had become a common self-description of Taiwan.

addition, many Han today openly claim that Aborigines are in fact ge-
netically and culturally part of the Han individually thereby further blurring boundaries. On the other hand, we have seen how the "authentic
Aborigine" has in recent years constantly been reconstructed, by Han as
well as by Aborigines, who are mutually borrowing whatever seems useful from each other. All this shows that appropriation and demarcation
are – as in the past – actually still very much related today in a mutually
reinforcing process, albeit in reverse. As one of few Taiwanese anthropologists, Xie Shizhong (1994a) rightly noticed this complexity and ambiguity of the relationship of the two groups at a very early stage in Taiwan's nationbuilding process. In one of his studies on ethnic tourism in
Taiwan, he contends:

> While Han tourists are in search of "aboriginal culture" (*shandi
> wenhua*),[53] Aborigines assiduously assist them, eager to provide
> them with a most qualified cultural image. And the more fixed this
> image of the other group's culture becomes, the clearer it can rep-
> resent the ethnic boundary between Han and Aborigines. In other
> words, it is the interpretation of "aboriginal culture" from different
> sources – from government, entrepreneurs, academics, aboriginal
> tourists, and Han tourists – that further enforces the division of the
> social world of Han and Aborigines.[54]

---

[53] Until the mid-nineties, "*shandi wenhua*" (mountain culture) was the term that stood
for "aboriginal culture" in general. As Xie (1994a: 19; 165) makes clear, the term
was associated with an authentic culture as the opposite of non-traditional and non-
authentic urban culture (Xie 1994a).

[54] Xie 1994a: 166.

GLOSSARY (only Chinese equivalents to English terms)

Ami (Ameizu)	阿美族
Atayal (Tayazu)	泰雅族
Bailang	百郎
Bao gongcheng	保工程
Bentu wenhua	本土文化
Bentuhua	本土化
Bingcun hubu	並存　互補
Bingcun jingzheng	並存　競爭
Bunun (Bunongzu)	布農族
Caihong zhuan'an	彩紅專案
Chen Qinan	陳其南
Chiang Ching-kuo (Jiang Jingguo)	蔣經國
Chiang Kai-shek (Jiang Jieshi)	蔣介石
Chucao	出草
Chuqi minzu	初期民族
Ciji	慈濟
Cong buluo dao juchang	從部落到劇場
Cuozhe fanying	挫折反應
Dagangkou	大港口
Dahui	大會
Daozheng zhuan'an	導正專案
Dekedaya (Deqidayaqun)	德奇搭雅群
Delugu zhi sheng	德魯閣之聲

Dooda (Daozequn)	道澤群
Dulan	都蘭
Duoyuan shehui	多元社會
Duoyuan wenhua	多元文化
Fandao	番刀
Fanren (Hoklo-Dialekt: Huanna)	蕃人
Fengnian ji	豐年祭
Fushi	富世
fuzhen yundong	復振運動
Gan'enjie	感恩祭
Ganhua	感化
Gao Jin Sumei	高金素梅
Gaoshanzu yanjiu huigu yu qianzhan zuotanhui	高山族研究回顧與前瞻座談會
Gaoshanzu	高山族
Gaoxiong	高雄
Guanyin	觀音
Guo Jianping	郭建平
Guojia	國家
Guomindang (Chinese National Party, KMT)	國民黨
Guozu-guojia	國族-國家
Hai'an-Ami	海岸阿美
Hakka (Kejia)	客家
Han	漢
Hanhua	涵化

Hanren minzu	漢人民族
Hoklo	河洛
Hu Defu (Ale Lusuolaman)	胡德夫 (阿勒 路索拉滿)
Hualian huanbao lianmeng	花蓮環保聯盟
Hualian xian yuanzhumin wenhua jiyi huodong	花蓮縣原住民文化祭儀活動
Hualian	花蓮
Hualianxian Tailuge jianshe xiehui	花蓮縣太魯閣建設協會
Huan wo muyu yundong	還我母語運動
Huan wo tudi yundong	還我土地運動
Huang Yinggui	黃應貴
Huangminhua yundong	皇民化運動
Ji zuxian	祭祖先
Ji	祭
Jiafen zhidu	加分制度
Jie	節
Jieshoulu	介壽路
Jingying da Taiwan, jianli xin zhongyuan	經營大台灣, 建立新中原
Jinmen	金門
Jitong	乩童
Juluo fuhexing daji	聚落複合性大祭
Kaidagelan dadao	凱達格蘭

Kavalan (Gemalanzu)	葛瑪蘭族
Kejiaren	客家人
Ketagalan (Kaidagelan)	凱達格蘭族
Kominka (huangminhua)	皇民化
Kuaguo	跨國
Lanyu (Orchid Island)	蘭嶼
Li Denghui	李登輝
Lian Zhan	連戰
Lin Yanggang	林洋港
Ling'en yundong	靈恩運動
Liyijing Youma	麗依京 尤瑪
Lü Xiulian	呂秀蓮
Mabuchi Toichi	馬淵東一
Mazu (Matsu)	媽祖
Minjindang (Democratic Progress Party, DPP)	民進黨
Minnanren	閩南人
Minzu	民族
Nandao minzu	南島民族
Nandao yuxi minzu	南島語系民族
Nandao	南島
Nanshi-Amei	南勢阿美
Nantou	南投顯
Nanxiang zhengce	南向政策
Neizai zhiwo	內在制握
Neize fanying	內責反應

Paiwan (Paiwanzu)	排灣族
Peipohuan (Pingpufan)	平埔蕃
Peng Mingmin	彭明敏
Pianyuan diqu jumin	偏遠地區居民
Pideru Wuga	彼得洛 烏嘎
Pingdong	屏東
Pingpu	平埔族
Pudu	普渡
Puyuma (Beinanzu)	北南族
Puyuma (Beinanzu)	卑南族
Qigong	齊公
Qu Haiyuan	瞿海源
Quzhu e'ling	驅逐惡靈
Renjian fukan	人間副刊
Renjian	人間
Rentong de wuming	認同的污名
Rukai (Lukaizu)	魯凱族
Saguliu	撒古流
Saixiat (Saixiazu)	賽夏族
Sedek (Saidekezu)	賽得克亞族
Shanbao	山胞
Shandi wenhua	山地文化
Shandi wenhua	山地文化
Shandiren	山地人
Shaoshu minzu	少數民族

Shawen zhuyi	沙文主義
Shengji	省籍
Shenhua	神話
Shenling	神靈
Shenzhu	神豬
Shequ fazhan xiehui	社區發展協會
Shequ jianshe	社區建設
Shequ wenhua yishu fazhan xiehui	社區文化藝術發展協會
Shequ zongti yingzao jihua	社區總體營造計劃
Shezhang (tribal administrator)	社長
Shoufeng	壽豐鄉
Siraya (Xilayazu)	西拉雅族
Sun Yat-sen (Sun Zhongshan)	孫中山
Taibalang zhanwang xiehui	太巴塱瞻望協會
Taibalang	太巴塱
Tainan	台南
Taiwan daxue	台灣大學
Taiwan duoyuan / duo zuqun shehui	台灣多元／多族群社會
Taiwan jidu zhanglao jiaohui (PCT)	台灣基督長老教會
Taiwan mingyun gongtongti	台灣命運共同體
Taiwan minjian zongjiao	台灣民間宗教
Taiwan minzu	台灣民族
Taiwan shengming gongtongti	台灣生命共同體

Taiwan si da zuqun	台灣四大族群
Taiwan Yuanzhumin de jidian yishi: xiankuang pinggu	台灣原住民的祭典儀式: 現況評顧
Taiwan Yuanzhumin quanli cujinhui (ATA)	台灣原住民權力促進會
Taiwan Yuanzhumin	台灣原住民
Taiwan yuanzhuminzu quanli cujinhui (ATA)	台灣原住民族權利促進會
Taiwan zhutixing	台灣主體性
Takasagozoku (jap.)	高砂族
Tao (Dawuzu; once: Yameizu)	達悟族
Taroko (Tailugezu)	太魯閣族
Tong (communication)	通
Tongbao	同胞
Tonghua	同化
Tongmen	銅們
Tsou (Cao)	曹族
Tuobian	脫變
Tuosaiqun (Dooda)	托賽群 (= 道澤群)
Waishengren	外省人
Waizai zhiwo	外在制握
Waize fanying	外賣反應
Walisi Beilin (Cai Guicong)	瓦歷斯 (貝林 蔡貴聰)
Walisi Yougan	瓦歷斯 尤幹

Wanrong	萬榮鄉
Wenhua gongzuozhe	文化工作者
Wenhua zhenzhi yu zhanyan:	文 化 政 治 與 展：
Saixia, Paiwan jingyan	賽夏, 排灣經驗
Wu Feng	吳鳳.
Wu Micha	吳密察
Wushe	霧社
Wushi (Ami language: Chikawasay)	巫師
Wuze fanying	無責反應
Xiaman Lanbo'an (Shi Nulai)	夏曼 藍波安（施努來).
Xiangtu shenxue	鄉土神學
Xianzhumin	先住民
Xie Shizhong	謝世忠
Xindang (NCP)	新黨
Xiulin	秀林鄉
Xu Muzhu	許木柱
Yami (Yameizu, today: Tao)	雅美族
Yanhuang zisun	炎黃子孫
Yasukuni Shrine	靖國神社
Yazu	亞族
Yiguo qingdiao	異國情調
Yimin	義民
Yuanwuzhe	原舞者
Yuanzhumin de yangfen	原住民的養分

Yuanzhumin jingying	原住民精英
Yuanzhumin kangzheng jingying	原住民抗爭精英
Yuanzhumin wenhua chucao xuanyan	原住民文化出草宣言
Yuanzhumin xinwen zazhi	原住民新聞雜誌
Yuanzhumin yundong	原住民運動
Yuanzhumin zhengming yundong	原住民正名運動
Yuanzhumin zhengzhi jingying	原住民政治精英
Yuanzhumin zhiqing	原住民知青
Yuanzhumin zhishi fenzi	原住民知識分子
Yuanzhumin zhishi jingying	原住民知識精英
Yuanzhumin zhishi qingnian	原住民知識青年
Yuanzhumin zuqun	原住民族群
Yuanzhumin	原住民
Yushan shenxueyuan	玉山神學院
Zhen yesu jiaohui	真耶穌教會
Zeng Jinlan	曾金蘭
Zeng Yulan	曾玉蘭
Zhan jitou	占雞頭
Zheng Rongxiang	鄭榮祥
Zhenzhixing	真實性
Zhonghua minguo shequ yingzao xuehui	中華民國社區營造學會
Zhonghua minzu	中華民族
Zhongyuan	中原
Zhongzu	種族

Zhou (Cao)	鄒 (曹)
Zhuonghua wenhua fuxing yundong	中華文化復興運動
Zhutixing	主體性
Zizhiqu	自治區
Zongci	宗祠
Zongshexing de zongjiao yundong	綜攝性的宗教運動
Zu	族
Zui'e'gan	罪惡感
Zuling	祖靈
Zulingji	祖靈祭
Zuqun rentong	族群認同
Zuqun	族群
Zuxian	祖先
Zuyi qunti	族裔群體

BIBLIOGRAPHY

Abasiattai, Monday B., 1989, "The Oberi Okaime Christian Mission: Towards a History of an Ibibio Independent Church." In: *Africa* 59(4), 496-516.

Alliance of Taiwanese Aborigines (ATA), 1987, *Yuanzhumin: bei ya-pozhe de nahan* [Aborigines: Outcry of the suppressed]. Taibei: Taiwan Yuanzhuminzu quanli cujinhui. 台灣原住民族權利促進會, 1987, 原住民 - 被壓迫者的吶喊, 台灣原住民族權利促進會 成立 三週年專輯, (台灣原住民族權利 促進會) 台灣 1987.

Anderson, Benedict, 1988 [1983], *Die Erfindung der Nation*. Frankfurt a. M.: Campus Verlag.

Ardener, Edwin, 1989, *The Voice of Prophecy and other essays*. Oxford: Oxford University Press.

Arrigo, Linda Gail, with Si Jilgilan (Huan Ching-Wen) and Si Maraos (Chung Chi-Fu), 2002, "A Minority within a Minority: Cultural Survival on Taiwan's Orchid Island". In: *Cultural Survival Quarterly* 26 (2). Retrieved on 25.2.2006 from http://209.200.101.189/ publications/csq/ csq-article.cfm?id=1555.

Ashcroft, Bill, Gareth Griffiths and Helen Tiffin, 1989, *The Empire Writes Back: Theory and Practice in Post-Colonial Literatures*. New York: Routledge.

Assmann, Jan, 1999, *Das kulturelle Gedächtnis: Schrift, Erinnerung und politische Identität in frühen Hochkulturen*. München: C.H.Beck.

Barker, John ed., 1990, *Christianity in Oceania: Ethnographic Perspectives*. Lanham: University Press of America.

Bell, Catherine, 1992, *Ritual Theory, Ritual Practice*. New York, Oxford: Oxford University Press.

Bell, Catherine, 1997, *Ritual: Perspectives and Dimensions*. Oxford and New York: Oxford University Press.

Bellwood, Peter, 1991, "The Austronesian dispersal and the origin of languages". In: *Scientific American* 7, 88-93.

Bhabha, Homi K., 1994, *The Location of Culture*. London: Routledge, 1994.

Bhabha, Homi K., 1995, "Cultural Diversity and Cultural Differences" in: Bill Ashcroft, Gareth Griffiths, and Helen Tiffin eds., 1995, *The Post Colonial Studies Reader*. London, New York: Routledge.

Bloch, Maurice, 1977, "The disconnection between power and rank as a process: an outline of the development of kingdoms of Central Madagascar". In: *Achives Européennes de Sociologie* 18, 107-148.

Bloch, Maurice, 1989, "Symbols, Song, Dance and Features of Articulation: Is Religion an Extreme Form of Traditional Authority?". In: Bloch, Maurice, 1989, *History, Ritual and Power*. London: The Athlone Press, 19-45.

Bosco, Joseph, 1994, "Taiwan Factions: Guanxi, Patronage, and the State in Local Politics". In: Rubinstein (1994), *The Other Taiwan - 1945 to the Present*. N.Y.: M.E. Sharpe, 114-143.

Bourdieu, Pierre, 1977, *Outline of a Theory of Practice*. New York: Cambridge University Press.

Bourdieu, Pierre, 1987 [1980], *Sozialer Sinn*. Frankfurt: Suhrkamp.

Bradsher, Keith, 2006, "Ancient emperor or political pawn?". In: *The New York Times*, 5.4.2006. Retrieved on 5.4.2006 from http://iht.com/bin/print_ipub.php?file=/articles/2006/04/05/news/taiwan.php.

Brass, Paul, 1991, *Ethnicity and Nationalism: Theory and Comparison*. London: Sage.

Bureau of Cultural Park of the Council of Indigenous Peoples (CIP), Executive Yuan Taiwan, 2004, Official Website. Retrieved on 5.10.2004, from http://www.tacp.gov.tw/ (replaced by new version in November 2004). 行政院原住民族委員會文化園區管理局網頁.

Burt, Ben, 1984, *Tradition and Christianity: The Cosmological Transformation of a Solomon Islands Society*. Harwood Academic Publishers.

Butler, Judith, 1991 [1990], *Das Unbehagen der Geschlechter*. Frankfurt: Suhrkamp.

Butler, Judith, 1998 [1997], *Hass spricht. Zur Politik des Performativen.* Berlin: Berlin Verlag.

Cai Baiquan, 2003, "Taiwan Struggling for Independence: A Historical Perspective". Retrieved on 15.01.2004 from http://www.wufi.org.tw/eng/timvmnt1.htm.

Cao Qiuqin, 1998, *Jisi fenshi yu Tailugeren de qinshu guanxi* [Ritual sharing and the kinship relations of the Taroko]. Taiwan: Unpublished M.A. thesis at National Donghua University. 曹秋琴, 1998, 祭祀分食與太魯閣人的親屬關係. 台灣:國立東華大學碩士論文 (未出版).

Chan, Selina Ching, 2006, "Cultural Imagination and Nation Building in Taiwan". Paper presented at the *Conference of the Society for East Asian Anthropology* (SEAA) at The Chinese University of Hong Kong, 13-16 July 2006.

Chang Mao-kuei, 1996, "Political Transformation and the 'Ethnization' of Politics in Taiwan". In: Schubert / Schneider eds., *Taiwan an der Schwelle zum 21. Jahrhundert – Gesellschaftlicher Wandel, Probleme und Perspektiven eines asiatischen Schwellenlandes.* Hamburg: Mitteilungen des Instituts für Asienkunde 270, 135-152.

Chen Guangxing, 1994, "Diguo zhi yan: 'ci' diguo yu guozu-guojia de wenhua xiangxiang" ["The Imperialist Eye: The Cultural Imaginary of a Sub-Empire and a Nation State"]. In: *Taiwan shehui yanjiu jikan* 17, Taiwan, 149-222. 陳光興, 1994, "帝國之眼: '次' 帝國與國族--國家的文化現象", in: 台灣社會研究集刊, 17期, 台灣 1994: 149-222.

Chen Hua, 1998, "Shequ yingzao yu jiti jiyi [Community Construction and Collective Memory]. Paper presented at the *Third Annual Conference on the History and Culture of Taiwan* at Columbia University, New York, August 20-23, 1998. 陳華, 1998, "社區營造與集體記憶". 紐約 (未出版).

Chen Ruiyun, 1990, *Zuqun guanxi, zuqun rentong yu Taiwan Yuanzhumin jiben zhengce* [Ethnic relations, ethnic identity, and basic aboriginal policy]. Taiwan: Unpublished M.A. thesis at National Zhengzhi University. 陳瑞芸, 1990, 族群關係, 族群認同與台灣原住民基本政策. 台灣.國立政治大學碩士論文(未出版).

Chen Zhaoru, 1994: "Shilun Taiwan renleixue de Gaoshanzu yanjiu" [Preliminary Discussion of the Gaoshanzu Research in Taiwan's Cultural Anthropology]. In: *Taiwan Indigenous Voice Bimonthly* 6, 27-36. "試論台灣人類學家的高山族研究". In: 山海文化雙月刊, 6期, 台灣 9/1994: 27-36.

Chen Zhaoying, 1995, "Lun Taiwan de bentuhua yundong: yi ge wenhuashi de kaocha" [Discussion of the Taiwanization Movement: Examination of a Cultural History]. In: *Zhongwai wenxue* 23 (9), 8-43. 陳昭瑛, 1995, "論台灣的本土化運動: 一個文化史的考察", in: 中外文學, 23卷, 9期, 2/1995: 8-43.

Clifford, James, 1988, *The Predicament of Culture – 'The Pure Products Go Crazy'*. Cambridge (Mass.): Harvard University Press.

Cohen, Abner, 1993, *Masquerade Politics: Explorations in the Structure of Urban Cultural Movements*. Berkeley, CA: University of California Press.

Comaroff, Jean, 1985, *Body of Power, Spirit of Resistance: The Culture and History of a South African People*. Chicago: University of Chicago Press.

Connerton, Paul, 1989, *How Societies Remember*. Cambridge: Cambridge University Press.

Council for Cultural Affairs (Xingzhengyuan wenhua jianshe xiehui), 1995, *Shequ zongti yingzao yu shequ wenhua huodong jihua* [Plan for integrated community construction and cultural activities in the communities], Taiwan. 行政院文化建設委員會,1995, 社區總體螢造與社區活動計劃, 台灣: 行政院文化建設委員會.

De Vos, George, 1975, "Ethnic Pluralism: Conflict and Accomodation". In: De Vos, George/Romanucci-Ross, Lola eds., 1975, *Ethnic Identity*. California, 1975: 5-41.

Duo Ao Yougeihai / Adong Youpasi, 1991, *Pin'aras ke' na bnkis tayal - Taiya'er zu chuanshuo gushi jingxuanpian* [Selection of the legends of the Atayal]. Taiwan: Taiya'er zhonghui muyu tuixing weiyuanhui cbs. 多奧 尤給海 / 阿棟 尤帕斯, 1991, 泰雅爾族傳說故事精選篇. 台灣:泰雅爾族中會 母語推行委員會出版社.

Durkheim, Émile, 1915 [1974], *The Elementary Forms of the Religious Life*. Glencoe: Free Press.

Fanon, Frantz, 1952, *Peau Noire, Masques Blancs*. Paris: Editions de Seuil.

Fanon, Frantz, 1967, *The Wretched of the Earth*. Harmondsworth: Penguin.

Friedman, P. Kerim, 2005, *Learning "Local" Languages: Passive Revolution, Language Markets, and Aborigine Education in Taiwan*. Philadelphia (PA): Ph.D. dissertation at The Temple University.

Fu Dawei, 1993, "Bailang senlin li de wenzi lieren" [Hunters of Chinese Characters in the Forest of Han Rascals], in: *Con-Temporary* 83, 3/1993, 28-49. 傅大為, 1993, "白朗森林裡的文字獵人", in: 當代雜志, 83期, 3/1993: 28-49.

Furuno Kiyoto, 1945, *Kosagozoku no matsuri seikatsu* [The Ritual Life of Taiwan's Aborigines], Tokyo 1945. (Chinese Translation: Guye Qingren, 2000, *Taiwan Yuanzhumin de jiyi shenghuo* [The Ritual Life of Taiwan's Aborigines]). Taiwan: Taiyuan wenhua congkan. 古野青人 , 1945 , 高沙族の祭義生活 , 東京. (中文翻譯本:古野青人 , 2000 , 台灣原住民的祭義生活台灣:台原文化叢刊).

Gaenszle, Martin, 2000, "Sind Rituale bedeutungslos? Rituelles Sprechen im performativen Kontext". [Are rituals meaningless? Ritual speech in performative context]. In: Klaus-Peter Köpping & Ursula Rao eds., *Im Rausch des Rituals. Gestaltung und Transformation der*

Wirklichkeit in körperlicher Performanz. Münster, Hamburg, London: LIT.

Gao Deyi, 1994, "Jiben zhengce yantao: Maixiang 'duoyuan yiti' de zuqun guanxi: Yuanzhumin jiben zhengce de huigu yu zhanwang" [Discussion of basic politics: towards a 'pluralist entity' in ethnic relations]. In: Republic of China Association for Cultural Development of Taiwan's Aboriginal Peoples (Zhonghua minguo Taiwan yuanzhuminzu wenhua fazhan xiehui) ed., 1994, *Yuanzhumin zhengce yu shehui fazhan [Aboriginal politics and social development]*. Taiwan, 114-181. 高德義, 1994, "基本政策研討: 邁向 '多元一體' 的族群關係", in: 中華民國台灣原住民族文化發展協會 ed., 1994, 原住民政策與社會發展. 台灣, 114-181.

Gao Jin Sumei (Jiwas Ali) (alias "May Jin"), 2004, "Chucao xuanyan" [Head-hunting Proclamation]. Retrieved on 06.10.2004, from: http://www.abo.org.tw/maychin/epaper/maychin041.htm. 高金素梅, 2004,"出草宣言".

Gao Jin Sumei (Jiwas Ali) (alias "May Jin"), 2007, Gao Jin Sumei's Website "Taiwan's Aborigines". Retrieved on 01.10.2007, from: http://www.abohome.org.tw/eng/.

Gariyi Jihong (Kaji-Cihung), 2000, "Guoshou, jingmian yu Slbuxan" [Head-hunting, Tattoos and Slbuxan]. PPT-presentation retrieved on 20.03.2002 from http://www.fusps.hlc.edu.tw/side00.htm (not traceable after September 10, 2004). 沓日羿吉宏, 2001,"馘首, 鯨面与slbuxan".

Gariyi Jihong (Kaji-Cihung), 2001a, "Guoshou, jingmian yu slbuxan" [Head-hunting, Tattooing and Head-hunter Cloth]. In: *Paper-Compilation of the First Symposium of Aboriginal postgraduates in Taiwan*. Taiwan. 沓日羿吉宏, 2001a, "馘首, 鯨面与slbuxan". In: 第一屆原住民研究生研究論文及發表會論文集.台灣.

Gariyi Jihong (Kaji-Cihung), 2001b,"Tayazu dongsaidekequn chuantong yiliao gainian" [The traditional medical conceptions of the Atayal-Sedek]. In: Taiwan Yuanzhumin jijinhui, 2001b, *Paper-Compilation of the Symposium on the traditional medicine of Taiwan's Aborigines VS Western medicine*. Taiwan.. 旮日羿吉宏, 2001b, "泰雅族東賽德克群傳統醫療概念". In: 財團法人臺灣原住民文教基金會, 2001, 原住民傳統醫療VS現代醫療 研討會論文集. 台灣.

Gariyi Jihong (Kaji-Cihung), 2002, "Yishi, zaizao yu bianqian: Taya dongsaidekequn liang ge cunluo yishi tanxi" [Revitalization and change of ritual: analysis of the rituals of two villages of the Sedek-Atayal]. In: *Paper-Compilation of the papers presented at the 3rd Aborigines' M.A. candidates symposium* 24.5.2002. Taiwan. 旮日羿吉宏, 2002, "儀式、再造與變遷：泰雅東賽德克群兩個村落儀式探析". In: 第三屆人類學相關系所研究生論文發表會論文集. 台灣 24.5.2002.

Gariyi Jihong (Kaji-Cihung), 2003, "Zuling, shengling yu jisi de chaoyuexing: Saidekequn cunluo jidian gainian fenxi" [The transcendence of ancestor-spirits, god and the ritual leader: An analysis of the ritual conception in villages of the East-Sedek]. In: Paper-Compilation of the papers presented at the "*Symposium on the encounter of Aborigine's traditional culture and rituals with Christianity*"]. Taiwan: Taiwan World Vision Association. 旮日羿吉宏, 2003, "祖靈、聖靈與祭詞的超越性：東賽德克群村落祭典概念探析." In: 臺灣世界展望會, 2003, 原住民傳統文化: 祭儀與基督教福音的對遇 研討會論文集. 台灣 21-22.7.2003.

Gariyi Jihong (Kaji-Cihung), 2004, *Jixing yu chaoyue: Seejiq Truku cunluo jidian yu zuling xingxiang* [English title of thesis in Chinese language: Improvisation and Transcendence: The Seejiq Truku Village Ritual and Ancestral Images]. Taiwan: Unpublished M.A. thesis

at Ciji University. 旮日羿吉宏, 2004, 即興與超越:Seejiq Truku村落
祭典與祖靈形像. 台灣: 慈濟大學碩士論文 (未出版).

Geertz, Clifford, 1982, Negara: The Theater State in Nineteenth-Century Bali, Princeton University Press.

Giddens, Anthony, 1994, "Living in a Post-Traditional Society". In: U.Beck, A.Giddens, S.Lash eds., 1994, *Reflexive Modernization. Politics, Tradition and Aesthetics in the Modern Social Order.* Oxford: Oxford University Press.

Green, Edwin C., 1978, "Winti and Christianity: A Study in Religious Change". *Ethnohistory* 25(3), 225-251.

Grice, H.P., 1957, Meaning. In: *Philosophical Review.*

Grimes, Ronald, 2001, "Ritual and the media". In: Hoover, Stewart M., Schofield Clark, Lynn, 2001, *Practicing religion in the age of the media: explorations in media, religion, and culture.* New York: Columbia University Press, p. 219-234.

Guan Xiaorong, 1992, *Cunyan yu quru* [Dignity and insult]. Taiwan: Shibao wenhua cbs. 關曉容, 1992, 尊嚴與屈辱. 台灣: 時報文化出版社.

Guan Xiaorong, 2000, "Dawu minzu dangjia zuozhu" [The Tao are the masters in their own home]. In: *Yuanzhuminzu* 2. Retrieved on 20.2.2006 from http://web.my8d.net/m5a07/volem002/. 關曉容, 2000, "達悟民族當家做主". In: 原住民族, 第 2 號.

Habermas, Jürgen, 1981, *Theorie des kommunikativen Handelns.* Frankfurt am Main: Suhrkamp.

Hall, Stuart, 1994, *Rassismus und kulturelle Identität.* Hamburg: Argument-Verlag.

Hamayon, Roberte Nicole, 2001, "Shamanism: Symbolic System, Human Capability and Western Ideology". In: Francfort, Henri-Paul & Hamayon, Roberte N. eds., 2001, *The Concept of Shamanism: Uses and Abuses.* Budapest: Akademiai Kiado, 1-30.

Handelman, Don, 1977, "Play and Ritual. Complementary Frames of Metacommunication". In: Antony J. Chapman & Hugh C. Foot eds., *It's A Funny Thing, Humour*. London: Pergamon Press, 185-192.

Handler, Richard, 1984, "On Sociocultural Discontinuity: Nationalism and Cultural Objectification in Quebec". In: *Current Anthropology* 25(1): 55-71.

Hayu Yudaw Chuang, 1999, *A Preliminary Study of Contextual Liturgy: The Saejiq Presbyterian Tradition in Taiwan*. Canada: Unpublished M.A. thesis at Vancouver School of Theology.

Hobsbawm, Eric and Ranger, Terence, 1983, *The Invention of Tradition*. Cambridge: Cambridge University Press.

Houseman, Michael and Severi, Carlos, 1998, *Naven or the Other Self: A Relational Approach to Ritual Action*. Leiden: Brill.

Hsieh Shih-chung, 1994, "Tourism, Formulation of Culture, and Ethnicity: A Study of the Daiyan Identity of the Wulai Atayal". In: Harrell, Stevan / Huang Jun-chieh eds., 1994, *Cultural Change in Postwar Taiwan*. Colorado: Westview Press, 184-201.

Hsu Mutsu, 1991, *Culture, Self, and Adaption: The Psychological Anthropology of Two Malayo-Polynesian Groups in Taiwan*. Taiwan: Academia Sinica 1991.

Hu Defu 2000, "Yuanzhumin Yundong zaiqi" [The Comeback of the Aboriginal Movement]. In: *Zuoyi zazhi* 4, 2/2000. 胡德夫, 2000, "原住民族運動再起". In: 左翼雜誌, 第 4 號.

Hu Taili, 2003, *Wenhua zhanyan yu Taiwan Yuanzhumin* [Cultural Performance and Taiwan Aborigines]. Taiwan: Lianjing cbs. 胡台麗, 2003, 文化展演與台灣原住民. 台灣：聯經出版公司.

Hu Taili, Liu Binxiong eds., 1987, *Taiwan tuzhu jiyi ji gewu minsu huodong zhi yanjiu* [The rituals and the singing and dancing customs of Taiwan's Aborigines]. Taiwan: Institute of Ethnology, Academia Sinica.. 胡台麗, 劉斌雄 eds., 1987, 台灣土著祭儀及歌舞民俗活動之研究. 台北：中央研究院民族研究所.

Huang Guochao, 2001, *'Shensheng' de wajie yu chongjian: Zhenxibao Tayaren de zongjiao bianqian* [Erosion and restauration of the "sacred": religious change of the Atayal of Zhenxibao]. Taiwan: Unpublished M.A. thesis at National Qinghua University. 黃國超, 2001, '神聖'的瓦解與重建: 鎮西堡泰雅人的宗教變遷. 台灣:國立清華大學碩士論文 (未出版).

Huang Meiying, 1995, "Quzhu shiji de eling" [Exorcizing the evil spirits of the century]. In: Huang Meiying, 1995, *Wenhua de kangzheng yu yishi* [Cultural resitance and ritual]. Taiwan: Qianwei cbs. 黃美英, 1995, "驅逐世紀的惡靈". In: 黃美英, 1995, 文化的抗爭與儀式. 台灣: 前衛出版社.

Huang Shiun-wey, 2003, "Accepting the Best, Revealing the Difference: Borrowing and Identity in an Ami Village". In: Clart, Philip and Jones, Charles B. eds., 2003, Religion in Modern Taiwan: Tradition and Innovation in a Changing Society. Honolulu: University of Hawai'i Press.

Huang Yinggui, 1984, "Taiwan tuzhu de liang zhong shehui leixing ji qi yiyi" [Two Types of Social Systems among Taiwanese Aborigines and their Implications]. In: *Bulletin of the Institute of Ethnology at Academia Sinica* 57, 1984, 1-30. 黃應貴, 1984, "台灣土著的兩種社會類型及其意義". In: 中央研究院民族學研究所 季刊, 57期, 1984: 1-30.

Huang Yinggui, 1986, "Dongpushe de zongjiao bianqian" [Religious change in Dongpu]. In: Huang Yinggui ed., 1986, *Taiwan tuzhu shehui wenhua lunwenji* [Society and Culture of Taiwan's Aborigines]. Taiwan: Lianjing cbs.. 黃應貴, 1986, "東埔社的宗教變遷: In: 黃應貴, 1986, 台灣土著社會文化論文集. 台灣：聯經出版公司.

Huang Yinggui, 1992, *Dongpushe Bunongren de shehui shenghuo* [The social life of the Bunun of Dongpu]. Taiwan: Academia Sinica. 黃應貴, 1992, "東埔社布農人的社會生活". 台灣：中央研究院.

Huang Yinggui, 2001, *Taidong xianshi Bunongzupian* [The Bunun of Taidong County]. Taidong: Taidong County Government. 黃應貴, 2001, 台東縣史布農族篇. 台灣：台東縣政府.

Huang Yinggui, Jiang Bin, Chen Maotai, Shi Lei, Qu Haiyuan, 1993, "Zunzhong Yuanzhumin de zicheng" [Paying respect to the name Aborigines gave to themselves]. In: Zhang Maogui ed., 1993, *Zuqun guanxi yu guojia rentong* [Ethnic Relations and National Identity]. Taiwan: Yeqiang, 191-197. 黃應貴, 蔣斌, 陳茂泰, 石磊, 瞿海源, 1993, "尊重原住民的自稱". In: 張茂桂, 1993, 族群關係與國家認同, 台灣: 業強出版社, 191-197.

Humphrey, Caroline and Laidlaw, James, 1994, *The Archetypal Actions of Ritual: A Theory of Ritual Illustrated by the Jain Rite of Worship.* Oxford: Claradon.

Hymes, Dell, 1975, "Breakthrough into Performance". In: Dan Ben-Amos & Kenneth S. Goldstein eds., 1975, *Folklore. Performance and Communication*, (Approaches to Semiotics 40). The Hague, Paris: Mouton, 11-74.

Jian Dongyuan, Shen Huisheng, Xie Mingzheng, Xu Huijiu, 2002, "Quan tai yuanmin zhushou – qi jiang ganlin" [Taiwan's Aborigines pray for blessing and timely rainfall]. In: *China Times* 20.5.2002. 簡東源、沈揮勝、謝敏政、許惠就, 2002, 全台原民祝禱: 祈降甘霖. In: 中國時報 20.5.2002.

Jian Hongmo, 2003, „Wufeng tianzhutang bei saixia chuanjiaoshi chutan [Preliminary discussion of the mission history of the North Saixiat at the Catholic Church of Wu Feng] (1955-1970). In: *Website of Institute for Religious Studies, National Fujen University Taiwan.* Re-

trieved on 25.11.2006 from http://www.indigen.fju.edu.tw/ arti-
cle/article06.asp. 簡鴻模, 2003, ”五峰天主堂北賽夏傳教史初探
(1955-1970)”.

Jiang Guanming, 1994, "Chucao xuanyan shi Yuan/Han duihua de qidian
- ping 1994 Yuanzhumin wenhua huiyi" [The head-hunting-
proclamation is the beginning of a dialogue between Aborigines and
Han: A critical commentary on the Aboriginal Culture Congress of
1994]. In: *Taiwan Indigenous Voice Bimonthly* 6, 37-44. 江冠明,
1994, "出草宣言是原漢對話的起點 - 評 1994 原住民文化會議", in:
山海文化雙月刊, 6期, 台灣, 37-44.

Jinnslim 2005/2006, "Taibalang de zulingji" [The ancestor-spirits-ritual
of Taibalang]. Retrieved on 25.08.2006 from http://blog.yam.com/
jinn1975/archives/445296.html. Jinnslim, 2005/2006, 太巴塱的祖靈
祭.

Kammerer, Cornelia Ann, 1990, "Customs and Christian Conversion
among Akha Highlanders of Burma and Thailand". *American Ethnologist* 17(2), 277-291

Katz, Paul R., 2004, "Fowl Play: Chicken-Beheading Rituals and Dispute
Resolution in Taiwan." In: David K. Jordan, Andrew D. Morris, and
Marc L. Moskowitz eds., *The Minor Arts of Daily Life: Popular Cul-
ture in Taiwan*. Honolulu: University of Hawai'i Press, 35-49.

Keesing, Roger M., 1989, "Creating the past. Custom and identity in the
contemporary pacific". In: *The Contempory Pacific* I (1 and 2), 19-42.

Kehoe, Alice Beck, 1989, *The Ghost Dance: Ethnohistory and Revitalization*. Holt: Rinehart and Winston

Kempf, Wolfgang, 1992, "The Second Coming of the Lord: Early Christianization, Episodic Time, and the Cultural Construction of Continuity in Sibog". *Oceania* 63, 72-86

Kertzer, David I., 1988, *Ritual, Politics, and Power*. New Haven (Conn),
London: Yale University Press.

Keyes, Charles, Laurel Kendall & Helen Hardacre eds., 1994, *Asian Visions of Authority: Religion and the Modern States of East and Southeast Asia*, Honolulu: University of Hawai'i Press.

Köpping, Klaus-Peter & Ursula Rao eds., 2000, *Im Rausch des Rituals. Gestaltung und Transformation der Wirklichkeit in körperlicher Performanz*. Münster, Hamburg, London: LIT.

Köpping, Klaus-Peter & Ursula Rao, 2003, "Einleitung: Autorisierungsstrategien in ritueller Performanz". In: E. Fischer Lichte, C. Horn, S. Umathum, M. Warstat eds., *Ritualität und Grenze*. Tübingen/Basel: A. Francke-Verlag, 211-218.

Köpping, Klaus-Peter, 2004a, "Geborgte Autorität: Die Macht der Form in ritualisierten Performanzen in Japan". In: Wulf, Christoph & Joerg Zirfas eds., *Die Kultur des Rituals*. München: Wilhelm Fink Verlag, pp. 62-90.

Köpping, Klaus-Peter, 2004b, Ritual und Theater im Licht ethnologischer Theorien: Interperformativität in Japan. In: Harth, Dietrich & Gerrit Jasper Schenk eds., *Ritualdynamik*. Heidelberg: Synchron Verlag 2004, 339-361.

Köpping, Leistle, Rudolph, 2005, Teilprojekt A1 "Dynamik und Effektivität ritueller Performanz und die Konstituierung soziokultureller Identität in Japan, Taiwan und Marokko". In: *Finanzierungsantrag des Sonderforschungsbereichs 619 Ritualdynamik: Soziokulturelle Prozesse in historischer und kulturvergleichender Perspektive*. Heidelberg: Ruprecht-Karls-Universität Heidelberg, 89-118.

Köpping, Leistle, Rudolph, 2006, *Ritual and Identity: Performative Practices as Effective Transformations of Social Reality?*, Hamburg/Münster/London: LIT.

Lai Shuya, 1994, "Tiaotuo xingshi zhuyi kejiu: cong buluo dao juchang – tan Yuanzhumin wenhua fazhan kunjing" [Escaping the set patterns of formalism: From the tribe to the stage – discussing the dilemma of aboriginal culture's development]. In: *Libao* 12.12.1994. 賴淑雅,

1994, "跳脫形式主義窠臼:從部落到劇場 - 談原住民文化發展困境". In: 立報 12.12.1994.

Lane, Christel, 1981, *The Rites of Rulers: Ritual in Industrial Society – The Soviet Case*. Cambridge: Cambridge University Press.

Lee, Ilya Eric, 1997, "Taiwan Yuanzhumin wenhua ziliao wanglu" [Web for materials on the culture of Taiwan's Aborigines]. Retrieved on 28.03.1997 from http://erac.ndhu.edu.tw/~culture/announce.html.

Li Jingchong, 1998, *Ameizu lishi* [The history of the Ami]. Taiwan: Shida shufan. 李景崇, 1998, 阿美族歷史. 台灣: 師大書範.

Li Junzhang, 1995, Taiwan Yuanzhuminzu lishi de xin tantao [New Investigation Upon Historicism of Taiwan Indigenous People]. Paper presentation at *"UN World Group of Indigenous Peoples"* (WGIP), Geneva 24.-28.7.1995.

Li Laiwang, Wu Mingyi, Huang Dongqiu eds, 1992, *Qianyuan – Ameizu minsu fengqing* [Qianyuan: about the folk customs of the Ami]. Taiwan: Dongbu hai'an fengjing tedingqu. 李來旺, 吳明義, 黃東秋 eds., 1992, 牽源 – 阿美族民俗風情. 台灣: 東部海岸國家風景區管處.

Li Yiyuan, 1982, "Shehui wenhua bianqian zhong de Taiwan gaoshanzu qingshaonian wenti" [The problems of the adolescents of Taiwan's high mountain people in times of socio-cultural change]. In: Li Yiyuan ed., *Taiwan tuzhu minzu de shehui yu wenhua* [Society and Culture of Taiwan's Indigenous Peoples]. Taiwan, 425-460. 李亦園, 1982, "社會文化變遷中的台灣高山族青少年問題", in: 李亦園 (ed.), 1982, 台灣土著民族的社會與文化, 台灣, 425-460.

Li Yiyuan, 1986, *Jubian yu tiaoshi: 1985 Taiwan wenhua pipan* [Abrupt Change and Adaptation: Criticique of Taiwanese Culture 1985]. Taiwan. 李亦園, 1986, 劇變與調適 - 1985 台灣文化批判, 台灣.

Liao Baoyi, 1994, Cong buluo dao juchang – xinhun xianglian? Dang Yuanzhumin wenhua chengle yishu zhanyan de qucai, chuli de taidu yu fenji youdai tansuo [From the tribe to the stage: The linking together of heart and soul? As aboriginal culture becomes source material for art performances, the adequate management and categorizaton still remain unclear]. In: *Zili wanbao* [Independent Evening News] 12.12.1994. 廖抱一, 1994 ,"從部落到劇場 -心魂相連?當原住民文化成了藝術展演的取材處理的態度與分際有待探索". In: 自立晚報12.12.1994.

Limond, Andrew, 2002, "Ethnicity on Orchid Island (Lanyu): The Yami-Tao Identity Crisis". In: *Yuanzhumin jiaoyu jikan* 28, 5-43.

Lin Jiancheng, 2002, *Taiwan Yuanzhumin yishu tianye biji* [Taiwan Aboriginal Art Field Study]. Taiwan: Yishujia cbs. 林建成, 2002 ,台灣原住民藝術田野筆記. 台灣:藝術家.

Lin Qingsheng, 1998, *Ameizu wuyi zhiliao yu xiandai jidujiao lingyi zhiliao zhi bijiao yanjiu: Yi Taibalang buluo wei li* [Comparative Study of Ami Shamanist Healing and Ami Protestants' Charismatic Healing: The Case of the Ami-tribe of Taibalang]. Taiwan: Unpublished M.A. thesis at Yushan Theology College. 阿美族巫醫治療與現代基督教靈醫治療之比較研究:以太巴塱部落為例. 台灣:玉山神學院碩士論文 (未出版).

Lin Suzhen, 1992, *Taiwan jidu zhanglao jiaohui dui Yuanzhumin xuanjiao zhi yanjiu (1912-1990)* [Study on the PCT mission in Taiwan's aboriginal society (1912-1990)]. Taiwan: M.A. thesis at National Donghai University. 林素珍, 1992, 台灣基督長老教會對原住民宣教之研究. 台灣:國立東海大學歷史學研究所碩士論文.

Linton, Ralph, 1943, "Nativistic Movements". In: *American Anthropologist 45(2)*, 230-240.

Liu Huanyue, 2001, *Taiwan Yuanzhumin jidian wanquan daolan [A Comprehensive Guide to the Rituals of Taiwan's Aborigines]*. Taiwan: Changmin wenhua. 劉還月, 2001, 台灣原住民祭典完全導覽. 台灣:常民文化.

Liu Shaohua, 1993, "Yuanzhumin wenhua yundong de lishi weizhi" [The historical importance of the cultural movement of Taiwanese Aborigines]. In: *Taiwan Indigenous Voice Bimonthly* 1, 48-55. 劉紹華, 1993, "原住民文化運動的歷史位置", in: 山海文化雙月刊, 1期, 台灣 11/1993:48-55.

Liyijing Youma, 1995, *Chuancheng - zouchu kongsu* [Passing on tradition: enunciate the charges]. Taiwan: Yuanzhu minzu shiliao yanjiushe. 麗依京 尤瑪, 1996, 傳承 – 走出控訴.台灣: 原住民史料研究社.

Ma Tengyue, 1998, *Tayazu wenmian tupu* [Pictures of Atayal Facial Tattoo], Taiwan: Sheying tiandi zazhishe. 馬騰嶽, 1998, 泰雅族文面圖譜, 1998年. 臺北: 攝影天地雜誌社.

Mabuchi Toichi, 1935, *Chupu Kosagozoku no matsudan* [Ritual Groups of the Aborigines of Central Taiwan]. Tokyo: *Minken III*, 1-29. 馬淵東一, 1935, 中部高沙族の祭典. 東京: 民間 III, 1-29.

Meyers, Birgit, 1994, "Beyond syncretism: Translation and diabolization in the appropriation of Protestantism in Africa". In: Stewart, Charles & Rosalind Shaw eds., 1994, *Syncretism/Anti-Syncretism: The Politics of Religious Synthesis*. London and New York: Routledge.

Ming Liguo, 1991, *Taiwan Yuanzhuminzu de jili.* [The Rituals and Ceremonies of Taiwan's Aborigines]. Taiwan: Taiyuan. 明立國, 1991, 台灣原住民的祭禮. 台灣: 台原出版社.

Mircea Eliade, 1968 , *The Sacred and the Profane : The Nature of Religion*. Australia: Harcourt Australia.

Munsterhjelm, Mark, 2002, "Happy Aborigines Dance for Benign Patriarchs: Ideologies Implicit in Some Recent Institutional Constructions of Taiwan Aborigines". Paper presented at *CASCA 2002*, University of Windsor, May 4, 2002.

Norton, Robert, 1993, "Culture and Identity in the South Pacific: A Comparative Analysis". In: Man 23 (4): 696-717.

Pan Chaocheng (Bauki Angau), 2003, "Jinian Diwayi Sayun [=Li Laiwang]" [Commemorating Li Laiwang]. Retrieved on 2.8.2006 from http://www.cyberbees.org/blog/archives/ 001696.html. 潘朝成, 2003, 紀念帝瓦伊 撒耘.

Pan Chaocheng (Bauki Angau), 2003, *Women wei tudi er zhan* [We fight for our land]. Documentary 56 min. Taiwan. 潘朝成, 2003, 我們為土地而戰. 台灣: 記錄片, 片長: 56分鐘.

Pan Inghai, 2000, "'Pingpu'Consciousness in Today's Taiwan: On History and Ethnicity". In: *China Perspectives* (Special Issue on Ethnic and National Identities in Taiwan) 28, 82-88.

Pan Meiling, 2001, "Quanqiuhua yu ruoshi laodong zuqun: Taiwan de Yuanzhumin yu waiji laogong" [Globalization and minority laborers: Taiwanese Aborigines and guest workers in Taiwan]. Retrieved on 15.01.2002 from http://home.kimo.com.tw/liutaho/A75.htm. 潘美玲, 2001, „全球化與弱勢勞動族群 — 台灣的原住民與外籍勞工". 台灣 (未出版).

Peters, Robert, 2002, "The Internet in China: The Harbinger of Democracy or Propaganda Tool Par Excellence". Retrieved on 5.10.2004 from: http://www.potomacinstitute.org/pubs/IT&World Politics_Ch9.pdf.

Pideru Wuga (Liao Jinsheng), 2002a, *Saideke – Saidekezu chuantong yinyue* [Sedek - Traditional Music of the Sedek] (CD) Taiwan 2002. 彼得洛 烏嘎.2000a, 賽德克 – 賽德克族傳統音樂.

Pideru Wuga (Liao Jinsheng), 2002b, Saideke wenhua wang [Sedek Culture Net]. Retrieved on 6.10.2004 from http://www.sedek.com/. 彼得洛 烏嘎, 2000b, 賽德克文化網.

Qiu Ruolong, 1990 [1995], *Wushe shijian* [The Wushe Incident]. Taiwan: Shibao wenhua cbs (2nd ed. 1995). 邱若龍, 1990, 霧社事件. 台灣: 時報文化出版社.

Qiu Ruolong, 1994, "Tayazu de jingmian wenhua" [The tattooing culture of the Atayal]. In: *Tayazu renwen lishi yantaohui lunwenji*, Taiwan 1994. 邱若龍, 1994, "泰雅族的鯨面文化", in: 泰雅族人文歷史 研討會, 台灣 1994.

Qiu Ruolong, 1999, *GaYa: 1930 nian de Wushe shijian yu Saidekezu* [GaYa: The Wushe incident of 1930 and the Sedek]. Documentary 100 min.. Taiwan. *GaYa:* 1930年的霧社時間與賽德克族. 台灣: 記錄片, 片長 : 100分鐘.

Qiu Yunfang, 2002, "Chuantong de jiangou yu wenhua de zhuanshi: Shixi Hualian Truku ren de zulingji" [Construction of Tradition and Change of Cultural Interpretations: Analysis of the Taroko Ancestor-Spirits-Ritual]. In: Paper-Compilation of the papers presented at the *"Symposium on Identity Construction, Ethnic Identification and the Breaking Up of the Atayal Ethnic Groups"*. Taiwan: Taiwan Yuanzhumin zhenxing wenjiao-Foundation, 1-18. 邱韻芳, 2002, "傳統的建構與文化的轉譯：試析花蓮Truku人的祖靈祭". In: 泰雅族族群意識之建構、認同與分裂學術研討會 (6.11.2002) 論文集. 台灣: 台灣原住民振興文教基金會, 1-18.

Qiu Yunfang, 2004, *Zuling, shangdi yu chuantong: Jidu zhanglao jiaohui yu Truku ren de zongjiao bianqian* [Ancestor-spirits, God and tradition: The PCT and religious change among the Truku]. Taiwan: Ph.D. dissertation at National Taiwan University. 邱韻芳, 2004, 祖靈、上帝與傳統：基督長老教會與Truku人的宗教變遷. 台灣: 國立台大人類學研究所博士論文.

Rao, Ursula, 2006, "Einleitung: Zwischen Struktur und Kontingenz". In: Rao, Ursula ed., *Kulturelle VerWandlungen*. Frankfurt: Peter Lang, 11-31.

Redfield, R., Linton, R., & Herskovits, M., 1936, "Memorandum on the study of acculturation". In: *American Anthropologist 38*, 149-152.

Republic of China Association for Cultural Development of Taiwan's Aboriginal Peoples (Zhonghua minguo Taiwan yuanzhuminzu wenhua fazhan xiehui) ed., 1994, *Yuanzhumin zhengce yu shehui fazhan* [Aboriginal politics and social development], Taiwan. 中華民國台灣原住民族文化發展協會 ed., 1994, 原住民政策與社會發展. 台灣.

Rouch, Jean, 1957, Les maitres fous [The Mad Masters]. Documentary. Frankreich.

Rubinstein, Murray A., 1991, "Taiwanese Protestantism in Time and Space, 1865-1988 ". In: E.K.Y. Chen ed., 1991, *Taiwan - Economy, Society and History*. Centre of Asian Studies Occasional Papers and Monographs, Hong Kong: University of Hong Kong, 251-281.

Rudolph, Michael forthcoming 3: "Failure of Ritual Reinvention? Efficacious New Rituals of Taiwan's Aborigines under the Impact of Religious Conversion and Elites' Competition. In: Ute Hüsken ed., *Getting it Wrong? Ritual Dynamics, Mistakes and Failure. Leiden: Brill.*

Rudolph, Michael, 1993, *Die Prostitution der Frauen der taiwanesischen Bergminderheiten: Historische, sozio-kulturelle und kulturpsychologische Hintergründe* [The prostitution problem of Taiwan's mountain-minorities: historical, socio-cultural and psycho-cultural factors]. Hamburg/Münster/London: LIT 1993.

Rudolph, Michael, 1994, "Taiwan shehui bianqian de shaoshu minzu funü changji wenti: shehui wenhua, shehui xinli, ji lishixing de yinsu" [Social change in Taiwan and the prostitution of the women of Taiwanese minorities: socio-cultural, psycho-cultural and historical factors]. In: *Taiwan Indigenous Voice Bimonthly* 4, 39-48.

Rudolph, Michael, 1996, "'Was heißt hier taiwanesisch?' - Taiwans Ureinwohner zwischen Diskriminierung und Selbstorganisation" ["Who has the right to call himself 'Taiwanese'? - Taiwanese Aborigines between discrimination and selforganization"]. In: Schubert, Gunter/ Schneider, Axel, 1996 eds.: *Taiwan an der Schwelle zum 21. Jahrhundert: Gesellschaftlicher Wandel, Probleme und Perspektiven eines asiatischen Schwellenlandes.* Hamburg: Mitteilungen des Instituts für Asienkunde 270, 285-308.

Rudolph, Michael, 2003a, *Taiwans multi-ethnische Gesellschaft und die Bewegung der Ureinwohner: Assimilation oder kulturelle Revitalisierung?* [Taiwan's Multi-Ethnic Society and the Movement of Aborigines: Assimilation or Cultural Revitalization?]. Hamburg/Münster/London: LIT 2003.

Rudolph, Michael, 2003b, "The Quest for Difference vs the Wish to Assimilate: Taiwan's Aborigines and their Struggle for Cultural Survival in Times of Multiculturalism". In: Rubinstein, Murray & Paul Katz eds., *Religion and the Formation of Taiwanese Identities.* New York: St. Martins/Palgrave, 123-156.

Rudolph, Michael, 2004a, "The Emergence of the Concept of 'Ethnic Group' in Taiwan and the Role of Taiwan's Austronesians in the Construction of Taiwanese Identity". In: *Historiography East and West: A multi-lingual on-line journal for studies in comparative historiography and historical thinking* 2:1 (Leiden: Brill), 86-115.

Rudolph, Michael, 2004b, "The Pan-Ethnic Movement of Taiwanese Aborigines and the Role of Elites in the Process of Ethnicity Formation". In: Christiansen, Flemming and Ulf Hedetoft eds., *The Politics of Multiple Belonging: Ethnicity and Nationalism in Europe and East Asia.* Hampshire, UK: Ashgate 2004: 239-254.

Rudolph, Michael, 2006b: (with K-P. Köpping und B. Leistle) „Introduction", in: Köpping, Leistle, Rudolph eds.: *Ritual and Identity: Per-*

formative Practices as Effective Transformations of Social Reality.
Hamburg/Münster/London: LIT, p. 9-32.

Rudolph, Michael, 2006c: "Elites' Competition, Ritual Restoration, and
Identity Formation: The Case of the 'Harvest Festivals' of Taiwan's
Ami". In: Köpping, Leistle, Rudolph eds., *Ritual and Identity: Per-
formative Practices as Effective Transformations of Social Reality.*
Hamburg/Münster/London: LIT, p. 209-248.

Rudolph, Michael, 2006d: "From Forced Assimilation to Cultural Revitalization: Taiwan's Aborigines and their Role in Taiwan Nativism",
in: Barry Sautman ed., *Cultural Genocide and Asian State Peripher-
ies*, New York: Macmillan Palgrave, p. 63-102.

Sahlins, Marshall, 1981, *Historical Metaphors and Mythical Realities:
Structure in the Early History of the Sandwich Islands Kingdom.* Ann
Arbor: University of Michigan Press.

Sahlins, Marshall, 2005 [1992], "The economics of develop-man in the
Pacific. In: Robbins, Joel, and Holly Wardlaw, 2005, The Making of
Global and Local Modernities in Melanesia: Humiliation, Transfor-
mation, and the Nature of Cultural Change. Burlington: Ashgate.

Sax, William S., 2002, *Dancing the Self: Personhood and Performance
in the Pandaw Lila of Garhwal.* Oxford University Press.

Sayama Yukichi, 1985 [1917], *Banzoku chosa hokokusho* [Research Report on the Barbarian Peoples]. Taiwan: Institute of Ethnology at
Academia Sinica [Tokyo 1917]. 佐山融吉, 1985 [1917], 蕃族慣習調
查報告書. 台灣中央研究院民族學研究所 [東京 1917].

Schechner, Richard, 1977, *Essays on Performance Theory, 1970-1976*;
New York: Drama Book Specialists.

Schechner, Richard, 1985, *Between Theatre & Anthropology.* Philadelphia.

Schieffelin, Edward, 1996, "On Failure and Performance: Throwing the
Medium out of the Seance". In: Laderman, Carol and Roseman, Ma-
rina eds., *The Performance of Healing.* London: Routledge, 59 - 89.

Shanhai zhuanji, 1998, "Qian ‚Ina' de shou: Ameizu Taibalang buluo
lewu" [Holding the hand of the 'Ina': The dances of the Ami-tribe of

Taibalang]. In: *Taiwan Indigenous Voice Bimonthly* 19, 4-34. 山海傳記, 1998, "牽 ,Ina' 的手:阿美族太巴塱部落樂舞". In: 山海文化雙月刊, 19期, 4-34.

Si Xiong, 2002, "Cong Baoluo zai gelinduo qianshu 12 zhi 14 zhang you guan fangyan de jiaodao ping yunzhumin jiaohui de fangyan yundong [Criticizing the glossalalia-movement of the aboriginal Church by referring to Paulus' comments on glossalalia in Corinthians 12-40]. In: *Yushan Theology College Schoolpapers*, Taiwan 7/2002. 司雄, 2002, "從保羅在哥林多前書十二至十四章有關方言的教導評原住民教會的方言運動". In: 玉山神學院2000年第七期學報. 台灣: 玉山神學院 7/2002.

Simon, Scott, 2006, Formosa's First Nations and the Japanese: from colonial rule to postcolonial resistance. In: *JapanFocus.org*, retrieved on 15.01.2006 from http://japanfocus.org/article.asp?id=489.

Song Xiaokun, 2002, "Intellectual Discourses in the Taiwan Independence Movement". In: Coppieters, Bruno and Huysseune, Michel, 2002, *Secession, History and the Social Sciences*. Brussels: VUB Brussels University Press, 227-246.

Stainton, Michael, 1995, *Return our Land: Counterhegemonic Presbyterian Aboriginality in Taiwan*. Canada: Ph.D. dissertation at York University.

Stewart, Charles & Rosalind Shaw, 1994, *Syncretism/Anti-Syncretism: The Politics of Religious Synthesis*. London and New York: Routledge.

Stoller, Paul, 1995, *Embodying Colonial Memories: Spirit Possession, Power and the Hauka in West Africa*. New York: Routledge.

Sun Dachuan, 2005, "Shensheng de huigui: Taiwan yuanzhu minzu jiyi de xiankuang yu zaixian" [The return of the sacral: The contemporary situation and the revitalization of the rituals of Taiwanese Aborigines]. Taiwan: National Donghua University. Retrieved on 15.01.2006 from http://www.ndhu.edu.tw/~tcsun/documents/016.pdf. 孫大川,

2005, 神聖的回歸: 台灣原住民族祭儀的現況與再生. 台灣:國立東華大學.

Taiwan International Film Festival (TIEFF), *Website of Taiwan International Film Festival.* Retrieved on 5.10.2004 from http://www.tieff.sinica. edu.tw/. 台灣國際民族誌影展網頁.

Tambiah, Stanley J., 1979, "A Performative Approach to Ritual". In: *Proceedings of the British Academy* 65, 113-169.

Taussig, Michael T., 1980, *The Devil and Commodity Fetishism in South America.* University of North Carolina Press.

Thorne, John F., 1997, *Pangcah: the Evolution of Ethnic Identity among Urbanizing Pangcah Aborigines in Taiwan.* Hong Kong: Ph.D. Dissertation at the University of Hong Kong. Retrieved on 20.8.2004 from http://sunzi.lib.hku.hk/hkuto/record/B31236170.

Tian Guishi, 1996, (mostly in Chinese) "The Facial Tattoo of Tayal". Retrieved on 18.06.2000 from http://hledu.nhltc.edu.tw/~tayal/. 田貴實, 1996, 鯨面文化工作室.

Tian Guishi, 2004, (mostly in Chinese) "The Sedeq Facial Tattoo Culture Studio". Retrieved on 6.10.2004 from http://atayal.hihosting.hinet. net/ptasan/main.html. 田貴實, 1996, 賽德克文史工作室.

Tian Zheyi (Daxiwulawan Bima), 2001, *Taiwan de Yuanzhumin: Ameizu [Taiwan's Aborigines: The Ami].* Taiwan: Taiyuan wenhua congkan 11. 田哲益,2001, 台灣的原住民:阿美族. 台原文化叢刊 11.

Tien Hung-mao & Cheng Tun-jen, 1997, "Crafting Democratic Institutions in Taiwan". In: *The China Journal* 37, 1-27.

Tien Hung-mao ed., 1996, *Taiwan's Electoral Politics and Democratic Transition.* N.Y.: M.E. Sharpe.

Tsai Cheng-Liang, Futuru 2005, ""Amis Hip Hop": The Body Exhibitions of Contemporary Amis Youth in Taiwan". Paper presentation at the *"104th American Anthropological Association Conference"*, Washington DC, Dec 3, 2005. Retrieved on 25.5.2006 http://www.oz.nthu.edu.tw/ ~d929802/amishiphop/index-2.htm.

Tung Chunfa, 1995, *The loss and recovery of cultural identity: a study of the cultural continuity of the Paiwan*. Japan: Ph.D. dissertation at Graduate School of International Christian University.

Turner, Victor, 1969, *The Ritual Process. Structure and Anti-Structure*. Chicago: Routledge & Kegan.

Turner, Victor, 1982, *From ritual to theatre: The human seriousness of play*. New York: Performing Arts Journal Publications.

Wagner, Rudolf, 1990, *The Contemporary Chinese Historical Drama*. Berkeley, CA: University of California Press.

Waldenfels, Bernhard, 1997, *Topographie des Fremden: Studien zur Phänomenologie des Fremden*, Bd. 1. Frankfurt.

Walisi Yougan, 1992, *Fandao chuqiao* [Taking out the savage's knife]. Taiwan: Daoxiang cbs. 瓦歷斯 尤幹, 1992, 番刀出鞘. 台灣: 稻鄉出版社.

Walisi Yougan, 1994, "Yuyan, zuqun yu weilai: Taiwan Yuanzhuminzu muyu jiaoyu de ji dian sikao" [Language, Ethnic Groups and Future Prospects: Some Reflections on Vernacular Language Education of Taiwan's Aborigines]. In: Taiwan Indigenous Voice Bimonthly, No.4, Taiwan 5/1994: 6-21. 瓦歷斯 尤幹, 1994, "語言, 族群與 未來: 台灣原住民族母語教育的幾點思考". In: 山海文化雙月刊, 4 期, 6-21.

Walisi Yougan, 2002, "Yuanzhumin de hou qiyu shidai" [Taiwan's Aborigines' post-rain-rites-times]. In: *Nanfang dianzibao,* 25.06.2002. Retrieved on 20.1.2006 from http://iwebs.url.com.tw/main/html/south/499.shtml. 瓦歷斯 尤幹, 2002, "原住民的後祈雨時代". In: 南方電子報 25.06.2002.

Wallace, Anthony F. C., 1956, "Revitalization Movements". In: *American Anthropologist* 58, 264-281.

Wallerstein, Imanuel, 1984, *The Politics of the World Economy*. Cambridge.

Wang Chongshan, 2001, *Taiwan Yuanzhumin de shehui yu wenhua* [Society and Culture of Taiwan's Aborigines]. Taiwan: Lianjing, 184-

210. 王崇山. 2001, 台灣原住民的社會與文化. 台灣：聯經出版公司.

Wang Yawei, 1999, "Hai you yuan lu yao zou" (There is still a long road ahead of us). Retrieved on 2.05.1999 from http://abori.pts.org.tw/reserve/writing/yawi2.html. 王亞維, 1999, "還有遠路要走".

Weller, Robert P., 2000, Religion and New Taiwanese Identities: Some First Thoughts. In: *Harvard Studies on Taiwan: Papers of the Taiwan Studies Workshop*, Volume 3.

Wu Gufeng, 2005, "Taiwan Yuanzhumin daibiao chuting chensu yaoqiu jingguo shenshe guihuan zuling" [Taiwanese Aborigines' representatives appear in court and require that the Yasukuni Shrine returns to them their ancestor souls]. In: *Xinhuawang* 17.6.2005. Retrieved on 25.2.2006 from http://news.xinhuanet.com/world/2005-06/17/content_3099398.htm. 吳谷奉, 2005, 台灣原住民代表出庭陳訴要求靖國神社歸還祖靈. In: 新華網大阪（日本）17.6.2005.

Wu Micha, 1994, "Pinglun Liao Binghui "Zuqun yu minzu zhuyi" [Commentary on Liao Binghui's contribution "Ethnic group and nationalism"]. In: Taiwan Association of University Professors, 1994, *Taiwan minzu zhuyi* [Taiwan Nationalism]. Taiwan: Qianwei, 101-120. 吳密察, 1994, "評論 廖炳惠: "族群與民族主義"". In: 台灣教授協會, 1994, 台灣民族主義. 台灣: 前衛, 101-120.

Wu Mingyi, 2002, "Ameizu de wenhua chuancheng yu chuantong jiaoyu" [The Cultural Heritages and Traditional Education of the Amis on Taiwan]. In: *Yushan Theology College Schoolpapers* 7/2002. 吳明義, 2002, "阿美族的文化傳承與傳統教育". In: 玉山神學院2000年第七期學報. 台灣: 玉山神學院 7/2002.

Wu Tiantai, 1993, "You jiaoyu de guandian tan Yuanzhumin chuji wenti" [Discussion of aboriginal adolescents' prostitution from the perspective of education]. In: *Guojiao yuandi* 44, 4-9. 吳天泰, 1993, "由教育的觀點談原住民雛妓問題", in: 國教園地, 44 期, 4-9.

Xie Shizhong, 1987a, *Rentong de wuming yu Taiwan Yuanzhumin de zuqun bianqian* [engl. Abstract: Ethnic contacts, stigmatized identity, and pan-Taiwan aboriginalism: A study on ethnic change of Taiwan Aborigines], Taiwan: Zili wanbao she. 謝世忠, 1987a, 認同的污名, 台灣: 自立晚報社.

Xie Shizhong, 1987b, "Yuanzhumin yundong shengcheng yu fazhan lilun de jianli: yi Beimei yu Taiwan wei li de chubu tantao" (engl. Abstract: Towards Dynamic Theories of the Origin and Development of Aboriginal Movements: The Cases of North America and Taiwan). In: *Bulletin of the Institute of Ethnology Academia Sinica* 64, 139-177. 謝世忠, 1987b, "原住民運動生成與發展理論的建立: 以北美與台灣為例 的初步探討", in: 中央研究院 民族研究所 集刊, 64期, 139-177.

Xie Shizhong, 1992a, "Pianli qunzhong de jingying: Shilun ‚Yuanzhumin' xiangzheng yu Yuanzhumin jingying xianxiang de guanxi" [Elites without people: Preliminary discussion of the relation between the symbol 'Yuanzhumin' and the elite phenomenon]. In: *Daoyu bianyuan* 5, 52-60. 謝世忠, 1992a, "偏離群眾的菁英: 試論 ' 原住民' 象徵與原住民菁英現象的關係". In: 島嶼邊緣, 5期, 台灣, 52-60.

Xie Shizhong, 1992b, "Guanguang huodong, wenhua chuantong de sumo, yu zuqun yishi: Wulai Daiyazu Daiyan rentong de yanjiu" (engl. Titel: Tourism, the Shaping of Tradition, and Ethnicity: A Study of Daiyan Identity of Wulai Atayal). In: *Kaogu renleixue kan* 48, 113-129. 謝世忠, 1992b, "觀光活動, 文化傳統的塑模, 與族群意識: 烏來泰雅族 Daiyan 認同的研究". In: 考古人類學刊, 48期, 113-129.

Xie Shizhong, 1994a, *Shanbao guanguang: Dangdai shandi wenhua zhanxian de renleixue quanshi* [Aboriginal tourism: An anthropological interpretation of contemporary Aborigine's cultural performance". Taiwan: Zili wanbao cbs. 謝世忠, 1994a, 山胞觀光:當代山地文化的人類學詮釋. 台灣: 自立晚報出版社.

Xie Shizhong, 1994b, "Guanguang guocheng yu 'chuantong' lunshu - Yuanzhumin de wenhua yishi" [Tourism and the discourse on `tradition`: the cultural consciousness of the Aborigines]. In: *Contemporary Monthly* 98, 10-29. Also in: Council for Cultural Affairs, 1994, *Yuanzhumin wenhua huiyi lunwenji*, 1-18. 謝世忠, 1994b, "觀光過程與 '傳統' 論述: 原住民的文化意識". In: 當代雜誌社, 98期, 10-29.

Xie Shizhong, 1994c, "Shandi gewu zai nar shangyan?" [Where are the songs and dances of the mountains staged?]. In: *Independence Morning Post* 19.12.1994. 謝世忠, 1994c, " 山地歌舞在哪兒上演?". In: 自立早報 19.12.1994.

Xie Shizhong, 1995, "Zuqun guanxi - yi ge zhishi shang de liaojie" [Ethnic Relations: an intellectual interpretation]. In: *Yuanzhumin wenhua gongzuozhe tianye shiyong shouce* 2. Taiwan: Taiwan Aboriginal Park, 107-140. 謝世忠, 1995, "族群關係: 一 個知識上的了解". In: 原住民文化工作者田野使用手冊 2. 台灣: 台灣原住民文化園區, 107-140.

Xie Shizhong, 1996, "'Chuantong wenhua' de caokong yu guanli: Guojia wenhua tixi xia de Taiwan Yuanzhumin wenhua" [The Control and the Management of 'Traditional Culture': aboriginal Culture under the National Culture System]. In: *Taiwan Indigenous Voice Bimonthly* 13, 85-101. 謝世忠, 1996, " '傳統文化' 的操控與管理: 國家文化體系下的台灣原住民文化". In: 山海文化雙月刊, 13期, 85-101.

Xie Shizhong, 2000, "Chuantong yu xin chuantong de xianshen: Dangdai Yuanzhumin de gongyi tixian" [Exposure of traditions and new traditions: Contemporary representations in aboriginal material culture]. In: *The I-lan Journal of History* 44, 7-40. 謝世忠, 2000, "傳統與新傳統的現身:當代原住民的工藝體現". In: 宜蘭文獻 44期, 7-40.

Xie Shizhong, 2004, *Zuqun renleixue de hongguan tansuo: Taiwan Yuanzhumin lunji* [engl. title: Makro research on ethnology: Taiwan Aborigines]. Taiwan: Taida chuban zhongxin. 謝世忠, 2004, 族群人類學的宏觀探索: 台灣原住民論集. 台灣: 台大出版中心.

Xu Muzhu and Li Yiyuan, 1978, "Shehui wenhua bianqian yu gaoshanzu qingshaonian wenti: Yi Huanshan Tayazu wei li de chubu yanjiu" (Socio-cultural change and the problems of aboriginal youth: the example of the Atayal from Huanshan). In: *Bulletin of the Institute of Ethnology Academia Sinica* 24, 281-297. 許木柱/李亦園, 1978, "社會文化變遷與高山族青少年問題: 以環山泰雅族為例的初步研究". In: 中央研究院民族學研究所 季刊, 24期, 1978: 281-297.

Xu Muzhu, 1987, *Amei zu de shehui wenhua bianqian yu qingshaonian shiying* [Social change of the Amei and the Adaptation of adolescents]. Taiwan. 許木柱, 1987, 阿美族的社會文化變遷與青少年適應. 台灣: 中央研究院民族學研究所.

Youbas Wadan, 2005, *Tayazu de zulingji ji qi bianqian* [The Atayal's ancestor-spirits-ritual and its change]. Taiwan: Unpublished M.A. thesis at National Donghua University. 台灣:國立東華大學碩士論文 (未出版). 尤巴斯 瓦旦, 2005, 泰雅族的祖靈祭及其變遷. 台灣: 國立東華大學碩士論文 (未出版).

Youlan Duoyou (Yulan Toyuw), 1995, "Jidian wenhua de zhutixing' [The subjectivity of ritual culture]. In: *Taiwan Indigenous Voice Bi-*

monthly 9, Taiwan, 52-56. 悠蘭 多又, 1995, "祭典文化的主體性".
In: 山海文化雙月刊, 9期, 52-56.

Zhang Maogui ed., 1993, *Zuqun guanxi yu guojia rentong* [Ethnic relations and national identity]. Taiwan: Yeqiang cbs. (Center for National Policy Research). 張茂桂 ed., 1993, 族群關係與國家認同. 台
灣: 業強出版社.

Zhang Maogui, 1996, "Taiwan zui cishou de zhengzhi wenti" [Taiwan's
most pressing political problem]. In: *Cai Xun* (Wealth Magazine) 168,
152-163. 張茂桂, 1996, "台灣最刺手的政治問題". In: 財訊, 168期,
152-163.

Zhang Weiqi, 1998, *Hedong buluo shequ yingzao: yi ge xiang yao biancheng shequ de buluo?* [Community Construction in the Eastshore-
tribe: a tribe that wants to become a community?]. Taiwan: Unpublished M.A. thesis at National Donghua University. 張瑋琦, 1998, 河
東部落社區總體營造: 一個想要變成社區的部落. 台灣:國立東華
大學碩士論文 (未出版).

Zhang Weiqi, 2003, Taibalang 'Ilisin' de lishi bianqian [Historical
change of Taibalang's 'Ilisin']. Taiwan: unpublished manuscript. 張
瑋琦, 2003, 太巴塱 'Ilisin' 的歷史變遷. 台灣 (未出版).

Zhang Weiqi, Ji Junjie, 1999, "Yi ge xiang yao biancheng shequ de buluo: Hedong buluo shequ yingzao" [A tribe that wants to become a
community: Community Construction in the Eastshore-tribe]. In:
1999 Compilation of papers of the conference on community aesthetics. Taiwan: Council for Cultural Affairs. 張瑋琦, 紀駿傑, 1999, "一
個想要變成社區的部落: 河東部落社區總體營造". In: 1999社區
美學研討會論文集. 台灣: 行政院文建會.

LIST OF FIGURES

Figure 21: Taibalang's shamans at unofficial ancestor worship in front of Taibalang's ancestor-stele

Figure 22: Ami shaman Zeng as San Taizi at Taiwanese folk religious Pudu (annual festival for the hungry ghosts) 2004

Figure 23: Ami shaman Zeng in her role as traditional Ami medium before Taibalang's ancestor stele 2003

Figure 24: Ami shamans at Academia Sinica, Taiwan, 2003

Figure 25: Ami shamans making pig drunk before divination

Figure 26: Ami shamans dancing on living pig before divination 2004

Figure 27: Taibalang's new Kakitaan with stone stele and inauguration text for the new Kakitaan head 2005

Figure 28: New building housing Taibalang's activity center 2005

INDEX

Performanzen / Performances

Interkulturelle Studien zu Ritual, Spiel und Theater / Intercultural Studies on Ritual, Play and Theatre
hrsg. von / edited by Christopher Balme, Klaus-Peter Köpping, Michael Prager und/and Christoph Wulf

Klaus-Peter Köpping; Ursula Rao (Hg.)
Im Rausch des Rituals
Gestaltung und Transformation der Wirklichkeit in körperlicher Performanz
Sind Rituale Dramen und können Dramen auch Rituale sein? Diese und ähnliche Fragen gehören zu den am häufigsten diskutierten Themen am Ende des Jahrhunderts auf einer breiten Front von Disziplinen, von der Ethnologie über die Theaterwissenschaften bis zu den Literatur- und anderen Kultur- und Sozialwissenschaften, die sich mit der Domäne des Performativen beschäftigen. Dahinter steht die Einsicht, daß nicht nur Individuen durch Handeln miteinander kommunizieren, sondern daß auch ganze Gruppen, Gemeinschaften und Kulturräume durch Darstellungs- und Aufführungsformen, die vom Theater über Sportveranstaltungen bis zu Ritualen reichen, ihre kollektiven Werthaltungen ausdrücken, reflektieren, legitimieren, aushandeln und verändern. Ritual als Performanz zeichnet sich dann dadurch aus, daß es einen konstitutiven Teil jenes kulturellen Gedächtnisses umfaßt, das in Körper inskribiert und durch Körper mitgeteilt wird. Eine besondere Pointe hat die Diskussion über kollektive kulturelle Performanzen durch die umstrittene und weithin debattierte Behauptung englischer Wissenschaftler erhalten, daß Rituale "bedeutungslos" seien. Mit diesen Problemen setzen sich die Beiträge dieses Bandes im deutschsprachigen Raum zum ersten Male in dezidierter Form auseinander. Das Für und Wider des Zugangs zu kollektiven und individuellen Identitäten über rituelle und theatrale Darstellungen wird an Hand von neuesten feldforscherischen Materialien, vor allem aus dem süd- und ostasiatischen, aber auch aus dem afrikanischen Kulturraum aus ethnologischer, indologischer und kunsthistorischer Sicht komparativ beleuchtet. Der vorliegende Band bietet damit einen prägnanten Überblick über und eine Anknüpfung an die gegenwärtige internationale Diskussion zu Problemen des Diskurses über Theatralität und Performanz und den Auswirkungen dieses Diskurses auf die europäischen Sichtweisen zu Primitivismus und Exotismus.
Bd. 1, 2000, 264 S., 20,90 €, br., ISBN 3-8258-3988-5

Alexander Henn
Wachheit der Wesen
Politik, Ritual und Kunst der Akkulturation in Goa
Die alljährlich im rituellen Theater des Jagar oder Zagor in Goa inszenierte 'Wachheit der Wesen' stellt eine symbolische und performative Begegnung von Menschen und Göttern dar, bei der sich hinduistische, indische und katholische, indische und portugiesische Traditionen auf vielfältige Weise miteinander verschränken. Über das rituelle Theater hinaus wird dabei eine Form der Mimesis sichtbar, die auf einen speziellen Modus von Akkulturation verweist. Dieser ist nicht grundsätzlich aus den von politisch-theologischen Mächten bestimmten historischen Prozessen der Selbstbehauptung, Konversion oder auch Synthese der kulturellen Unterschiede abgelöst. Doch weist die von der rituell-ästhetischen Handlung geleitete performative Inszenierung von Macht, Religion und Gesellschaft gleichermaßen über die Idee der kulturellen Polarisierung, wie der Verschmelzung hinaus, wenn die dabei zum Tragen kommende Mimesis ihr 'Original', das 'Andere' entweder auslöscht oder doppelt.
Bd. 2, 2003, 264 S., 30,90 €, br., ISBN 3-8258-5642-9

Julia Glesner
Theater für Touristen
Eine kulturwissenschaftliche Studie zum *Tjapukai Aboriginal Cultural Park,* Australien
„Theater für Touristen" versteht sich als Beitrag zu einer kulturwissenschaftlich orientierten Theaterwissenschaft. Seinem Gegenstand,

LIT Verlag Berlin – Hamburg – London – Münster – Wien – Zürich
Fresnostr. 2 48159 Münster
Tel.: 0251 / 620 32 22 – Fax: 0251 / 922 60 99
e-Mail: vertrieb@lit-verlag.de – http://www.lit-verlag.de

dem australischen *Tjapukai Aboriginal Cultural Park*, in dem die Kultur der Ureinwohner für Touristen aufgeführt wird, nähert sich die Arbeit über den Begriffskomplex der rhetorischen Strategien und bietet damit eine Methode zur Analyse performativer Repräsentationen an. Im Zentrum steht hierbei die Unterscheidung tropischer Strategien. Werden Metonymie und Synekdoche häufig synonym gebraucht, demonstriert „Theater für Touristen" die Notwendigkeit, zwischen beiden zu differenzieren, um so ideologische Inhalte in kulturellen Repräsentationen nachweisen zu können.
Bd. 5, 2002, 128 S., 17,90 €, br.,
ISBN 3-8258-6061-2

Nathalie Peyer
Death and Afterlife in a Tamil Village
Discourses of low caste women
Studies of death rituals and of beliefs about the afterlife in India have mainly been carried out from the perspective of male members of high castes following the Sanskritic tradition. Contrary to this, the present study focuses on rural low caste women's discourses about death and afterlife. Their talk about death and afterlife is analyzed in a wider social context. This reveals that death is symbolically related to and meaningful for the social order, the re-creation of life, and the status of women. It is important to control death as it is considered a vulnerable state of transition that is constantly endangered by impurity and by attacks of malign ghosts.
Bd. 6, 2004, 120 S., 19,90 €, br.,
ISBN 3-8258-6991-1

Klaus-Peter Köpping; Bernhard Leistle; Michael Rudolph (Eds.)
Ritual and Identity
Performative Practices as Effective Transformations of Social Reality
It is a contested question whether rituals must be considered as mere structures of representation that preserve and strengthen social, cultural and personal identities, or whether rituals should be seen as performative practices that negotiate, change and reconstitute these identities, thereby transforming and subver-

ting social reality. This book pays attention to the latter approach, deepening insights with theoretical discussions and new ethnographic material from Africa, Asia, and Europe.
Authors: K. Neves-Graca, L. Kendall, K.-H. Kohl, M. Lackner; M. Nijhawan, M. Rubinstein, E. Schieffelin.
Bd. 8, 2006, 304 S., 29,90 €, br.,
ISBN 3-8258-8042-9

Esther Messmer-Hirt; Lilo Roost Vischer (Hg.)
Rhythmus und Heilung
Transzendierende Kräfte in Wort, Musik und Bewegung
Aus dem Inhalt: Messmer, Musik und ihre Wirkfaktoren; Boesch, Schamanisches Heilen in der Psychiatrie; von Ins, Possession in Senegal and France; Signer, Afrikanische Heilrituale; Fatoba, Healing Energies in Yoruba Ifa Religion; Lühning, Candomblé - therapeutische Erfahrung; Hoffmann-Axthelm, Heilung durch Musik?; Messmer-Hirt, Intuition in Lehr- und Lernprozessen
Bd. 9, 2005, 168 S., 19,90 €, br.,
ISBN 3-8258-7849-x

Ulrich Demmer; Martin Gaenszle (eds.)
The Power of Discourse in Ritual Performance
Rhetoric and Poetics
This volume focusses on the ways discourse is used in ritual performances as an important medium of power, enabling speakers/actors to construct, redefine and transform interpersonal relationships, cultural concepts and worldviews. The various case studies gathered here, from South Asia, South East Asia, Africa and South America, show that recent developments in linguistic anthropology, ritual theory and performance studies provide new conceptual tools to take a fresh look at these issues. Foregrounding pragmatic approaches to language and discourse, they explore the social dynamics of rhetorical discourse, text and context, normativity and creativity, the poetics of dialogue and speech, as well as the manifold interactions of speakers, addressees and audience. The volume thus embraces both the micro-level of speech activities as well as

LIT Verlag Berlin – Hamburg – London – Münster – Wien – Zürich
Fresnostr. 2 48159 Münster
Tel.: 0251 / 620 32 22 – Fax: 0251 / 922 60 99
e-Mail: vertrieb@lit-verlag.de – http://www.lit-verlag.de

the macro-level of social and political relationships and brings out the subtle workings of control, authority, and power in situations marked as ritual. The contributions, all based on extensive fieldwork, include many concrete samples of speech and discourse which give an authentic impression of the different voices and make for vivid reading.
Bd. 10, 2007, 216 S., 24,90 €, br.,
ISBN 978-3-8258-8300-3

Henrik Jungaberle; Jan Weinhold (Hg.)
Rituale in Bewegung
Rahmungs- und Reflexivitätsprozesse in Kulturen der Gegenwart
Rituale sind in Bewegung. Jahrhundertealte Traditionen verändern sich rasant. Globalisierung und neue Kommunikationsmedien beeinflussen diesen Prozess ebenso wie die weltweite Migration. Im vorliegenden Band wird dies auch aus Sichtweise der Akteure dargestellt. Zu diesem Zweck verwenden die Autoren aus verschiedenen Kultur- und Sozialwissenschaften den Framing-Ansatz (Rahmung) nach Gregory Bateson und Erving Goffman – und entwickeln diesen weiter. Interdisziplinäre Brücken werden geschlagen, die es möglich machen kulturpsychologische Aspekte der Veränderung von Ritualen zu erfassen. Wie orientieren sich der Einzelne und seine Gruppe in Ritualen? Wann beginnt „Ritual" und wann endet es? Und wie wandelt sich das Geschehen manchmal plötzlich zu „Spiel"?, „Theater"?, „Kampf"?, „Show"? oder „Improvisation"?? Ritualdynamik erweist sich als spannendes Feld sozialer Entwicklung, das Einblick in den Wandel von Individuen und Gesellschaften ermöglicht.
Bd. 11, 2006, 264 S., 29,90 €, br.,
ISBN 3-8258-9265-4

Nadine Sieveking
Abheben und Geerdet Sein
Afrikanisch Tanzen als transkultureller Erfahrungsraum
Afrikanisch Tanzen ist seit Mitte der 80er Jahre in Deutschland zum festen Bestandteil einer urban geprägten Körper- und Freizeitkultur geworden. Auf der Basis einer empirischen Studie von Kursen und Workshops

in Berlin bei international bekannten Tänzerinnen wie Norma Claire, Nago Koité, Koffi Kôkô und Elsa Wolliaston, analysiert die Autorin die körperliche Erfahrungsrealität beim Tanzen als eine Verflechtung von physischen, sozialen und imaginären Bedeutungsebenen. Dabei nimmt sie die Perspektive der Tanzenden ein und hebt die poly-rhythmischen Interaktionsstrukturen hervor, die bei Live-Trommelbegleitung zwischen Tanz und Musik entstehen.
Bd. 12, 2006, 360 S., 24,90 €, br.,
ISBN 3-8258-9592-0

Ethnologie: Forschung und Wissenschaft

Wim van Binsbergen
Intercultural Encounters
African and anthropological lessons towards a philosophy of interculturality
This book brings together fifteen essays investigating aspects of interculturality. Like its author, it operates at the borderline between social anthropology and intercultural philosophy. It seeks to make a contribution to intercultural philosophy, by formulating with great precision and painful honesty the lessons deriving from extensive intercultural experiences as an anthropologist. Its culminating section presents an intercultural philosophy revolving on the tenet 'cultures do not exist'. The kaleidoscopic nature of intercultural experiences is reflected in the diversity of these texts. Many belong to a field that could be described as "meta-anthropology", others are more clearly philosophical; occasionally they spill over into belles lettres, ancient history, and comparative cultural and religious studies. The ethnographic specifics supporting the arguments are diverse, deriving from various African situations in which the author has conducted participatory field research (Tunisia, Zambia, Botswana, and South Africa).
Bd. 4, 2003, 616 S., 40,90 €, br.,
ISBN 3-8258-6783-8

LIT Verlag Berlin – Hamburg – London – Münster – Wien – Zürich
Fresnostr. 2 48159 Münster
Tel.: 0251 / 620 32 22 – Fax: 0251 / 922 60 99
e-Mail: vertrieb@lit-verlag.de – http://www.lit-verlag.de

Gerhard Kubik
Zum Verstehen afrikanischer Musik
Aufsätze
Gerhard Kubiks bahnbrechendes Werk "Zum Verstehen afrikanischer Musik" gibt eine Einführung in die Grundbegriffe der neueren afrikanischen Musikforschung. Wesentliche Fragen der Ikonologie in der afrikanischen Musikforschung werden behandelt und Querverbindungen der Musikforschung zur bildenden Kunst, zur Tanzwissenschaft und dem Jazz aufgezeigt. Der Autor macht so auf transkulturative Prozesse zwischen Afrika und der Westlichen Welt aufmerksam. Ferner widmet sich der Band historischen Arbeiten zum Xylophonspiel in Buganda, der Harfenmusik bei den Azande in der Zentralafrikanischen Republik und den mit Liedern verbundenen 'al´ǫ-Yoruba-Märchen in Nigeria. Ein aktualisiertes Vorwort und eine Liste mit neuerer, weiterführender Literatur runden das Werk ab.
Bd. 7, 2., aktualis. u. erg. Aufl. 2004, 448 S., 19,90 €, br., ISBN 3-8258-7800-7

Wim van Binsbergen; Peter L. Geschiere (Eds.)
Commodification: Things, Agency, and Identities
(*The Social Life of Things* revisited)
The empirically rich and analytically provocative contributions to this volume focus on Africa and on the process through which commodities come into being. Commodifcation is shown to be a powerful tool towards understanding the modern world, especially South economies and South-North interactions today. It greatly illuminates the three central concepts things, agency, and identities, and thus is conducive to the much-needed dialogue between anthropology and economics. In the book, some of the original contributors of A. Appadurai's edited collection from 1986 *The Social Life of Things: Commodities in Cultural Perspective* meet with today's prominent names in the field (Jean & John Comaroff, Paul & Jennifer Alexander, R. Dilley, M. Rowlands, and award-winning N. Rose Hunt) and with scholars of the next generation: B.

Weiss, R. van Dijk, J. Roitman, J. Leach, and I. Stengs. Together with W. van Binsbergen and P. Geschiere, this team explores the dynamics of Commodification.
Bd. 8, 2005, 400 S., 34,90 €, br., ISBN 3-8258-8804-5

Eveline Dürr
Identitäten und Sinnbezüge in der Stadt
Hispanics im Südwesten der USA
Die Studie, die auf ethnographischer Feldforschung basiert, untersucht kollektive Identitäten, Repräsentationen und interethnische Beziehungen in zwei hispanischen Vierteln von Albuquerque, New Mexico (USA). Während im pittoresken Stadtteil Old Town Identitäten durch symbolische Praktiken öffentlich gemacht werden und zur Aneignung des Raumes dienen, sind im sozial schwachen Viertel Barelas kollektive Identitäten wesentlich weniger ausgeprägt und präsent. Die Studie geht den Gründen für diese Unterschiedlichkeit nach und stellt historische Entwicklungen, strukturelle Merkmale und räumliche Bedingtheiten in den Mittelpunkt der Analyse. Neben theoretischen Diskussionen liefert das Buch auch umfassende Daten zur Geschichte und Gegenwart von Albuquerque.
Bd. 9, 2006, 248 S., 19,90 €, br., ISBN 3-8258-9041-4

Julia Reuter; Corinne Neudorfer; Christoph Antweiler (Hg.)
Strand Bar Internet
Neue Orte der Globalisierung
Strände und Straßen in Afrika, indonesische Internetcafés und laotische Bergdörfer gelten bislang nicht als die zentralen Schauplätze der Globalisierung. Kritiker und Befürworter der Globalisierung schauen lieber auf das Treiben an internationalen Finanzmärkten oder in die Chefetagen multinationaler Konzerne. Materielle Infrastruktur oder gänzlich informalisierte, transnationale Räume werden hier weitgehend ausgeblendet. Der Band wirft einen Blick auf diese neuen Orte der Globalisierung, deren Bewohner ihren eigenen Umgang mit globalen Themen gefunden haben: Sie entwickeln Strategien, um die

LIT Verlag Berlin – Hamburg – London – Münster – Wien – Zürich
Fresnostr. 2 48159 Münster
Tel.: 0251 / 620 32 22 – Fax: 0251 / 922 60 99
e-Mail: vertrieb@lit-verlag.de – http://www.lit-verlag.de

Lebensbedingungen vor Ort zu verbessern, ihre (Minderheiten-)Identitäten zu vernetzen oder weltweiten Protest zu organisieren. Neben empirischen Fallstudien gelingt es den Beiträgen aus Soziologie, Ethnologie und Politik die neuen Orte unter Zuhilfenahme postkolonialer, praxistheoretischer und weltsystemtheoretischer Argumente auch theoretisch zu ‚verorten'.

Bd. 10, 2006, 218 S., 19,90 €, br.,
ISBN 3-8258-9294-8

Franz von Benda-Beckmann;
Keebet von Benda-Beckmann
Social Security Between Past and Future
Ambonese Networks of Care and Support

Social security is a particularly precarious issue where states hardly provide any services in periods of need and distress. The book analyses the arrangements relationships through which food, shelter and care are provided on the island of Ambon, famous spice island in Eastern Indonesia. It also shows how relations of support tie Ambonese migrants in the Netherlands to their home villages, and how normative conceptions of need and care among kinsmen and villagers change over time. Though special in their own historical setting, Ambonese networks of care and support are illustrative of poor rural populations in the Third World. Focusing on the precursors of the violent conflict that erupted in 1998, the book shows that social security is like a magnifying glass linking past, present and future.

Bd. 13, 2007, 344 S., 29,90 €, br.,
ISBN 978-3-8258-0718-4

Comparative Anthropological Studies in Society, Cosmology and Politics

ed. by
Prof. Dr. Josephus D. M. Platenkamp (University of Münster/Germany) and Prof. Dr. Bruce Kapferer (University of Bergen/Norway)

Guido Sprenger
Die Männer, die den Geldbaum fällten
Konzepte von Austausch und Gesellschaft bei den Rmeet von Takheung, Laos

Die seit 50 Jahren erste Monographie zu den Rmeet (Lamet), einer Hochlandgesellschaft in Laos, kreist um die Frage: Welche Beziehungen werden für notwendig erachtet, um die Gesellschaft zu reproduzieren? Dabei werden Rituale und der sozio-kosmische Gabentausch, der Personen, Häuser und Dörfer konstituiert, ebenso angesprochen wie Handel, Nationalstaat und interethnische Beziehungen. Durch die Verbindung klassischer ethnographischer Themen mit einer geschichts- und globalisierungsbewussten Perspektive entsteht das dynamische Bild eines lokalen Wertesystems.
Ausgezeichnet mit dem Förderpreis des Frobenius-Instituts 2004

Bd. 1, 2006, 344 S., 29,90 €, br.,
ISBN 3-8258-8043-5

John Christian Knudsen
Capricious Worlds
Vietnamese Life Journeys. With a Foreword by E. Valentine Daniel

"Capricious Worlds" covers a period of 20 years of exile. Through the life journeys of Vietnamese refugees, the book presents a world rich in experience and wisdom, where the will to survive is complemented by the skills to do so. Individuals must learn to conquer systems that transform human beings into numbers, and men, women and children into de-personalized figures. The transformations render an unsettling peace that refugees struggle against, inspired by a search for recognition, a search not only for what is lost, but also for what might yet be. The book is about refugees en route to, and in, Norway. It also speaks to the challenges of being exiled in general: a reality for 40 million refugees and internally displaced persons worldwide.

Bd. 2, 2005, 224 S., 24,90 €, br.,
ISBN 3-8258-8108-3

LIT Verlag Berlin – Hamburg – London – Münster – Wien – Zürich
Fresnostr. 2 48159 Münster
Tel.: 0251 / 620 32 22 – Fax: 0251 / 922 60 99
e-Mail: vertrieb@lit-verlag.de – http://www.lit-verlag.de

Paul van der Grijp
Passion and Profit
Towards an Anthropology of Collecting
Collecting is a matter of authenticity, of creating new identities, both of the objects collected and, by extension, of the collector. Passion and Profit provides a range of ethnographic examples, both historical and contemporary, and also includes a selective analysis and personal evaluation of the increasingly rich and varied literature on collecting. The collectibles discussed in Passion and Profit are not only elitist cultural objects such as works of art (ancient, modern or tribal), antiques and books, but also non-elitist objects such as stamps, postcards, plants, and other mass-produced items. The central research question is: What is the cultural phenomenon of collecting all about? Or, more specifically: What moves collectors? In addressing this question, this book aims to be a substantial contribution to the collecting literature from an anthropological point of view.
Bd. 3, 2006, 336 S., 29,90 €, br.,
ISBN 3-8258-9258-1

Soziologie und Anthropologie
Kulturwissenschaftliche Perspektiven
hrsg. von Prof. Dr. Detlef Pollack,
Prof. Dr. Werner Schiffauer und
Prof. Dr. Anna Schwarz (Europa-Universität
Viadrina, Frankfurt/Oder)

Rebecca Budde
Mexican and Central American L.A.
Garment Workers
Globalized Industries and their Economic Constraints
Studying the urban agglomeration of Los Angeles County, CA is on the one hand very interesting, exciting, as there is such a wide variety of people living there. This not only concerning ethnic origins but also in view of social classes, (haves and have nots), sub cultures, 'Lebenswelten' and milieus. On the other hand, studying L.A. empirically, i.e. living, working and more than anything else talking to people while observing them, gives an insight into how a society so full of discrepancies works and operates. „To live from day to day. That is life in L.A." Mirna, Los Angeles Garment Worker from Guatemala. Undocumented migration to the USA and the US- American textile and garment industry are examples that demonstrate well the interconnectedness of international economic interests, policy-making and migration flows.
Bd. 1, 2005, 160 S., 19,90 €, br.,
ISBN 3-8258-8397-3

Andrea Blaneck
Netzwerke und Kooperationen an der
deutsch-polnischen Grenze
Untersuchungen zum wirtschaftlichen Milieu in der Grenzregion an der Oder
Das Buch zeigt regionale Entwicklungskontexte an der deutsch-polnischen Grenze auf und themati- siert die in ihnen wirksamen Verhaltens- und Interaktionsmuster regionaler Wirtschaftsakteure. An- hand von umfassenden Interviews mit Unternehmer/innen der Informationstechnologiebranche und mit Vertreter/innen von Wirtschaftsfördereinrichtungen wird untersucht, inwieweit man im deutsch- polnischen Grenzgebiet von einer integrierten Wirtschaftsregion sprechen kann. Grenzüberschreiten- den unternehmerischen Netzwerken und Kooperationen wird dabei eine besondere Bedeutung beige- messen.
Bd. 2, 2005, 120 S., 19,90 €, br.,
ISBN 3-8258-8934-3

Sarah Dornhof
Weder Huren noch Unterworfene
Geschlechterkonstruktionen und Interkulturalität in der französischen Gesellschaft
Im Jahr 2003 wird in einem Pariser Vorort ein junges Mädchen lebendigen Leibes verbrannt. Dies wird zum Auslöser für eine landesweite Protestbewegung „Weder Huren noch Unterworfene", die das patriarchale, sexistische System in den Banlieues thematisiert, das auf dem Gesetz des Stärkeren und einem bestimmten, um die Sexualität der Frauen zentrierten Ehrenkodex gründet. Das Buch analysiert die Bewegung sowie die Interdependenzen von Geschlecht, Klasse, Ethnizität

LIT Verlag Berlin – Hamburg – London – Münster – Wien – Zürich
Fresnostr. 2 48159 Münster
Tel.: 0251 / 620 32 22 – Fax: 0251 / 922 60 99
e-Mail: vertrieb@lit-verlag.de – http://www.lit-verlag.de

und Religion im französischen Migrations-
kontext.
Bd. 3, 2006, 112 S., 19,90 €, br.,
ISBN 3-8258-9681-1

Anke Draude
**Der blinde Fleck der Entwicklungs-
theorie**
Von der Unüberwindbarkeit der Modernisierungstheorie im Korruptionsdiskurs
Die Modernisierungstheorie hatte als ent-
wicklungstheoretisches Paradigma bereits in
den 1970er Jahren ausgedient. Alternativen
liegen jedoch nicht auf der Hand. Was soll
gesellschaftliche Entwicklung sein, wenn
nicht Modernisierung? Am Beispiel des Kor-
ruptionsdiskurses zeigt sich, dass trotz einer
oberflächlichen Ablehnung modernisierungs-
theoretische Argumentationsmuster die ent-
wicklungstheoretische Diskussion bis heute
dominieren.
Bd. 4, 2007, 112 S., 14,90 €, br.,
ISBN 978-3-8258-0248-6

Soziologie und Anthropologie
Kulturwissenschaftliche Perspektiven
hrsg. von Prof. Dr. Detlef Pollack,
Prof. Dr. Werner Schiffauer und
Prof. Dr. Anna Schwarz (Europa-Universität
Viadrina, Frankfurt/Oder)

Rebecca Budde
**Mexican and Central American L.A.
Garment Workers**
Globalized Industries and their Economic
Constraints
Bd. 1, 2005, 160 S., 19,90 €, br.,
ISBN 3-8258-8397-3

Andrea Blaneck
**Netzwerke und Kooperationen an der
deutsch-polnischen Grenze**
Untersuchungen zum wirtschaftlichen
Milieu in der Grenzregion an der Oder
Bd. 2, 2005, 120 S., 19,90 €, br.,
ISBN 3-8258-8934-3

Sarah Dornhof
Weder Huren noch Unterworfene
Geschlechterkonstruktionen und Interkulturalität in der französischen Gesellschaft
Im Jahr 2003 wird in einem Pariser Vorort ein
junges Mädchen lebendigen Leibes verbrannt.
Dies wird zum Auslöser für eine landesweite
Protestbewegung „Weder Huren noch Unterworfene", die das patriarchale, sexistische
System in den Banlieues thematisiert, das
auf dem Gesetz des Stärkeren und einem
bestimmten, um die Sexualität der Frauen
zentrierten Ehrenkodex gründet. Das Buch
analysiert die Bewegung sowie die Interdependenzen von Geschlecht, Klasse, Ethnizität
und Religion im französischen Migrations-
kontext.
Bd. 3, 2006, 112 S., 19,90 €, br.,
ISBN 3-8258-9681-1

Anke Draude
**Der blinde Fleck der Entwicklungs-
theorie**
Von der Unüberwindbarkeit der Modernisierungstheorie im Korruptionsdiskurs
Die Modernisierungstheorie hatte als ent-
wicklungstheoretisches Paradigma bereits in
den 1970er Jahren ausgedient. Alternativen
liegen jedoch nicht auf der Hand. Was soll
gesellschaftliche Entwicklung sein, wenn
nicht Modernisierung? Am Beispiel des Kor-
ruptionsdiskurses zeigt sich, dass trotz einer
oberflächlichen Ablehnung modernisierungs-
theoretische Argumentationsmuster die ent-
wicklungstheoretische Diskussion bis heute
dominieren.
Bd. 4, 2007, 112 S., 14,90 €, br.,
ISBN 978-3-8258-0248-6

LIT Verlag Berlin – Hamburg – London – Münster – Wien – Zürich
Fresnostr. 2 48159 Münster
Tel.: 0251 / 620 32 22 – Fax: 0251 / 922 60 99
e-Mail: vertrieb@lit-verlag.de – http://www.lit-verlag.de